hollow

kids

hollow kids

Recapturing the Soul of a
Generation Lost to the Self-Esteem Myth

Laura L. Smith, Ph.D.
Charles H. Elliott, Ph.D.

FORUM
An Imprint of Prima Publishing

Published by Prima Publishing, Roseville, California. Member of the Crown Publishing Group, a division of Random House, Inc.

Random House, Inc. New York, Toronto, London, Sydney, Auckland

PRIMA PUBLISHING, FORUM, and colophons are trademarks of Random House, Inc., registered with the United States Patent and Trademark Office.

Library of Congress Cataloging-in-Publication Data

Smith, Laura L.
   Hollow kids : recapturing the soul of a generation lost to the self-esteem myth / Laura L. Smith, Charles H. Elliott
    p. cm.
   Includes index.
   ISBN 0-7615-1674-3
   1. Youth. 2. Self-esteem—Social aspects. 3. Social values. I. Elliott, Charles H. II. Title.
HQ796 .S553   2001
305.235—dc21   2001033468

01 02 03 04 HH 10 9 8 7 6 5 4 3 2 1
Printed in the United States of America

First Edition

Visit us online at www.primapublishing.com

CONTENTS

PREFACE

Hollow Kids is a personal book, not just a story about the many kids who lead hollow lives today. We were adolescents during the 1960s, the decade that opened with a focus on politics, the Vietnam War, the civil rights movement, and the dawn of the women's movement. Heated discussions and debates consumed the attention of Americans. As the decade unfolded, the self-esteem movement gained momentum and began to envelop our culture, slowly shifting the focus from larger issues to the pursuit of personal happiness.

Few growing up at that time failed to hear seductive messages of "Free love," "Tune in, turn on, drop out," "Do your own thing," and "Take the easy way out." Songs and media, directed at kids, promoted the ideas of self-indulgence and feeling good.

We'd like to claim that we embraced only the solid messages of the time and discarded the hollow ones. We can't. In retrospect, both of us realize that the fledgling self-esteem movement inspired too many decisions in our lives. Decisions that regrettably put transient pleasures ahead of family and friends. Decisions we would make differently today—if we could.

Yet rather than feeling like victims of the self-esteem movement, we have come to accept our own considerable imperfections with humility. And, as we expose the flawed ideas of those who profited from the marketing of self-esteem, we accept that promoters of the movement were as imperfect as we were. We now welcome our opportunity to make a difference today, for our kids.

This book is intended to demonstrate how we can all help our children discover the deeper joy found in connecting with others and looking outward rather than seeking the shallow pleasures of self-indulgence. Nevertheless, we face a formidable obstacle: the entrenched perspective of the self-esteem movement that firmly grips our collective psyche. The movement captured our souls with its alluring, intuitively appealing theory that raising self-esteem could provide a painless remedy for a panoply of problems, from depression to violence. With the self-esteem "solution" in hand, the movement infiltrated our homes, schools, and businesses.

Unlike the purveyors of self-esteem, we promise no easy answers or quick solutions. Nor do we expect you to uncritically accept our alternative perspective. We hope you will instead examine our argument with both skepticism and an open mind. As you review our logic and evidence, we encourage you to assess the actual impact the self-esteem movement had on you and others and consider joining us in recapturing the souls of our young, and perhaps even our own.

Hollow Kids opens with a surprising look at the problems seen in adolescents today as compared to 30 or 40 years ago, documenting the increases in depression, substance abuse, eating disorders, anxiety, and crime; the decline in values; and the diminishment of school achievement. Chapter 1 describes how self-esteem promoters pronounced low self-esteem as the *primary cause* of all these problems, a contention we all soon accepted as truth, thus opening the floodgates for thousands of books, videos, tapes, and lesson plans designed to bolster everyone's self-esteem.

Chapter 2 defines self-esteem, uncovers a number of important myths about the concept, and presents a new model for understanding the nature of self-esteem. Chapters 3 through 7 review specific problem areas that the Self-Esteem Movement declared were due to low self-esteem and examine the evidence for and against the self-esteem traffickers' contentions. You'll likely be surprised by what you discover.

Chapter 8 unwraps our alternative to the promotion of self-esteem—namely, acceptance—and discloses how those who can learn to accept their gifts *and* their flaws, their present *and* their past can turn from being victims toward becoming copers.

Chapters 9 and 10 reveal how parents and educators can foster the development of acceptance in children. We present what we hope you'll find to be an enlightened view of parenting and teaching based on the building blocks of acceptance: self-control and empathy.

Hollow Kids ends with a sense of cautious optimism. Our journey led us through an examination of our own values and beliefs to an appreciation of our connections and a reevaluation of our priorities.

We dedicate *Hollow Kids* to those we carelessly wounded along the way through our own self-absorption.

ACKNOWLEDGMENTS

We would like to thank and ask forgiveness from our families and friends, whom we have neglected for the past nine months. Especially: Brian, Allison, Sara, and Trevor. Many people contributed a great deal to our efforts. We also thank our agent, Ed Knappman, who recognized the potential of our proposal and persisted in getting it to market. In addition, we appreciate the efforts of Steve Martin, acquisitions editor at Prima Publishing, whose initial enthusiasm and poetic ideas inspired us. We also wish to thank David Richardson who continued Steve's work. Special thanks to John Bergez, who asked us hard questions and masterfully helped us express our ideas in a logical, organized manner. He creatively guided the development of the initial draft into its current form. We express considerable gratitude to Andi Reese Brady, Libby Larson, and Ruth Younger, all of whom skillfully tracked and edited the final product.

We also would like to acknowledge the impressive works of Roy F. Baumeister, social psychologist, whose ideas greatly influenced our work. In addition, Martin Seligman, Aaron T. Beck, Albert Ellis, David Myers, Robert Leahy, and John Rosemond have all provided us with inspiration and ideas.

Heartfelt thanks also to Lucille Vigil for painstakingly recording references, Tatiana Abras, Adele Evans, Trevor Wolfe, and David Weers for research, Colleen Weers for useful critique, Elizabeth Deardorff for educational curriculum materials, Scott

Love for keeping our computers humming, Audrey Hite for keeping us sane, and Martha Kaser and Juan Montoya for keeping us focused. Thanks for the efforts of Pat Henshaw, Prima publicist. And a special thanks to Karen Villanueva, our enthusiastic, energetic personal publicist.

Finally, to all of the kids we've talked to and worked with throughout the years, thanks for the insights and stories.

CHAPTER 1

THE SELF-ESTEEM MOVEMENT: THE SELLING OF AN ILLUSION

THE FOUR MOVED TOGETHER IN A PACK. STEPS SYNCHRONIZED, pace slow, hunting as they prowled through the food court. The youngest boy, age 12 or so, wore his baseball cap low over his face, hiding blemishes from his imaginary audience. The older boy, hair closely shaved on the sides with purple tips on top, found reasons to stick his pierced tongue out. Gold earrings shone from his ears and eyebrow. One girl, in front of the others, shuffled backward, chatting and laughing. Her low-cut halter-top exposed a blue butterfly tattooed between her breasts. The other girl flipped her wavy black hair and giggled.

We approached them, clipboards in hand. Dr. Smith held up her hand to get their attention and asked if they had a few minutes of time in return for some mall coupons. The girls agreed and convinced the boys to do the same. We had five questions:

1. Do you feel good about yourself?

2. What's important to you?

3. What are your life goals?

4. What values are important to you?

5. How are you doing in school?

Nicole, the girl with the tattoo, spoke first. When asked how she felt about herself, she told us she thought she was just great. Nicole said she was very popular, but that maybe she could lose a couple of pounds. The most important things in her life were her friends and having enough money to buy clothes. She had to think about her goals for a few moments. Nicole related that she wanted to have a lot of money, but didn't care much about how she got it.

Like other young people we've interviewed, Nicole seemed confused by the question regarding values. She asked us what we meant. We clarified by telling her values mean standards you live by, your sense of morality, how you decide what is right and wrong, and how you relate to others. Nicole said she tries not to hurt other people except when they get in her way. She couldn't elaborate. Finally, regarding school, she informed us she was doing fine. We asked what fine meant; what grade point average had she accumulated? Nicole didn't really know, but thought she got mostly B's and C's.

Fifteen-year-old Adam, the one with the purple hair, volunteered to answer our questions next. He declared himself a "bad dude," which he clearly intended as a positive self-description. Adam said nothing was especially important to him. His goals? He grinned and said he just wanted to get by, kick back, and smoke bud (marijuana). When we asked him about values, his face exuded a flat, hollow expression. He told us values don't mean anything to him and school was a total drag. He planned on dropping out and getting his GED.

Jason, the 12-year-old wearing the baseball cap, looked down at his sneakers and told us he felt okay about himself. He couldn't say what he found important, just hadn't thought about it. When we pressed him, Jason said he liked to watch TV a lot—he guessed that was important—and he liked his video games. He planned on designing video games for a living someday. He responded to our question about values by stating that he wanted to make a lot of money. Of course, he found school boring, but he usually passed his classes. We then asked Jason if he had any experience with computers other than playing games. He said he'd surfed the Web a little and sent friends messages. Mostly, he liked playing games.

Jocelyn, the one with wavy black hair, spoke last. She too seemed to feel pretty good about herself but worried about her weight. She said having a good time with her friends was the most important thing to her. She'd thought about college but didn't know what she wanted to study. Jocelyn valued friendship more than anything else. Her grades in school had gone up and down at times, but she remembered doing very well in grade school.

We've posed these questions to many teenagers. Some provided us with thoughtful, reflective answers, describing substantive goals, along with a realistic appraisal about what it takes to achieve them. These kids voiced concerns beyond a narrow focus on their own lives. They expressed interest in such things as politics, the environment, and spirituality. But too many of the kids' responses, like those of the teens in the mall, seemed disturbingly shallow, reflecting a preoccupation with oneself and with superficial gratifications.

Collectively, the young people we have talked to felt quite good about themselves. They certainly seemed to possess high self-esteem. Self-doubt and feelings of inadequacy did not plague them. If they expressed dissatisfaction, it usually had something to do with their appearance. For girls, weight issues came up frequently; boys either said very little or denied having self-doubts. Most of our respondents pointed to their peer group, family, or money as the important things in their lives. A few spelled out specifics like their cars, video games, or CD collections. Their goals ranged from none to generic success to becoming an Internet entrepreneur, a doctor, a lawyer, and even "the richest person in the world." All too often, the loftier goals seemed out of reach, given their school performance.

By far, the most difficult question for all of the kids concerned values. Most seemed puzzled by the term and asked for clarification. When we explained that values were the morals they lived by, the rules of right and wrong, and standards that dictate how to treat other people, they still struggled.

When asked about his values, one bright, well-educated 14-year-old replied, "I just try to stay out of trouble." Another told us she valued the time she spent with her friends. Even many of the more thoughtful kids we talked with had trouble being specific when asked about values. A few spoke in clichés, such as "Live by the golden rule," "Be true to yourself," or "Do your best." Others articulated values related to personal achievement. For example, one related, "There's no doubting yourself," and another, "You can do whatever you set out to do." Rare indeed was the adolescent who spoke of grand or altruistic ideals, such as contributing to the good of the world, dedicating a portion of their lives to a higher power, or simply helping others. Fundamentally, the kids we've talked to seem concerned, first and foremost, with themselves.

Now, you might wonder whether this isn't a normal state of affairs. Haven't young people always focused primarily on themselves? Perhaps, but we contend that teens have never demonstrated as much self-focus as they do today. Survey data from a variety of sources indicate a relatively recent shift in values toward greater preoccupation with oneself and with material gratification. To take one example, psychologist David Myers reviewed data that demonstrated dramatic changes in college students' values between 1970 and 1998. These data reveal a rise in materialism and a precipitous drop in a desire to find meaning in life.[1] The University of California at Los Angeles asks college freshmen about their interests and values every year. Over 250,000 freshmen at more than 450 colleges admit to more boredom at school and less interest in social and political affairs than any other class in a generation.[2]

A recent survey of 33,534 younger teens reflected this self-preoccupation and lack of interest in finding meaning. When asked what they considered the biggest issues facing teens today, the number one response was "whether or not to have sex," and the second most frequent response was "popularity." The combined responses of "drugs," "violence in schools," and "grades" received fewer votes than "whether or not to have sex." Teens expressed no concern for issues such as global warming, poverty, the environment, war, or politics.[3]

On the other hand, teens today appear to have more self-confidence and self-esteem than ever before.[4] For example, when asked to rate their abilities in academics, leadership, intellectual pursuits, writing, and public speaking, college freshmen expressed confidence levels more than 50% higher than levels reported in 1971.[5] The experiences of today's youth contrast sharply in this respect to those of most of their parents, for whom adolescence was a time of tremendous personal growth accompanied by self-doubt, awkwardness, social discomfort, and painful introspection. This, at least, might seem like a cause for celebration. Why would we want our children to feel as badly as many of us did?

So maybe we can forgive a little academic, social, and political apathy, materialism, shallowness, and self-centeredness if it means that our kids are at least happier and emotionally healthier. Yet, depression, rarely diagnosed in children prior to

1960, has flourished among our youth. A recent study found 9% of children suffering from depression in a sample of 3,000 12- to 14-year-olds.[6] Psychologist Martin Seligman reviewed the literature and concluded that children born after the baby boom of the 1950s and 1960s "were suffering from depression roughly ten times the rate of people born in the first third of this century."[7] In fact, the National Institute of Mental Health has estimated that more than 1.5 million Americans under the age of 15 suffer from serious depression.[8] Of even greater concern, the suicide rate among our nation's youth soared 155% from 1962 to 1996.[9] About a fifth of all high school students seriously contemplated suicide in 1998. In fact, suicide has become the third leading cause of death for teenagers.[10] Our youth certainly don't appear to be getting any happier.

Well, perhaps our kids aren't getting happier, but what about other areas of psychological adjustment? Not great either. Today, the prevalence of child psychopathology—that is, serious emotional or behavioral disorder—is estimated at 15%. One study found that the number of impaired children nearly doubled over the 13-year period from 1976 to 1989. These children showed greater sullenness and stubbornness. They were more likely to lie, cheat, and destroy property.[11] Furthermore, since the 1950s anxiety in children has shown dramatic increases. In recent years, average children report more symptoms of anxiety than children who were actual psychiatric inpatients in 1957. And since anxiety often predates depression, these findings suggest that depression levels will continue their alarming rise.[12] In addition, the incidence of two potentially deadly forms of eating disorders, anorexia and bulimia, has risen substantially over the years.[13]

So maybe they aren't so happy or well-adjusted, but one might assume they've learned more. After all, technology allows us to communicate across the globe in seconds. We routinely access the libraries of the world sitting at our computers. Former president Clinton made a goal of giving Internet access to every school in America. At least our children must have benefited from advances in technology at the schools.

Of course they have. In fact, you may have read in the newspaper that SAT scores of our students have increased in recent years. From 1990 to 2000, verbal test scores eked out a 5-point gain, while math scores rose 13 points. *However, the full story reveals that verbal scores on the SAT decreased an astonishing 49 points between 1960 and 2000. Math scores decreased 7 points in that time. Total test scores dropped by 56 points.*[14]

It is possible that some of this decrease could be chalked up to greater numbers of high school students, especially those of diverse ethnicity, taking the test over the years. More students of differing abilities started applying to colleges, which may have lowered scores a bit. However, the College Board, administrators of the SAT, reports that although the proportion of minorities taking the test continues to rise every year, over the past 10 years, most ethnic groups' scores have risen significantly. Furthermore, if decreased scores since the 1960s were simply due to larger percentages of students taking the test, one would expect to see at least the same, if not higher, top scores. Yet, that's not what happened *during the time period in which SAT scores dropped the most.* In 1966, 33,200 students received a score of 700 or above on the SAT verbal test. In 1983, although more took the test, only 11,638 achieved scores of 700 or better.[15]

Well, so they aren't happier, better adjusted, or smarter. But at least crime has gone down. We've all read about significant reductions in juvenile arrest rates in the past few years. In fact, from 1994 to 1999, the Violent Crime Index juvenile arrest rate declined by 36%, leaving it just 4% over the level in 1988.[16] However, the surgeon general surveyed juveniles and found that they are engaged in violent acts at the *highest rate since records have been kept.* The surgeon general also contends that arrest rates have declined merely because fewer youths are carrying weapons and, therefore, are less likely to attract police attention.[17] Furthermore, the decreases in arrest rates may have also been partially due to the fact that we've locked so many kids in jail. Never before have such numbers of young people been incarcerated. On October 29, 1997, 125,805 American teenagers lived in jail, which represents more than a 50% increase since 1983.[18] And consider that overall, from 1965 to 1998, the number of serious crimes—murder, rape, robbery, and aggravated assault—committed by juveniles soared 114%.

And we're experiencing violence of a kind never seen before. Privileged children from high-income, intact families have amassed arsenals of weapons and mercilessly killed their classmates. Eric Harris and Dylan Klebold, the teen killers who murdered 15 people and injured more than 40 others at Columbine High School in April 1999, left behind videotapes depicting their schemes and philosophies. They spoke of being superior, more evolved, and above human.[20]

What happened? During an era in which our youth experienced deteriorations in moral values, personal adjustment, mental health, and educational achievement, the human genome project unraveled many secrets of health, disease, and life itself. Nanotechnology soon promises the development of tiny machines that can clean out human arteries like miniature plumbers. Agricultural advances are producing disease-resistant plants with a higher yield and greater nutritional value. We've even re-engineered some fruits and vegetables to produce their own natural insecticides. In time, these developments may finally feed the world's hungry. It seems the impossible has become possible.[21]

How could we have accomplished so much in the areas of science, technology, and medicine while the souls of our youth withered? Did we so focus on innovations that we neglected to nurture the character of our children? Did we fail to care to such an extent that we created hollow children, who are self-centered and morally vapid?

No, not at all. We cared a lot. So much so that during the past 40 years or more, we virtually went to war on the problems experienced by our children. During this era of meteoric technological progress, we devoted massive efforts to improving psychological adjustment and well-being. The science of psychology attempted to eliminate depression and anxiety while increasing personal satisfaction. We worked to reduce teenage pregnancy, drug addiction, divorce, suicide, and eating disorders. Educators fought academic mediocrity and worked to increase standards. Society struggled to decrease crime, from minor shoplifting to murder. We also enlisted an army of mental health professionals to accomplish these goals. The ranks of this force swelled to well over 500,000 psychologists, social workers, psychiatrists, counselors, psychotherapists, lay counselors, and various other magicians in the United States alone.

THE SELF-ESTEEM WAR

The amassed armies of mental health professionals searched for the enemy of adjustment and well-being in many quarters. They looked at poverty, abuse, biology, oppression, and distorted thinking. However, these armies converged on one target above all others: *low self-esteem*. The campaign against low self-esteem, which is also known as the self-esteem movement, has spanned close to half a century.

Professionals in the field of mental health attributed depression, suicide, drug abuse, alcoholism, teenage pregnancy, poverty, school failure, abuse, delinquency, and violence to low self-esteem. The professionals indicted low self-esteem for all of these crimes and found it guilty beyond a reasonable doubt. They then accumulated an arsenal of weapons for combating low self-esteem and recruited teachers and parents to aid in the fight. Educators and authors rewrote textbooks, curriculums, and parenting manuals in order to boost children's self-esteem.

Yet, the war waged by the self-esteem movement has been lost. The statistics cited a moment ago on young people's emotional health, academic achievement, and violence leave no doubt that the self-esteem movement has utterly failed to ease our social concerns. How did the idea that improving self-esteem could redress most of our social ills come about? Fifty years ago, self-esteem was a rather obscure idea. Today, it occupies center stage in child-rearing practices, social sciences, education, and mental health. In spite of failing to fulfill any of its promises, it remains revered by many social scientists and mental health professions as the panacea for a host of maladies. In fact, self-esteem has become a societal mantra. In the words of Professor William Damon:

> Teachers, clinicians, and guidance counselors everywhere speak first and foremost about the primary importance of self-esteem. They see a lack of self-esteem at the root of every problem and an increase in self-esteem as the hope for every recovery. Many professionals believe self-esteem to be the key engine of both intellectual and personality growth.[22]

Truly, the self-esteem movement has permeated our society. You are a rare parent, educator, or professional if the idea of self-esteem has not penetrated your thinking and attitudes, altering in subtle or dramatic ways your approach to raising, teaching, or working with children. Self-esteem has achieved the status of an unquestioned value. High self-esteem is good, and we must promote it in our children. Low self-esteem is bad, and we must prevent our kids from experiencing the horrors associated with it.

Just about all of us bought this message. It seemed so convincing at the time. At the least, most of us assumed that raising self-esteem couldn't do any harm and it just might help a lot.

Yet the evidence suggests that raising self-esteem as a cure for all that ails us is simply a myth—and one that, we will argue, has not only failed to deliver on its promises but had serious negative consequences. It is time to wean ourselves from our attachment to the myth of self-esteem and seek out a better alternative, one that promotes the kinds of values and healthy social and emotional adjustment we want for our children.

Disabusing ourselves of the illusions promoted by the self-esteem movement won't be easy. Let's begin by exploring how the movement came to have such a grip on our thinking about children despite the lack of scientific evidence supporting its claims.

THE SEEDS OF THE SELF-ESTEEM MOVEMENT

The interest in self-esteem took several decades to reach its current crescendo. We investigated the evolution of this interest by accessing a database available on the Internet. PsychInfo contains abstracts and titles of most articles written in psychology since 1887. We found only 26 articles containing the keyword "self-esteem" between the years 1887 and 1940, with all of these appearing after 1928. As you can see in Figure 1, it wasn't until the 1960s that interest began to pick up steam. The decades that followed witnessed an explosion of academic interest in the concept of self-esteem. Clearly, self-esteem has become a staple of psychological research. Where did the concept come from, and how has it achieved such exalted status?

The first psychologist to cite the term "self-esteem" was the eminent and highly influential William James, who wrote about it in 1890.[24] Although James himself devoted relatively little attention to the concept of self-esteem, his remarks planted seeds—seeds that took over 50 years to germinate.[25]

During the 1940s, humanistic psychologist Abraham Maslow contributed to the interest in self-esteem by investigating the relationship between self-esteem and women's sexuality. In his early work, Maslow also related self-esteem to marital happiness and frequency and type of orgasm.[26] Later, Maslow provided more fertilizer for the seedlings of the self-esteem

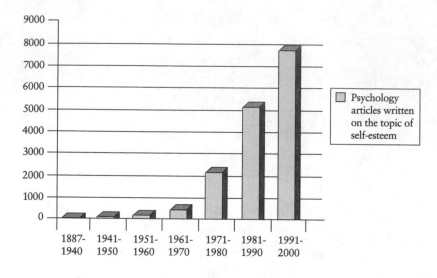

FIGURE 1
SOURCE: *PSYCHINFO/APA*[23]

movement by developing his concept of self-actualization. He believed that self-actualized people have reached the highest possible level of human development—they have fulfilled their potential. Compared to people who have not achieved this level of development, they have higher values and display greater autonomy, personal growth, and capacity for love. Sadly, he believed, most people never reach this level. He contended that brilliant artists and scientists achieved self-actualization more often than others. However, he thought most of us could achieve self-actualization if it weren't for inhibitions imposed by society. Thus, he called for schools to create conditions that favor spontaneity and unbridled expression of the self. Self-actualization evolved into the ultimate goal pursued by many followers of the self-esteem movement.[27]

Alfred Adler, a contemporary of Sigmund Freud, also focused on the self. He believed people possess a self-concept based on their early life experiences. People struggle to live up to a self-ideal. Adler believed that the root of neurosis lies in the attempt to overcome feelings of inferiority that people develop because of earlier life experiences. Adler believed that this attempt often overshoots the mark and leads to feelings of superiority over others.

Adler's ideas provided some of the first hints of the problems that might arise from an emphasis on self-esteem alone. He essentially recognized that an overabundant focus on the self could lead to emotional problems. In fact, he declared, "All neurosis is vanity."[28] Thus, Adler realized that positive or negative self-views involve a neurotic preoccupation with how one compares to others.

In the 1940s and 1950s, Carl Rogers also celebrated the self in his development of client-centered therapy. He agreed with Maslow that self-actualization represents the ultimate goal for everyone. Rogers believed that one of the ways a person can reach a self-actualized state is through unconditional positive regard from a therapist. Just what does unconditional positive regard mean? It means that no matter what a client says or does, the therapist responds with kindness, empathy, and compassion. Presumably, if a client lies, cheats, or steals, the route to overcoming these impulses is to be found through warmth and acceptance on the part of the therapist. In all fairness, we doubt Rogers would go that far. And some of his ideas about empathy, genuineness, and positive regard do have merit; many studies show, for example, that psychotherapy works better when the therapeutic relationship includes empathy.

Over the years, however, Rogers's client-centered therapy has not enjoyed much empirical support (support derived from controlled scientific studies) for its effectiveness as compared to many other types of psychotherapies. However, that lack of support did not dampen the enthusiasm for Rogers's ideas in the field of education. Rogers virtually equated education with therapy. He exhorted teachers to provide unconditional positive regard for every student. He wrote that schools need to free students of inhibitions and constraints. Learning, he said, comes from within.[29] Curriculums should conform to the dictates of students' needs. Content is secondary to freedom and creativity. Teachers should give authority to students in deference to their need for attaining self-actualization. He felt schools should be "a place where students would come to prize themselves, would develop self-confidence, and self-esteem."[30] Many educators responded deliriously to Rogers's prescriptions.

A number of psychologists also responded with enthusiasm to the writings of Rogers, and to Maslow and Adler as well. Editors of psychology journals devoted increased journal space to investigating the relationship of self-esteem to a dizzying array of subjects. In order to study self-esteem, psychologists developed tests or measurements of the attribute, which, in turn, provided additional fuel for the study of self-esteem. Some of these measures were surprisingly simple, consisting of as few as 10 items, to which people indicated how much they agreed on a five-point scale.[31] Nevertheless, these rather superficial tests had the effect of turning self-esteem from a concept to a reality.

Once someone develops a measure for a concept, it becomes "reified"—that is, it changes from a mere idea into something that can be measured; and if it can be measured, it must therefore exist. And the more people measure and study it, the more important it must be. Due to the development of these scales, the number of studies and the range of their topics burgeoned. For example, articles looked at how self-esteem might affect a person's susceptibility to persuasion, how self-esteem might affect memory, and how it relates to ethnocentrism, gossiping behavior, social class, alcoholism, cigarette smoking, stress, modesty, and even factors leading one to assume the life of a hippie.[32] Scientists also implicated low self-esteem as the cause of hostility and delinquency.[33] Later, self-esteem provided reasons for why children cheat at games, why students fail to achieve in school, how males feel about women's liberation, and what causes women to be assertive. One treatise actually declared low self-esteem responsible for homosexual foot fetishes![34]

This proliferation of studies ultimately elevated self-esteem to the status of a panacea for a host of societal ills. The scientific community's zeal soon spread into the popular press. In 1952, Norman Vincent Peale introduced his smash hit, *The Power of Positive Thinking,* with "BELIEVE IN YOURSELF. Have faith in your abilities! It is appalling to realize the number of pathetic people who are hampered and made miserable by the malady popularly called the inferiority complex. But you need not suffer from this trouble."[35]

Peale preached that financial success and happiness would come simply from thinking highly of yourself and your abilities, using positive thoughts to cancel out negative thoughts, and mindlessly repeating affirmations and visualizations. His promises of achieving a better life by simply thinking positive thoughts held great allure, as attested to by the over five million eager purchasers of his book. The breathtaking triumph of *The Power of Positive Thinking* foreshadowed the wholesale trafficking of self-esteem starting in the 1960s.

SELF-ESTEEM BLOSSOMS: THE SELF-ESTEEM TRAFFICKERS

By the 1960s, the stage was set for an onslaught of self-esteem promoters, authors, and gurus. Sociologist John Hewitt has described this collage of professionals, pseudo-professionals, and laypersons as "self-esteem entrepreneurs."[36] Indeed, marketers of the self-esteem movement managed to find audiences in business, churches, corporations, farms, hospitals, homes, and schools. The promoters promised a cornucopia of benefits, including academic achievement, happiness, good health, increased sales and profits, friendship, popularity, mental health, tranquility, satisfaction, resilience, the ability to overcome almost any obstacle, and even love. To peddle their message, the self-esteem entrepreneurs have exploited every imaginable venue: television and radio shows, videotapes, audiotapes, workshops, weekend seminars, popular magazines, infomercials, books, individual therapy, and group therapy. Society has become saturated with the notion of a nirvana of self-love, as reflected in these current book titles:

- *I Love Me!*

- *We're All Special*

- *Love Yourself First*

- *The Ultimate Miracle: You!*

- *Be Full of Yourself: The Journey from Self Criticism to Self Celebration*

- *The Complete Idiot's Guide to Enhancing Self-Esteem*

- *Affirm Yourself Day by Day: Seed Thoughts for Loving Yourself*

- *ABC I Like Me*

- *Ten Days to Self-Esteem*

Nathaniel Branden, from Beverly Hills, California, stands out among those who have made a very good living preaching the self-esteem sermon. Many consider Branden the most influential contemporary writer about the topic of self-esteem. His career began in the late '60s and has spanned more than 30 years. He has stayed quite busy, writing 20 books in all, with titles such as *How to Raise Your Self-Esteem, Nathaniel Branden's Self-Esteem Every Day, The Power of Self-Esteem, The Psychology of High Self-Esteem, Self-Esteem at Work, The Six Pillars of Self-Esteem, A Woman's Self-Esteem,* and *Honoring the Self.* He's also recorded audio versions of many of his books and created original tapes, such as *Strengthen Your Ego* and *Succeeding Through Inner Strength*. In addition to writing, he consults with corporations throughout the world and, not surprisingly, serves as the executive director of the Branden Institute for Self-Esteem.

In 1969 Branden wrote, *"I cannot think of a single psychological problem—from anxiety and depression to fear of intimacy or success, to spouse battery, or child molestation—that is not traceable to the problem of poor self-esteem"* (emphasis added).[37] This statement exemplifies the breathtaking audacity of the self-esteem movement, invoking a single, simplistic, global construct as the primary cause of most human maladies. Of course, sound bites sell. Deliver a hopeful message in an easily understood package and people flock to hear it, buy it, and digest it. And it doesn't hurt if you make a few references to the "scientific" literature. Branden, like almost all of the self-esteem traffickers, cites scientific findings to support *and sell* his products. After all, people have learned to believe in science. Whether the science being cited is solid or contains conceptual cracks down to its foundation is not something most people are in a position to judge.

A case example from one of his books illustrates Branden's version of honoring the self.[38] He wrote about a man, married for 30 years, who had an affair. The man came to Branden for advice. He was passionate about his new love and indifferent to his wife. However, he felt that his wife was a good woman who had been loyal to him for 30 years. She was the mother of his three children and had never done anything reproachable. Branden asked the man to imagine that he had only six months to live. What would he do? The man replied that he would leave his wife and live with the other woman. A year later, Branden lamented the fact that the man had remained with his wife. "I have never been able to escape the conviction that had he a higher level of self-esteem, a greater conviction of his own lovability and of his right to be happy, the story would have ended differently."[39]

Nowhere did Branden discuss how the man might have considered improving his marriage or the value of keeping a family together. The clear message: If you are at all unhappy and you think well of yourself, leave forthwith; don't give it another thought. How far Branden will go in treating self-esteem as a be-all (and cure-all) is demonstrated by the advice he has given to women who suffer from sexual inhibitions. Branden suggested the following remedy: "Sometimes, working with a woman who is dissociated from her own body, and, more specifically, blocked in the pelvic area, I will ask her to perform bump-and-grind movements while saying aloud, over and over again, 'I am a good girl.'"[40] We'd like to see the scientific data supporting this therapeutic technique.

SELF-ESTEEM AS A CURE-ALL: SCIENCE OR SNAKE OIL?

The self-esteem movement has flourished in spite of the lack of scientific data to support it. This point is best demonstrated by what happened when advocates of higher self-esteem looked for the evidence that would support their nostrums.

In 1984, California legislator John Vasconcellos introduced legislation—eventually passed and signed by the governor—funding the California Task Force on Self-Esteem. The legislature approved a budget of $735,000 and directed the task force to compile research on the relation of self-esteem to crime and violence, alcohol and drug abuse, teenage pregnancy, child abuse, chronic welfare dependency, and educational failure. Next, they were to find out how self-esteem is developed, damaged, or enhanced. The extraordinarily high hopes that by now were associated with self-esteem resonate in the words of Vasconcellos, who compared this work to unlocking the secret of the atom and exploring the mysteries of outer space. Said Vasconcellos, "Developing self-esteem and responsibility—a potential 'vaccine' against the social problems we face—may be the most compelling of human ventures."[41]

The task force hired academic experts to validate the belief that self-esteem stands out as a primary cause of most social problems. Their findings appeared in *The Social Importance of Self-Esteem,* published by the University of California Press in 1989. In fact, most of the findings suggest that a quite different title would have been more appropriate—*The Social Unimportance of Self-Esteem.* The introductory chapter concluded, "One of the disappointing aspects of every chapter in this volume . . . is how low the associations between self-esteem and its consequences are in research to date. . . . The news most consistently reported . . . is that the associations between self-esteem and its expected consequences are mixed, insignificant, or absent."[42]

Not only was the association between social problems and self-esteem weak, but the vast majority of the research utilized correlational statistics only, a practice that seriously limits the conclusions that can be drawn from the findings. Briefly, correlations describe observed relationships between two or more things under study, called variables. If two variables are positively correlated, then high levels of one tend to be associated with high levels of the other. To take a simple example, you'd probably find a positive correlation between people's height and the size of their feet. In general—though you might find lots of exceptions—taller people have bigger feet, and shorter people have smaller feet. By the same token, if you took a large sample of people and looked at number of cigarettes smoked and the incidence of lung cancer, you would likely see that the more cigarettes smoked, the more cases of lung cancer. Thus, a positive correlation, or relationship, exists between cigarette smoking and lung cancer. Again, though, there are exceptions; not all heavy smokers get lung cancer, and not all people with lung cancer smoke.

Now, here's the problem. For years, bands of lawyers for the tobacco companies argued that the observed correlation between smoking and cancer was not proof that smoking cigarettes *causes* lung cancer. They contended that other variables, such as genes or stress, might have caused *both* an increased tendency to smoke *and* an increased risk of lung cancer. And they were absolutely correct, to the extent that it's true that a correlation alone doesn't establish that variable *x* causes variable *y*. After all, being tall doesn't cause you to have big feet, any more than having big feet causes you to be tall. There are other variables (such as your genes) that account for both your height and the size of your feet.

Now, at this point, we have much better evidence that smoking really does increase the chances of getting lung cancer. That evidence comes from more sophisticated research designs in which the level of intake of cigarette smoke could be manipulated in various laboratory animals. In general, establishing a causal relationship, as opposed to a mere association between variables, requires experimental research in which variables can be controlled in such a way that other possible causes can be ruled out. Thus, correlational studies certainly raised our suspicions about smoking and lung cancer, but it took experimental studies to establish scientifically that the relationship between these variables was a causal one.

To clarify with another example, suppose you read a report showing a high correlation between time spent playing video games and arrest rates for juvenile delinquency. Let's say that arrested juveniles averaged 15 hours a week of video game playing, compared to 4 hours a week for teenagers in general. You might be tempted to conclude that playing video games greatly influences the likelihood of juveniles' committing crimes. But the evidence doesn't entitle you to draw that conclusion. Perhaps excessive leisure time leads kids to play more video games *and* get into more mischief. Or perhaps the quality and amount of parental supervision are responsible for kids being drawn to both video games and crime. In fact, we know that teenagers who commit crimes are less likely to be involved in after-school activities such as sports teams or clubs and are less likely to have adult supervision. So, the fact that arrested teenagers play more video games may not at all be a cause of their delinquent behavior.

When someone tosses "scientific" evidence your way, keep this principle firmly in mind: Correlations are useful, but they do not prove causation. In the case of self-esteem, a variety of studies have shown a modest correlation between self-esteem and various social problems such as low achievement. So, does low self-esteem *cause* low achievement? Or does low achievement cause low self-esteem? Or does something else, such as poor self-control, cause *both* low self-esteem *and* low achievement? This type of correlational study simply can't answer these questions.

The paucity of data concerning the value of increasing self-esteem didn't slow down the California Task Force. Not at all. Instead, they blithely ignored the findings reported in their own book and spun off a group dedicated to the propagation of raising self-esteem in our schools, at home, and in society. The group was originally called the National Council for Self-Esteem; the directors changed the name to the National Association for Self-Esteem (NASE) in 1995. Early members included Jack Canfield (coauthor of the mega-selling Chicken Soup series who has worked prodigiously to infuse self-esteem into the schools), Gloria Steinem (feminist author), and Nathaniel Branden (self-esteem guru discussed above).[43]

NASE now has a presence on the World Wide Web; you can visit it at www.self-esteem-nase.org. On the Web site, you'll find guides to parenting, worldwide conferences, self-esteem links, a research center, a reference center, membership information, educational programs, and a listing of local chapters. Of particular interest is the research page, which blames low self-esteem for problems of school achievement, crime and violence, teenage pregnancy, drug and alcohol abuse, teen suicide, high school dropout rates, cheating and stealing, and poor health, including cancer.

If you look closely, however, you might notice a couple of things about the references upon which these claims are based. First, the references are generally over 10 years old. Second, most come from popular books or articles in small magazines rather than scientific journals, which are refereed by experts. Of particular note, NASE neglected to cite the 1989 book commissioned by the California Task Force on Self-Esteem. It's difficult to believe that the National Association for Self-Esteem omitted the reference because it didn't know about it. After all, the task force that inspired the creation of the association commissioned the book. The more likely reason for its omission is that the book painfully fails to support the group's cause.

CRITICISMS OF THE SELF-ESTEEM MOVEMENT

Not surprisingly, a few voices have quite recently started to question the self-esteem movement.[44] These critics have aptly cited a number of problems that come from the indiscriminate effort to increase everyone's self-esteem as a panacea for human problems. In particular, critics have zeroed in on three issues.

First, they say the movement has separated self-esteem from actual achievement and that doing so removes incentives for accomplishments. Too often, critics say, self-esteem promoters preach that all children require praise and we should always make them feel successful, no matter what they've actually accomplished.

Second, the critics argue that schools have emphasized self-esteem to the detriment of standards. They argue that social promotion, grade inflation, and unproductive time spent on vacuous boosting of self-esteem have led to degradation of curriculums and performance. For example, from 1988 to 2000, the percentage of college freshmen who reported "earning" A+, A, and A– grade averages when in high school climbed from 28% to 39%. It would be an awesome achievement if almost 40% of our high school students were attaining such levels of excellence. Of course, they aren't. During the same period that grades skyrocketed, a more objective measure—SAT scores—increased only marginally.[45]

Third, critics have condemned the promotion of self-esteem for causing parental overindulgence. When parents unduly concern themselves with their children's self-esteem, it becomes difficult to discipline. Discipline involves confrontation and temporary bad feelings. Sometimes kids feel guilty when they're reprimanded for their deeds. Their self-esteem might dip for a little while. On the other hand, guilt and bad feelings may generate better behavior the next time. But many parents feel discomfort in allowing their children's self-esteem to suffer, even if briefly.

We agree in part with these arguments. Certainly, it is appropriate to be concerned about children learning to "feel good" about themselves for no good reason or about students who no longer know what "outstanding" means because everyone expects, and too often receives, an A. But it is easy to target foolishness, such as the recommended incantations of "I am special; I am beautiful" or not allowing teachers to give grades to elementary students out of fear of damaging students' self-esteem. The question is, where does the self-esteem movement fundamentally go wrong, and what should replace self-esteem in the thinking of parents, educators, and professionals who work with children? And here, we think, many critics have missed the mark by failing to fully understand the nature of self-esteem and the far more serious problem the self-esteem movement represents.

First, to criticize the self-esteem movement should not mean giving up all concern for problems that may have a connection with low self-esteem. As we'll show you, excessively high self-esteem creates greater troubles, but that doesn't mean that we should sweep significant issues of low self-esteem under the rug.

Second, the critics have a point when they say that the movement encourages us to teach children to feel good about themselves for no reason, but the obvious alternative—tying self-esteem to accomplishments—also has problems. Basing self-esteem entirely on accomplishments means that failure must induce low self-esteem—and all of us fail some of the time. Moreover, when we do succeed, the boost to our self-esteem is fleeting. As author David Mills has commented, "When people base their self-esteem on specific behaviors or accomplishments, they must constantly strive for, and perpetually achieve, new goals if their ego intoxication is to continue."[46]

Mills's remark brings us to the heart of the issue about self-esteem. We contend that the central problem with placing excessive emphasis on developing high self-esteem is that doing so leads to increased *self-absorption*. This intense focus on the self lays a foundation for misery that manifests itself in more ways than many critics of the self-esteem movement have contemplated. It isn't just about decreasing educational standards or rearing overindulged children. As we will demonstrate in the coming chapters, self-absorption underlies eating disorders, distortions in body image, greed, anxiety, depression, narcissism, aggression, and violence. Self-absorption fuels disregard for others; it erodes moral development. Ironically, it can even lead to low self-esteem. This is the insidious way in which our preoccupation with self-esteem is failing our children and damaging their happiness, their emotional adjustment, and their sense of values and obligation to others.

Nobody intended to fill our kids with self-absorption and narcissism. The self-esteem movement started with a few good ideas and took them too far. People who came to maturity in the 1960s wanted to feel good, and they wanted the same for their kids. The self-esteem traffickers exploited these ideas and gradually turned them into distorted, costly prescriptions for living.

A BETTER WAY: ACCEPTANCE

In this book we propose an alternative to the misguided and destructive quest for higher and higher self-esteem. In its place, we recommend the idea of *acceptance*. Acceptance can provide our children a way of learning to become self-forgetful. It shifts the emphasis from internal preoccupation to a connection with others. It allows them to thrive with much less worry about their inevitable weaknesses, mistakes, and failures. Acceptance leads to improved emotional well-being.

Before we can fully describe acceptance as an alternative to self-esteem, we need to examine more closely exactly what is wrong with the logic of the self-esteem movement, and how preoccupation with self-esteem leads to the problems we have described. As someone concerned with children, you have a right to expect a careful analysis before you are asked to dispense with an idea so apparently reasonable as the notion of self-esteem. Moreover, we believe that one reason the critics of the self-esteem movement have made so little headway is that the concept of self-esteem has become so entrenched in all of our thinking that it takes a thorough reexamination of it to root it out. Consequently, in the next chapter we will take a closer look at exactly how current thinking about self-esteem is misleading. Along the way, we will develop a fuller and more accurate conception of self-esteem, one that helps explain what we actually observe in our children. In Part Two, we will explore in detail the serious problems caused by a distorted self-esteem and the self-absorption that accompanies it.

In Part Three, we will present the acceptance alternative and its implications for parents and teachers. This, we believe, is the antidote to self-absorption and narcissism. It is the way to reclaim a generation lost to the myth of self-esteem and fill the hollow places in our children's souls with humility, values, and grace.

CHAPTER 2

FOCUS ON SELF:
ESTEEM OR NARCISSISM?

A WEEK BEFORE THE HOMECOMING DANCE, MARIAN, A SENIOR IN high school, sat alone in her room flipping through a magazine. She'd resigned herself to spending the next weekend babysitting at a neighbor's house, knowing she'd never get a date. This was her last year in high school and she'd never been asked to a formal dance. Marian was mature for her age and more intelligent than most of her peers. Although attractive, she lacked the confidence to flirt with guys. For the most part, the boys at her school flocked toward the flashy, frivolous type. Marian desperately wanted to go to a dance, at least this once. But she had little hope. She felt sure no one would ever ask her.

When it came to getting a guy, you might say her self-esteem drooped like a flag on a windless day. So, when Brandon called, Marian's first thought was that he must need help on a homework assignment. She couldn't believe what she was hearing when he asked her to the homecoming dance. She figured he'd probably asked and been turned down by a dozen girls before, desperate, he gave up and reluctantly invited her.

Marian was even more surprised when, after a few dates, Brandon told her he really liked her. It didn't take long for Marian to think she was in love. She immediately started to worry. How would she ever manage to hold his interest? After all, Brandon was really cute, and Marian viewed herself as quite unexciting. Her worries compelled her to call Brandon incessantly for reassurance. If he wasn't home, she obsessed over where he might have gone. She queried him constantly concerning his whereabouts and sulked whenever he talked to other girls. She even pouted when he went out with the guys.

Not surprisingly, Brandon soon wearied of Marian's unrelenting nagging and questioning. He abruptly broke off the relationship after just a few weeks. This, of course, only convinced Marian of what she had feared all along: No boy would ever find poor Marian desirable.

Unlike Marian, Don never worried about dates. As the handsome, charming captain of the football team, he was always surrounded by girls. By his senior year, he bragged to his teammates about scoring with at least 25 different girls. But he never stayed with one for long; after each conquest, he lost interest. He certainly had no desire for companionship. Although Don thought of his teammates as his close friends, he spent more time bragging about his accomplishments than getting to know them.

The summer after he graduated, Don experienced some perplexing feelings of listless boredom. He tried to call a number of his "friends," but his former teammates were always too busy to see him. Several of the girls he called turned him down cold. He couldn't understand these rejections. Don became indignant. He couldn't fathom how those undiscerning babes could give up a chance to be with him, the one who had always been so special and idolized. Don figured he could live without high school girls; better game awaited in college. Nevertheless, uncomfortable feelings of loneliness tarnished his summer. He didn't know what to do with himself. Mostly, though, he was just mad.

Don and Marian—opposite ends of the self-esteem spectrum, one conceited and arrogant, the other insecure and self-deprecating. Funny, isn't it, how two opposites ended up so much alike? Both suffered. Both ended up disconnected and alone.

That isn't supposed to be what happens, is it? We all think we understand how low self-esteem can make us miserable and interfere with our relationships with others. But can an overly high self esteem produce similar problems of adjustment? And if so, what happens to the idea that the cure for whatever ails our youth is to raise their self-esteem? We may not want our kids to be like Marian, but do we really want them to be like Don?

These questions point to some of the profound problems in the way many of us have been led to think about self-esteem. The simplistic view that underlies so much of the self-esteem movement can't account for people like Don. It can't explain why Marian and Don end up in such similar straits. And it can't tell us what to do to raise and educate children who have a healthy attitude about themselves, fulfilling relationships with others, and a constructive engagement with life.

That's why we need a better way to think about self-esteem. And, as the example of Don shows, we also need to question whether high self-esteem is the bedrock of good adjustment, the be-all and end-all that we've been told it is.

Let's begin by asking what self-esteem really is. Then we'll explore some of the myths that have been propagated about self-esteem and why those myths are pernicious for how we think about our children. Next, we'll consider self-esteem from a new and more promising vantage point, one that explains both the anomalies in popular thinking about self-esteem and what we actually observe in our kids. With this perspective in mind, we can begin to see how the notion of acceptance provides a much better goal for our children to embrace.

WHAT EXACTLY IS SELF-ESTEEM?

Just exactly what are the self-esteem marketers selling? What is self-esteem and how can we explain it?

Synonyms for "self-esteem" readily come to mind: self-concept, self-regard, pride, self-image, self-importance, self-appreciation, self-ideal, self-worth, self-confidence. These terms imply a global evaluation of oneself: I am a good (or worthy or special) person. Or not. That's the way self-esteem traffickers describe self-esteem, as an all-encompassing judgment that we should support in our kids by constantly telling them how uniquely special they are. Yet that isn't the way self-esteem "works."

If we examine self-esteem more closely, we can see that it involves three components:

- an *observation or perception* of some quality of the self

- an *evaluation* of that quality

- an *emotional reaction* to the evaluation that depends on how much we care about the particular area in our life that we are evaluating

To illustrate, consider Joseph, a high school senior who worked as a clerk in a shoe store. He was quite bright but did poorly in school, barely passing his classes. He was not popular, had no athletic talent, and tended to be a loner. You might assume his self-esteem suffered from his relative lack of accomplishments, but you'd be wrong. Joseph felt great about himself and his life. He was an avid guitar player. He played with a local band every chance he got. Although he made little money playing his guitar, he considered himself a successful musician. He valued and enjoyed playing almost any gig that came his way. Joseph didn't attach emotional significance to academic success, athletic ability, or social pursuits. Thus, he felt great about himself, his life, and his ambitions.

Notice how Joseph's self-worth was based on the three components of self-esteem just described. First, he observed himself: He wasn't much of a student or an athlete, let alone a stud, but he enjoyed and cared about music. Next, he evaluated his musical talent in comparison to others'. Joseph believed he was a good musician, good enough to feel a lot of satisfaction in performing whether he made much money at it or not. Finally, the emotional component: Whereas Joseph was indifferent about a lot of things, he cared about musical talent above all else. Therefore, he felt good about himself. Joseph would have said he had high self-esteem.

Or consider Helen, who excelled at her studies in junior high. She was placed in the gifted program and belonged to the debate team. She was a talented athlete and a standout on the soccer team. It would be hard to find a more popular student. You might assume Helen had high self-esteem. You'd be wrong. Helen was a lot like Marian—she believed she was unalluring. She was sure that no boy would ever ask her out. In fact, boys didn't pay much attention to her. Despite her talents and accomplishments, Helen felt lousy about herself. Like Joseph, she based her self-esteem on observation, evaluation, and an emotional reaction. She focused on her attractiveness, judged it inadequate, and was emotionally upset by her judgment because she cared about that aspect of herself intensely.

THREE MYTHS ABOUT SELF-ESTEEM

The third component of self-esteem, emotional reaction, fueled the excitement and passion of the self-esteem movement. No one would care about self-esteem if it didn't generate a lot of feelings. The self-esteem traffickers exploited the public's emotions by peddling the bounty of good feelings to be derived from high self-esteem and issuing dire warnings of the horrors of low self-esteem. Since people have strong feelings about self-esteem, it was easy to be convinced. The movement did not need to rely on data and scientific studies to advance its cause. In the process, the movement also successfully generated a number of beliefs that remain widely accepted today. Specifically, the self-esteem movement has helped promote three myths about self-esteem that have deeply influenced the thinking of parents, teachers, and others who are concerned about kids. Looking at why these ideas are misconceptions will help pave the way for an assault on powerful forces in our culture, forces that have stripped too many of our kids of the values necessary for a productive and fulfilling life.

Myth 1: Self-Esteem Is a Global Rating of One's Total Self

Is the emotional investment in self-esteem made in one grand, sweeping judgment of overall worth? In other words, if you have high self-esteem, do you feel good about every aspect of yourself? In turn, if you have low self-esteem, do you loathe every part of your being? That's how the self-esteem traffickers often describe the way self-esteem works, but a little thought will show that this notion is absurd.

Think back to the examples of Joseph and Helen. Joseph's high self-esteem wasn't based on the delusion that he excelled in every part of life. He knew very well that he wasn't much of an athlete or a student, but that didn't bother him. What mattered to him was his music, and it was his self-evaluation in this area that led to his high self-esteem. By the same token, Helen was popular, a skilled athlete, and an excellent student. She knew all those things about herself, but she still suffered from low self-esteem because of her emotional investment in a single area of her life—namely, her perceived unattractiveness to boys.

Over a hundred years ago, William James presented a more sophisticated view of self-esteem. He suggested that our self-esteem rests on the evaluations we make about specific personal qualities or areas of our lives. In 1890, James wrote, "I, who for the time have staked my all on being a psychologist, am mortified if others know much more psychology than I. But I am contented to wallow in the grossest ignorance of Greek. My deficiencies there give me no sense of personal humiliation at all."[1]

Notice that James's view is consistent with the three-part model of self-esteem that we described a moment ago: self-esteem involves a perception of one or more qualities in ourselves, an evaluation of those qualities, *and* an emotional investment in the evaluations we make. True, the resulting feeling is a global one: Joseph felt good about himself, and Helen felt bad about herself. But that global feeling rests on specific perceptions and evaluations that we care about, not on an undifferentiated judgment that "I'm terrific in every way" or "I'm hopeless in every way."

Myth 2: The More Self-Esteem, the Better

The usual approach to self-esteem is simplistic in another way as well. It assumes that, if self-esteem is a good thing, then more of it is always better. For example, Nathaniel Branden describes self-esteem as a fundamental human need, analogous to good health; one can never have too much. Yet most of us recognize that there is such a thing as conceit and arrogance. In other words, self-esteem isn't like good health in the sense that more is always better. How, then, do self-esteem promoters rationalize this myth?

This issue is a real problem for people like Branden, who are committed to the idea that high self-esteem is an unqualified good. Branden has responded with a truly ingenious solution. In order to propose you can never have too much self-esteem, Branden turns what most people would call excessive self-esteem on its head. He has decided that a feeling of superiority over others, boastfulness, arrogance, and self-glorification all represent *inadequate* self-esteem "rather than, as some people imagine, too high a level of self-esteem."[2] If this seems illogical to you, it should. It is difficult to juxtapose boastfulness, arrogance, and self-glorification with Branden's description of low self-esteem, which includes lack of confidence, self-deprecation, and feelings of worthlessness. Are we really to believe that we should help conceited, self-absorbed boors raise their withered self-esteem? Is that the cure for people like Don, who felt so superior to others that when they rejected him he could respond only with bafflement and anger? Logic aside, no research exists to support this notion.

While Branden seems to say that excessively high self-esteem is actually a masquerade for low self-esteem, other self-esteem promoters have taken a different angle. They contend that overly high self-esteem rests on mistaken, excessively positive ideas about oneself. Yet, remarkably, they have argued this self-delusion is a good thing.

This was the tack taken in the late 1980s by Dr. Shelley Taylor and Dr. Jonathan Brown. They stunned the mental health field by asserting that various types of positive illusions and self-enhancement (essentially overly high self-esteem) actually *improve* mental health. Taylor and Brown purported that distortions of reality—believing things are better than they really are—actually help people. In other words, thinking you are better than you really are is good for you.

Taylor and Brown actually managed to amass some data and quite a bit of pseudo-logic to support their argument that unrealistically positive self-evaluations contribute to well-being. They suggested that individuals who are stuck on themselves are more able to care about others and to engage in productive work. In fact, they said, these people are generally happier and more contented than the rest of us.[3] Incredibly, more than a few academic types bought their cleverly contrived arguments.

Pretentiousness and conceit were in. Some proponents of this perspective even suggested that we start teaching depressed patients to distort reality and deny negative but realistic information about themselves. In other words, depressed persons should pretend that everything about their lives is fine, even if it isn't. What depressed people need to learn is to *distort* their views of themselves and others so that they will feel better— never mind that their original perceptions were accurate. Following the publication of Dr. Taylor's popular book, *Positive Illusions: Creative Self-Deception and the Healthy Mind,* a radio show picked up on her ideas. "Feeling blue? Doctors now say you can lie yourself into happiness."[4]

Thankfully, the prevailing tide of opinion soon began to turn. Thoughtful, comprehensive, and scathing reviews of the positive self-illusions perspective emerged. And a group of researchers turned the logic of valuing positive illusions into mulch.[5] For example, Drs. Taylor and Brown stated that people who demonstrate overly positive illusions about themselves also report feeling more psychologically healthy than people who hold realistic self-views. However, most of the studies they depended on for this conclusion based "psychological health" on self-report alone. In other words, they asked people to say if they were psychologically healthy or not. This choice for how to assess psychological health is a problem. Ask people who see themselves more positively than justified by reality whether they have emotional problems. Obviously, they will tell you no, they feel fine. In the trade, we call this denial. Other researchers have established that possessing positive illusions is not healthy.

For example, Dr. Jonathan Shedler and colleagues studied a group of people who claimed to be psychologically healthy. They found some of these people were indeed free from emotional distress. And they found another group who self-reported psychological well-being, but who, on closer examination, demonstrated significant emotional problems, covered up by repression and denial. These repressors also had excessive physiological reactions to stress, which could lead to later health problems.[6]

Additional evidence found that "self-enhancement" (overly positive self-evaluation) actually has a *negative* impact on psychological adjustment. A variety of such studies convincingly demonstrated what should have been obvious all along: Most of us don't like people who think too highly of themselves. As a result, "self-enhancers" have poor relationships, much like Don, who found himself alone after years of self-focused bragging and lack of concern for others.[7]

Myth 3: Low Self-Esteem Is the Cause of Everything That Ails Us

We've already touched on the third myth about self-esteem in Chapter 1. It is the idea that low self-esteem is not only a bad thing, but the primary cause of every problem we observe in our children, from shoplifting to poor academic performance to violence. It follows that the solution to all these problems is to raise children's self-esteem. Thus, we should teach children they are special, wonderful, and unique in every way, no matter what their actual qualities or accomplishments are. That's the "cure" that follows from the diagnosis that low self-esteem is at the root of virtually every problem of adjustment.

This myth is so pernicious, and so entrenched, that we'll be dissecting it further in the chapters to come as we explore the relationship of self-esteem to a variety of issues and problems. Along the way we'll discover not only the emptiness of this myth, but also that the supposed cure—raise self-esteem at all costs—is worse than the "disease."

CONSEQUENCES OF THE THREE MYTHS

The three myths about self-esteem are important because, rolled up together, they lead to advice that is not only misguided but toxic. Thus, the self-esteem traffickers deceive you into buying the idea that you can't get too much of their product. Even those who appear to already possess an exorbitant amount of self-esteem need more. This fuzzy logic is no accident. It allows the wholesale, unrestrained marketing of the self-esteem movement. The movement comes with no FDA warning label stating that too much self-esteem could be harmful to your health.

So, books, parenting classes, and media preach self-esteem above all else; they urge us to tell children they are wonderful no matter what. As a result, children receive praise and compliments for everything they do. Never mind whether the self-evaluations we encourage are unrealistic or false. Never mind that, in reality, people's self-esteem rests on specific evaluations of their personal qualities, not fuzzy, global evaluations of their total self. Never mind that the whole proposition that low self-esteem is the primary cause of every observed problem is a doctrine, not a fact.

By the same token, challenging children is frowned on because of the danger of frustration or failure. It won't do to put too much pressure on kids; they must, above all else, feel good about themselves. At least that's what many of the entrepreneurs say. Let's take a look at some of their advice.

From *The 10 Greatest Gifts I Give My Children,* by Steven Vannoy:

> *If I could give my child no other gift in the world, my top choice would be self-esteem. Without it, we wither. With it, we thrive. When you have high self-esteem, you are nearly invincible.*[8]

This author gives some good advice about focusing on children's strengths instead of weaknesses. But some of what he says could easily lead to a false, inflated self-esteem. For example, he suggests asking your children these questions at the dinner table:

- What did you do better today than you've ever done before?

- What did you do today that let you know how special you are?[9]

Come on. How many days do you do anything at all that's better than you've ever done before? How often do you do something that demonstrates how "special" you are? You know that's not what life is really like. But when you ask kids questions like these, they will come up with something, real or made up. They might believe what they tell us, or they might not. If they do believe it, we're encouraging them to accept fictions about themselves and to feel superior to others. If they don't believe it, we're encouraging them to tell *us* fictions while meanwhile they feel bad because at some level they know that their claims to being "special" rest on sand. Either way, the ironic result is that by telling kids they have to be special to be okay, we're encouraging either a false self-regard or a feeling of coming up short of our expectations. *That's what comes of putting positive illusions ahead of accurate self-perception.*

Furthermore, the self-esteem movement makes parenting more complicated than it needs to be. It gets people to question their own good sense. For instance, the self-esteem traffickers often give detailed prescriptions for what to say to your kids and how to say it. In her book, *Self-Esteem: A Family Affair,* Jean Clarke advises, "Telling an older child what a high jumper he is or telling the baby he can yell louder than anybody else can be a self-esteem–building message if the message is delivered in an admiring tone."[10] Praise a child for jumping or a baby for yelling? That's like praising them for breathing. Praising ordinary behavior saps praise of its meaning and value. How can a child later appreciate real accomplishments that are followed by the same messages?

Clarke also tells parents how to discipline. In doing so, she robs parents of their basic instincts. Everyone tells children not to do things, and sometimes it needs to be said sharply. But not according to Clarke. She tells us, "Saying, 'Stop that!' or 'Don't do that!' or 'Not that way!' does not invite a child to have positive self-esteem."[11] To preserve our children's self-esteem, Clarke declares, *all* discipline messages should come complete with thorough explanations. However, most of the time when parents say no, their kids know very well why. After all, what kinds of things do parents tell their kids not to do? "Don't run into the street," "Don't hit your sister," "Don't play with matches," "Don't scream so loud."

This is not to deny that sometimes explaining the "why" of things to kids is a good idea. The point is that making something like this notion of discipline into a commandment of parenting *on the grounds that it serves kids' self-esteem* is plainly silly. Worse, it communicates the wrong message—not that there are good reasons to do some things and to refrain from others, but rather that what *really* matters is how self-important our kids feel, whether they deserve to or not.

The ultimate result of the self-esteem myths—with their relentless promotion on radio, morning television, prime time talk shows, and even the nightly news—is that too many parents start to think they aren't measuring up to the gold standard of self-esteem–based parenting. Thus, they lose confidence in their abilities and judgments, their common sense and parental instincts. It's pretty intimidating for most people to hear low self-esteem blamed for every imaginable social ailment, from teenage pregnancy to school dropout rates. And, with the message coming from supposed experts, it becomes all too plausible that our mission must be to raise our kids' positive feelings about themselves, despite our misgivings about whether positive illusions are a good thing or whether people should feel good about themselves in every possible way.

It's time to restore some common sense to our thinking about these issues. To do that, we need a better and more accurate model of self-esteem that doesn't fall prey to the myths we've described. Let's now consider such a model.

A NEW PERSPECTIVE ON SELF-ESTEEM

Everyone who knows little Gerald says he's honest. When Gerald finds lunch money dropped on the playground, he promptly returns it to the teacher. He dutifully informs his teacher when other kids cheat, lie, steal, or cut in line. He also gives his undiluted opinion when asked about anything. He lets his older sister know when he thinks she looks ugly before she leaves on a date. And when Aunt Ruth asks if he likes her peach cobbler, he forthrightly declares, "It stinks!" Is it possible to be *too* honest?

At age 15, Cynthia is one of the most dependable kids we've ever known. She is always on time, is a reliable baby-sitter, gets straight A's in school, and sings in the church choir. Terrific, right? But Cynthia also obsesses about doing everything right and fulfilling every single obligation. One evening, the church choir had a performance scheduled at the same time her debate team had a tournament. Cynthia couldn't stand the prospect of disappointing anyone. Her parents found her sobbing in her room, unable to decide what to do. Is it possible to be *too* dependable?

Great qualities, honesty and dependability. Everyone knows the problems caused by dishonesty or undependability, and it seems as though you couldn't have too much of their opposites. That's exactly the kind of argument we hear in regard to self-esteem: You can't have too much. Yet other kids hated Gerald for his punctilious honesty and called him a snitch. Even Aunt Ruth had a hard time liking him. Cynthia came unglued when trying to balance her life. She came to our office for treatment of an anxiety disorder.

Self-esteem, honesty, dependability, courage, generosity, and trust all sound like things to strive for. However, more is not always better. Something happens when personal qualities become extreme. An excess of courage makes us rash; an excess of generosity makes us a mark for the unscrupulous; an excess of trust makes us dupes. Even good qualities can often turn into bad ones. Like all these other qualities, self-esteem lies on a continuum, from low to high. We don't deny that you can have too little self-esteem. A person with extremely low self-esteem may indeed wallow in self-loathing. However, that doesn't mean that more is always better. Those with excessively high self-esteem may indulge in disgusting delusions of grandeur. Both extremes create problems.

Moreover, although self-esteem lies along a continuum, in our view that continuum doesn't travel along a straight line, from low to high. Rather, we conceptualize the self-esteem continuum as nonlinear, almost circular. As you can see in Figure 2, the

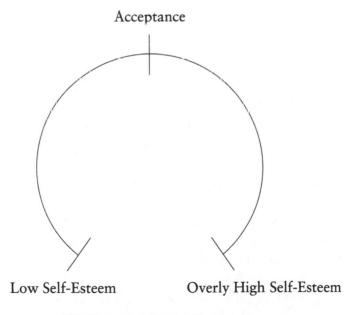

FIGURE 2   The Self-Esteem Continuum

extremes approach each other and nearly converge. In fact, extremely low and extremely high self-esteem are closer to each other than to the center point. That's because, as you will see, the extremes of self-esteem have some surprising similarities.[12]

The Similarities of Self-Esteem Extremes

Although we contend that both self-esteem extremes have unexpected commonalities, we're not endorsing Nathaniel Branden's claim that overly high self-esteem is actually low self-esteem. We think the differences are obvious. Grandiosity isn't the same as inadequacy, and conceit doesn't look like self-degradation. That's absurd. Nevertheless, there are striking similarities in the effects of the self-esteem extremes.

For example, people with overly high or low self-esteem look similar in the way they *deal with feedback*. Both rigidly distort information they receive from others. We opened this chapter with a description of Marian, the 16-year-old who thought she'd never attract a guy. As you may recall, she could barely believe that Brandon really wanted to ask her out. Whenever guys flirted with her, she interpreted their attention as at best benign, and at worst cruel, teasing. Her low self-esteem colored her view of anyone's possible interest in her. She responded to advances with aloofness and even irritation. Boys learned to see her as rather strange.

By contrast, Don, the good-looking football player, viewed himself as God's gift to women. He assumed all of his dates wanted sexual intimacy with him. He found himself confused when one young woman resisted his moves. She said no. Don truly believed in his irresistibility; therefore, "no" meant "yes" to Don. He didn't stop; he kept pushing for more. Don was shocked when the girl burst into tears, slapped him sharply in the face, and ran out of his car.

Why do people at the extremes of self-esteem distort or even ignore feedback? Because our self-views are powerful filters of incoming information.[13] In effect, we see the world through the glasses of our self-views, and the result can be either a clear picture of the world or a distorted one. People whose self-views are largely accurate perceive feedback for what it is. In contrast, Marian's negative self-view blocked her from accepting a basic, sincere show of interest, and Don's inflated self-view prevented him from understanding the meaning of "no." Self-views work like that, by letting in information that is consistent with the self-perception and rejecting information that contradicts it.

Not only do our self-views filter what gets in; they also affect what we remember.[14] For example, Don told a teammate about his disastrous date. His version of the story was that the girl came on to him and, for no reason, abruptly changed her mind. He concluded the girl must have been, in his words, "on her period." Thus, Don's excessively high self-esteem both filtered out negative information about his behavior and interfered with his recall of events. Such bias in information processing and recall makes self-views very hard to change.

Social psychologists have verified that extreme self-views function in this manner. For example, in one study, researchers measured the self-esteem of college students. The researchers presented students with a long list of adjectives that supposedly described their unique personalities. In reality, all the students were given the same list to review. The researchers used words like "friendly," "rude," "kind," "nervous," "likable," and "disagreeable." Later, they asked the students to remember as many adjectives as they could. Those with low self-esteem more often remembered negative adjectives and those with high self-esteem were more likely to remember positive adjectives, even though negative and positive adjectives appeared in the same proportion on the lists presented to both groups.[15]

A further similarity between those with extremely high or extremely low self-esteem is that both demonstrate *hypervigilance to criticism*. Those with low self-esteem are extremely hurt by criticism, whereas those with inflated self-esteem usually respond to criticism—when they can't just filter it out—with defensiveness or anger. In other words, both groups possess a kind of brittleness and rigidity. They have little capacity for flexibly responding to the demands of the world. When stressed, they reflexively respond with excessive emotion; it's just that they each bring different emotions to the table. Under conditions of threat, criticism, or challenge, those with low self-esteem usually feel sad, guilty, anxious, and depressed, while those with puffed-up self-esteem experience tension, hostility, and anger.

Finally, both groups *struggle to find good friendships*. Intimate relationships, as well as casual relationships, flounder. People with low self-esteem are very anxious and insecure in their close relationships, whereas those with high self-esteem tend to have superficial, distant relationships. As Don and Marian illustrate, the similarity of self-esteem extremes explains how two young people with such "opposite" self-esteem could both end up lonely and rejected.[16]

At the root of these similarities between low and excessively high self-esteem is *self-absorption*. This exorbitant self-focus causes people with either low or overly high self-esteem to ruminate about how they stand in relation to others. In short, they both suffer from self-centeredness. People with either low or overly high self-esteem are alike in spending lots of time thinking about their accomplishments or lack thereof, or in dwelling on their appearance, their possessions, or their skills. Whether they obsess about having too much of these things or too little, both are obsessed with themselves.

Just how harmful is self-absorption? Far more than you might think. Dr. Rick Ingram reviewed the numerous independent investigations concerning self-focused attention and emotional problems. He found heightened *self-absorption is associated with depression, anxiety, alcohol abuse, anger, vulnerability to unpleasant feelings, psychopathy, and mania*.[17] The term "associated" indicates correlations, or relationships, between variables rather than direct causation. Astute readers may recall that correlation studies cannot establish causation. Are we doing what we accused the self-esteem movement of doing? That is, are we relying exclusively on correlational studies to make our case?

Although correlational studies provide a starting point, the research on self-absorption goes further. For example, one predictive study measured the tendency of college students to ruminate about (focus on) themselves. Later, an earthquake occurred. The investigators went back to the students they'd previously assessed. They found that students who had earlier exhibited self-focused rumination, had developed significantly higher levels of depression right after the earthquake, as well as almost two months later.[18] Dr. Nolen-Hoeksema reviewed a large number of other longitudinal, predictive studies that collectively demonstrated that those who self-ruminate have higher levels of depressive and anxious symptoms over time than those who do not engage in so much self-focus.[19]

Of course, the most definitive type of research involves experimental manipulation of variables. Quite a few studies have shown that increasing subjects' self-focus causes increases in depressive and anxious feelings as well as reduced ability to solve problems. How did the experimenters induce increased self-focus? They did so in various ways, such as asking subjects to spend eight minutes reflecting about their current personal characteristics and physical and emotional states. Other experimenters had participants look at themselves in a mirror or write essays with many references to the self. All of these methods of increasing self-focus caused negative feelings to intensify and/or lowered problem-solving ability.[20] *You will see in later chapters how these experimental inductions of self-focus have an eerie similarity to exercises found in many popular books on raising self-esteem.*[21]

The intense focus on self sculpts the parallel problems inherent with high and low self-esteem. Once we realize this, we can see how a superficial, mindless promotion of self-esteem simply exacerbates the underlying cause of the problems experienced by those with low self-esteem *and* those with excessive self-admiration. What happens when we bombard our kids with the message of how important it is to feel wonderful about themselves, whether deserved or not? It's not just that we puff up the ones who are prone to conceit and arrogance. It's also the wrong solution for the kids whose self-esteem is low. Think about the effects of making self-esteem all-important for kids who don't think they belong at the top of the totem pole, who feel they don't measure up to the standard of feeling wonderful about themselves all the time. It isn't much of a stretch to think they feel even *worse* about themselves for failing to achieve the high self-esteem so valued by textbooks, teachers, and parents. After all, there must be something wrong with them when they try to fill out those self-esteem exercises and struggle to come up with answers to questions like "What I like about me."

Excessively High Self-Esteem and Narcissism

Although the consequences of extreme self-esteem run parallel in many ways, they also diverge. In particular, the self-esteem traffickers have ignored the perils of overly high self-esteem, and for good reason. What parent would ever buy the book *Lower Your Child's Self-Esteem in Ten Days?* Yet, in many cases, that's exactly what needs to happen.

The ancient Greeks had a story that illustrates what we mean. In Greek mythology, Narcissus was a strikingly handsome young man who thought quite highly of himself. Today, we would call him conceited. Beautiful women courted him, and he met them with haughty rejection. He considered himself too good for them. Among his admirers was the nymph Echo. Narcissus cruelly rejected her as well. The gods punished him by condemning him to contemplate his own beauty reflected in a pond. Narcissus lovingly watched his reflection until he wasted away and died.

From this story comes the modern concept of narcissism. A narcissistic personality demonstrates a broad pattern of grandiosity, an unusual desire for admiration, and a lack of empathy for others. Such persons are excessively preoccupied with themselves. They consider themselves superior human beings, special and unique. Their needs always come first. They feel entitled to unreasonably favorable treatment and often take advantage of others. They believe that others envy them, but they can be extremely jealous themselves. They demand control and can be arrogant and haughty.[22]

Of course, there are degrees of narcissism, but at the core, narcissism is self-esteem gone awry. Narcissism is the hazard encountered by the "self-enhancers" we referred to earlier. Remember Drs. Taylor and Brown, who recommended that an overly positive self-image is a good thing, that it helps people form better relationships with others? In reality, the reverse is true. For example, in one study researchers asked college students to rate their own personalities. Then professionals and friends who knew the students also rated them. One group of students—the self-enhancers—thought better of themselves than either their friends or the professionals did. Friends of the men in this group described them as hostile, unable to delay gratification, and condescending. Basically, these men acted like angry, selfish jerks. Friends depicted self-enhancing women as hostile, self defeating, and defensive. Don't forget, the people who rated these folks were their friends.

Another related study asked college students to engage in a debate. Observers described the self-enhancing men as speaking rapidly, interrupting, bragging, and showing hostility. Self-enhancing women were described as irritable, seeking reassurance, and socially awkward. Clearly, self-enhancement, which is roughly equivalent to our notion of overly high self-esteem, doesn't lead to good mental health. It doesn't win friends and influence people.

These data support common sense. People are far better off if they have *accurate* self-perceptions that can acknowledge and accept inevitable human foibles and frailties. As the research team that conducted the above two studies put it:

> *One can then still like oneself and find rewarding social validation. Driven, suppressive, narcissistic claims of self-perfection, as our findings indicate, do not dispose one toward social adaptations that warrant being called mentally healthy.*[23]

In other words, the old virtues of modesty and humility are not only good things, but also good for you. But, you might object, surely people who appear extremely confident, competent, and socially skillful gain by believing fully in their capacities, even if they think more highly of themselves than justified by reality. Don't others look up to them, in awe of their unshakable conviction in their own self-worth? Perhaps you've even known people like this and thought well of them simply because they thought so well of themselves.

The fact is, recent studies suggest that self-enhancing people do sometimes make positive early impressions. At a first meeting, others often see them as particularly well-adjusted, agreeable, and competent. Predictably, however, as others get to know them better over time, reality sets in. People start to view self-enhancers more as the arrogant, egotistical people they really are. Thus, the latest findings support the idea that self-enhancers are indeed seen negatively—it just takes a while sometimes.[24]

For instance, when Sherry transferred to Taylor Middle School, most of the seventh-grade class took immediate notice. Sherry was striking, well dressed, and socially skillful. Everyone wanted to be her friend, and all the guys wanted to take her out. Her lunch table was crowded with admirers. She talked about her accomplishments and conquests at her former school, and she amused her classmates with stories and anecdotes. After a few months, however, her popularity waned.

Rarely did she show interest in others, and her temper flared at any slight, whether real or imagined. One day, Jody confronted Sherry about exaggerating her supposed conquest of a high school boy. Sherry reacted with fury and threw her soda in Jody's face. Classmates were shocked at Sherry's brazen behavior. Eventually, Sherry's lunch table crowd thinned out.

Ultimately, then, people see through narcissists. In the end, self-enhancers like Don, the young man we described at the start of this chapter, lose friends and popularity. Yet, as was true of Don, they persist in their actions even in the face of rejection. Why? Because they can't put themselves in other people's shoes. They truly have no idea how they affect others. They rarely spend much time actively listening and learning about someone else. Instead, they work to defend themselves against feared challenges and rejection. Ever vigilant for possible assaults on their self-esteem, narcissists respond with tension and rage.

You see, the narcissistic self-esteem balloon is filled too full. It could burst at the slightest touch. At some level, narcissists know that, so they aren't about to let people get too close. The balloon of their self-esteem must be protected at all costs. That's why the narcissist lashes out when criticized, whether with rage, angry words, sullen silence, or physical aggression. Most of us, when faced with disappointment or criticism, react with sadness or varying degrees of discomfort, but narcissists and those with overly positive self-esteem get mad.

When we pump our kids up with self-esteem messages of hollow praise, we risk creating little narcissists. Teaching kids to repeat affirmations such as "I like me" and "I am special" is not a benign exercise. These messages contain a real danger. They fill the self-esteem balloon with untruths and distorted expectations—and those untruths and distortions must then be defended. As we'll discuss in the chapters to come, kids with overly high self-esteem may protect their precious self-image through conspicuous consumption: designer clothes or the latest electronic gizmos. They may obsess over achievement to an un-healthy degree, driven to perfectionism. Some of these kids may preoccupy themselves with appearance, investing in body pierc-ing, cosmetic surgery, and diets. When they don't get what they want, they may resort to aggression. And if that doesn't work, they may succumb to depression.

This is the hidden danger lurking in reckless promotion of self-esteem. At the same time, let's not forget that *both* self-esteem extremes are problematic. An overinflated balloon may be in constant danger of bursting, but a balloon with no air is useless. So extremely low self-esteem causes problems, too, and, as we've already suggested, some of those problems resem-ble those associated with overly high self-esteem. Children with low self-esteem generally feel worthless. They feel unimportant and less deserving than others. Often they are shy and timid. They lack confidence and experience depression more often than other kids. Sometimes, to escape this gloomy view of themselves, children with low self-esteem will also seek solace in conspicuous consumption. Like those with overly high self-esteem, they may obsess over achievement to an unhealthy de-gree and be driven to perfectionism. Although most kids with extremely low self-esteem remain mired in their self-loathing, a few undoubtedly seek to escape those feelings. However, they choose a treacherous escape route by trying too hard. They crave a perfect body and end up anorexic. Or they ache to achieve status through hollow possessions. In effect, they reach for an overly high self-esteem, and, in promoting the culture of narcissism, we simply speed them on their way.

Keep in mind our model of self-esteem that shows the end points tending to converge. What the extremes of self-esteem have in common is an excessive preoccupation with self. We contend that the self-esteem movement has likely increased self-absorption in our kids. This intense focus on the self has dis-tracted children from the kind of meaningful life satisfaction and fulfillment that require self-control, values, balance, and connectedness with others. The simplistic pursuit of self-esteem has kidnapped the soul of a generation.

CHANGING THE FOCUS: FROM SELF-ESTEEM TO ACCEPTANCE

Not too long ago, we were sitting in the stands half-watching warm-ups for a high school soccer tournament. The schools had long been fierce rivals, and students and parents rapidly filled the stands. Each team formed a close circle, getting last-minute instructions from the coach. Low voices erupted into cheers as athletes ran out to the field.

The game began. The sounds of players and coaches shouting encouragement and bawling their frustration at each other competed with the cheers and groans from the stands. The noise made it hard to talk, and the intensity of the contest was contagious.

It was easy to see that the game was about much more than the joy of exercise or having fun. Although there was no bonus for the winner or fine for the loser, the stakes of winning seemed high for every player on the field. Is it too much to say that, as much as anything else, the kids were playing for the sake of their self-esteem?

As the game continued scoreless, Dr. Elliott pointed at a curly-haired baby, standing wide-legged on a blanket next to the stands. The toddler, probably just about a year old, was oblivious to the competition on the field. His face was intense with concentration. He looked forward at some unobservable goal and took two wobbling steps. His expression changed to joy and delight, and he lost his balance. Over he toppled and then, with the same determination, pulled himself up, ready to begin anew.

Loud cheers snapped our focus back to the game. Our team had a shot at the goal and finally scored. When we looked back at the baby, his parents beamed as he staggered toward them.

We realized that the juxtaposition of the game and the infant told us a lot about self-esteem. The soccer players were keenly concerned with their performance. When a player missed a pass that ended up in his opponent's control, his face filled with anguish and self-loathing. Sometimes the coach reinforced these feelings with harsh criticism. At times of glory, a great pass or a save, pure joy lit up a player's face. To a significant degree, the game wasn't just about the pleasure of exercising and developing skills. It was about oneself and how one stacked up against others.

When the game was over, the losers weren't about to celebrate how much fun they had had playing. They would be crestfallen (and so would many of their parents). As we said earlier, self-esteem generates powerful feelings.

Our baby had no such concerns. Happily and clumsily, he toddled about—no doubt the worst walker around that day. He couldn't run or dance intricate steps around a soccer ball. He could barely ambulate, and he certainly didn't evaluate his walking. But he wasn't thinking about his performance, and still less was he comparing it to anyone else's. He wasn't embarrassed about falling down. He just kept on going. No self-reflection, just pure behaving. The joy on his face was the reflection of accomplishment and mastery without self-evaluation. He could experience success and failure without concern for his worth. He was absorbed by living and learning, not with himself.

Our toddler demonstrated what we call acceptance. Acceptance is a state that allows both positive and negative qualities without self-aggrandizement or degradation. *It is either an innocent or an enlightened path away from obsession and focus on the self.* Acceptance lies at the top of our circular self-esteem model, far removed from the self-absorbed extremes.

As the following chapters demonstrate, self-absorption has cost us too much. It has bred greed, aggression and violence, declining standards, frantic "drivenness," eating disorders, and preoccupation with shallow status symbols. *Both low self-esteem and overly high self-esteem represent the antithesis of humility.* We call for the abandonment of a preoccupation with self-esteem and the self-absorption that a focus on self-esteem promotes. We ask for a return to the wisdom and grace of acceptance and humility.

CHAPTER 3

MIRROR, MIRROR ON THE WALL: SELF-ESTEEM AND OBSESSION WITH APPEARANCE

MICHAEL'S SKIN LOOKED GRAY. HE WAS EXHAUSTED, COLD, AND weak, His slowed heart rate and low blood pressure made the simple act of standing a chore. He'd lost 45 pounds in the past few months. Dry, damaged hair fell out in clumps each time he tried to comb it.

Teams of specialists gathered to treat Michael. Despite desperate measures, Michael died of cardiac arrest. He was only 15 years old.

Michael did not die from cancer, AIDS, or some exotic virus; he died because of his diet. During his last months, he scrupulously avoided consuming any fat. He dreaded the idea of corroding his arteries and dying of a heart attack. So he ate thin slices of fat-free lunch meat, drank water, and completed his diet with pita bread. No fat or plaque lined the walls of his arteries. As a result of his obsession, Michael starved to death; the muscles in his heart gave out.

Michael suffered from anorexia nervosa, an eating disorder characterized by an abnormal fear of becoming obese, a distorted self-image, a persistent unwillingness to eat, and severe weight loss. Ironically, anorexia nervosa caused the very thing Michael feared the most: cardiac arrest.[1]

For 16-year-old Kimberly, the feelings began shortly after a chemistry quiz. Kimberly fought hard to resist, but once her defenses weakened, thoughts of binging overwhelmed her. She felt anxious and empty, and she needed to fill the void. Unable to wait a second longer, she bought three candy bars at a vending machine. While driving, Kimberly frantically shoved the candy into her mouth. Her anticipation and excitement mounted when she stopped her car at a local market. Quickly pushing her cart through the aisles, she tossed in four rolls of refrigerated cookie dough, two containers of fudge brownie ice cream, and a large bag of chips. The clerk smiled and remarked that Kimberly must be preparing for a party. She was.

At home, Kimberly turned on the oven and opened the package of cookie dough. The chips were already half-eaten by the time she put the first batch into the oven. She needed two rolls of dough to fill one cookie sheet because she ate every other slice. Craving still more, she ravenously tore open the ice cream. Ritualistically, she ate two chips, then one spoonful of ice cream, followed by a slice of cookie dough. When the oven timer buzzed, her distended stomach ached. The discomfort turned to shame and despair. She'd lost control. Her parents would find out if she didn't hide the evidence, so she rapidly finished the ice cream and choked down the hot cookies.

Depression, sickness, and guilt accompanied Kimberly to the bathroom. Kneeling in front of the toilet, she jammed her finger down her throat. Her body reflexively responded and puked again and again, until green bile streaked the bowl. Soon dry heaves ceased, and only tears streamed down her red, swollen face. It was over—until the next time.

Like Michael, Kimberly suffered from an eating disorder. The disorder that afflicted Kimberly, called bulimia, is characterized by episodic binge eating followed by feelings of guilt, depression, and self-condemnation.

Sadly, Michael's and Kimberly's stories are all too common. Look around, and you'll see evidence of a plague of eating disorders among our youth. Consider Sia and Shane Barbi (aka the Barbi twins), who rose to fame when they appeared on the cover of two issues of *Playboy* magazine. Their eating problems started with binging on Girl Scout cookies. They yearned to indulge in whatever they wanted without getting fat. They thought of a solution: starvation, obsessive exercise, and laxatives. It worked for a while, but Sia relentlessly increased her laxative doses and eventually overdosed on almost 100 tablets. The doctor told her she would surely die if she continued consuming excessive laxatives. Today, the twins write and speak about eating disorders, hoping to dissuade others from the ravages of the disease.[2]

There seems to be no limit to the lengths some young people will go to in their obsession with body image, especially weight. And once eating disorders start, they seem to spread like the flu. At one college in spring 1996, plastic Baggies started to disappear from a sorority house kitchen. The sorority's president launched an investigation that ended with a shocking finding. Hundreds of sandwich bags filled with vomit lay hidden in a dark basement bathroom. Not all of the vomit ended up in Baggies. Incredibly, many gallons of stomach acid contained in the vomit eroded the building's pipes, which had to be replaced. Most of the 45 members obsessed about their weight and competed to see who among them could consume the fewest calories.[3]

What lies behind such grotesque, tragic eating disorders? In our view, the epidemic of anorexia nervosa and bulimia, as well as other types of obsessive behavior related to appearance that we will discuss in this chapter, reflects the culture of narcissism that has been fueled by the self-esteem movement. Although there are other contributing causes to specific cases of these disorders, there is no denying that the fetish of self-esteem has persuaded children to contemplate their bodies and appearance more than ever.

Consider the messages promoted by the self-esteem movement. The movement tells children and teens, "Look in the mirror and declare, 'I love me.' Now give yourself a hug." Nathaniel Branden even recommends standing in front of a mirror naked for two minutes twice each day while declaring messages of self-love.[4] Now, those messages may not sound particularly pernicious. In fact, it might seem that they would discourage a preoccupation with appearance. After all, the idea is to tell kids they are beautiful no matter how they look. Branden, for example, intended to increase self-esteem by encouraging folks to accept their bodies. Isn't that a noble goal, to encourage people to feel good about everything and to think of themselves as beautiful independent of their actual appearance? Don't we all want our kids to feel beautiful?

Unfortunately, it isn't that simple. The message not only fails to accomplish its goal; it boomerangs. Just think about staring in the mirror at your naked body twice a day. We don't know about you, but many of us would notice each and every imperfection in our bodies, whether we were instructed to make self-affirmations or not. How do you not notice that blemish on your face, the bulge at your hips, the slight dimpling in the thighs, or the new wrinkles around your eyes? It's just human nature. *The real effect of this kind of advice is to increase people's focus on their bodies, and specifically their appearance.* By encouraging so much self-observation, the "I am beautiful" message leads not to self-acceptance, but to a *self-centered perspective*. And from there it's a short step to narcissistic self-absorption.

Forcing our children's attention to their reflections in the mirror is malignant in other ways as well. In the first place, it focuses attention on a superficial aspect of the self. Sure, the intention might be to raise self-esteem by giving a different meaning to "beautiful" than conventional attractiveness. But let's be real. Beauty is primarily an external, culturally defined concept that is literally skin-deep. So telling children they are and must be beautiful *is a dirty trick* because the message insidiously promotes the supreme importance of beauty and self-admiration.

Furthermore, telling our children they are beautiful regardless of reality doesn't fool them. Children who fall short of the cultural standards of beauty are painfully aware of their deficits. When told to feel good about their looks, they feel defeated. The message only leads them to measure their worth with the yardstick of external image. What you look like takes precedence over who you are. It's a seductive message, not easily resisted—especially when the media fortify the unintended consequences of the self-esteem movement by bombarding young girls with images of thinness and boys with pictures of bulked-up bodies. Finally, in its misguided attempt to keep kids from feeling bad *about anything at all*, the self esteem move ment directs attention away from the community and the family and channels it toward the almighty self. In this way the preoccupation with raising self-esteem, no matter how well-intentioned, leads straight to the obsessive behavior discussed in this chapter. And as you'll see, the costs are frightening.

EATING DISORDERS

We've already mentioned one manifestation of a narcissistic obsession with one's body image—eating disorders. It's little wonder that, as we'll see, eating disorders are increasingly common among kids today, especially—though by no means exclusively—girls. Slick magazines aimed at preteens display emaciated models representing the pinnacle of glamour. The standard model has long, thin legs, boyish hips, and full breasts. She stands 5 feet 7 inches tall, weighs 100 pounds, and wears a size 2.[5] Miss America's weight has plummeted over the past several decades, to the point that health officials worry about the nutritional status of current beauty pageant contestants.[6] Painfully thin pop stars, actresses, and models detail their exercise and diet regimens in magazines and tabloids, and on television. And more than ever our youth look to models as their guide for feminine perfection. In the words of author Jill Zimmerman, "All they want is to feel good about themselves in a sea of doubt and turmoil encouraged by a multi-billion-dollar-a-year beauty industry. And they think the panacea is to look like a supermodel: perfectly thin, tall, sculpted, and commanding—our cultural epitome of feminine success."[7]

Thinness has evolved into the standard by which our young girls and women measure their worth. Yet even a 50-billion-dollar-a-year weight-loss industry has failed miserably at helping people slim down. Americans grow more obese every year. Many wonder how they will ever achieve thinness. A reporter asked supermodel Cindy Crawford, speaking at Princeton University, whether the unrealistic image projected by models causes eating disorders. She replied, "Do you look at pictures of me and want to puke?"[8] She appeared coldly oblivious to ravages inflicted by our cultural obsession with appearance.

As models shrink, the average American woman stands 5 feet, 4 inches tall and weighs 140 pounds. No wonder 75% of American women express dissatisfaction with their bodies. Even more alarming are the effects of this narcissistic self-focus on our children. Fifty percent of 9-year-old girls and, astonishingly, 80% of 10-year-old girls have dieted. Ninety percent of high school girls diet as a part of their lifestyle.[9]

One study found that more than half of all girls between the ages of 9 and 15 either exercised or dieted to lose weight. Another study found half of the girls and about a third of the boys expressed discontent with their weight. These kids were between the ages of 8 and 10! Five percent of those little girls used laxatives or diet pills. Furthermore, young girls form the biggest group of new smokers—and they're doing it in order to curb their appetites.[10]

Findings like these show up in study after study. For example, the Centers for Disease Control surveyed over 16,000 ninth through twelfth graders on their eating habits. They found that about 60% of all female high school students and almost a fourth of the male students were trying to lose weight. Among girls, 7½% either used laxatives or vomited to prevent weight gain; 8% took diet pills.[11]

Dieting and excessive interest in body image easily turn into full-blown eating disorders. Many of those with eating disorders report starting with dieting accompanied by intensified fears of becoming fat. Just how important all this is will become clearer as we explore more closely what eating disorders are, their prevalence among young people, and the terrible costs associated with them.

Anorexia Nervosa and Bulimia Nervosa

The Diagnostic and Statistical Manual of the American Psychiatric Association lists two major categories of eating disorders, anorexia nervosa and bulimia nervosa. We cited examples of them at the start of this chapter. Anorexia nervosa, which killed young Michael, often begins between ages 14 and 18. It comes in two forms, restricting type and binge-eating/purging type. People with the restricting type of anorexia keep weight off by zealous dieting, ardent fasting, or merciless exercise regimes. Those with the binge-eating/purging type of anorexia regularly binge on unthinkable amounts of food followed by purging—abuse of laxatives, diuretics, enemas, or self-induced vomiting.[12]

People with either form of anorexia *weigh less than 85% of normal* for their age, sex, and height. Even though thin, they have an intense fear of being fat or gaining any weight. When anorexics look in the mirror, they don't see their bony, emaciated reflection. Rather, they amazingly contort the reflection into a bloated, overweight body. Where others perceive a sunken-eyed figure resembling a corpse, anorexics genuinely see corpulence.

The most common eating disorder, bulimia nervosa, generally starts in adolescence, as it did for 16-year-old Kimberly. Bulimia nervosa usually begins when a dieter loses control and starts secretive, frenzied binge eating. Bingers can devour as many as 20,000 calories at a time and commonly consume up to a full gallon of ice cream at a single sitting. By the way, 20,000 calories equals about 210 brownies or five layer cakes. As you can imagine, binges cause considerable discomfort, both physical and emotional. People with this type of bulimia (known as nonpurging type) follow the binging with fasting or excessive exercise.

Those with the purging type of bulimia, ashamed of their gluttonous session, turn to laxatives, diuretics, enemas, and/or self-induced vomiting to rid themselves of calories and shame.[13] Bulimics indulge in binging/purging quite frequently, averaging 14 episodes each week. Of those people with purging-type bulimia, 80 to 90% resort to vomiting. They induce vomiting by stimulating the pharynx with a finger or an instrument such as a toothbrush or spoon. After a while, they acquire proficiency at vomiting and can provoke it at will. Unlike anorexics, however, bulimics do not manage to lose weight significantly below the norms. Despite desperate efforts, their weight goals remain elusive. The only difference between purging anorexics and the purging type of bulimic is their weight. Bulimics weigh within the average range for their height or are overweight, whereas anorexics weigh well below the norm.[14]

How Common Are Eating Disorders?

Experts universally agree that recent decades have witnessed an epidemic of eating disorders.[15] In a 50-year study conducted by the prestigious Mayo Clinic in Rochester, Minnesota, the incidence of anorexia nervosa declined in the 1940s and 1950s. Since then, it has increased about 35% for each five-year period.[16] Similarly, a number of studies have demonstrated dramatic increases in bulimia. One renowned authority has concluded, "If anorexia nervosa, once a rare disorder, has increased in prevalence to the point where it is considered not uncommon, the sudden ascendancy of bulimic syndromes seems nothing short of spectacular."[17]

Of particular concern is the prevalence of eating disorders in younger children. Examples are all too easy to find. One 7-year-old weighing 57 pounds complained about her big thighs. She told her doctors if she could only get down to 50 pounds, other kids would like her better. A 10-year-old recently had to use ponytail holders to secure the straps on her bathing suit after losing 10 pounds. Fourteen-year-old Amelia Greenberg's meals consisted of a cracker, a mushroom, and a grape. Due to her malnourished state, her heart had slowed to 31 beats per minute when she arrived at Children's Hospital in Denver, Colorado.[18] Normal pulse for children over 10 and adults is 60 to 100, while a trained athlete usually has a rate between 40 and 60.[19]

The National Association of Anorexia Nervosa and Associated Disorders has reported that 10% of eating disorders begin at the age of 10 years or younger. And a full third begin between the ages of 11 and 15. To disguise their problems, children sneak their meals to the dog under the table and turn up stereos to drown out their vomiting.[20]

Once thought of as exclusively affecting girls, eating disorders increasingly occur in boys. Women have always thought of their bodies in ornamental terms. Throughout time, most cultures have encouraged women to adorn themselves with jewels, clothing, and makeup. In contrast, cultures emphasized what men's and boys' bodies could accomplish in hunting, sports, or other physical endeavors. Thus, most males fostered their self-esteem through their athletic successes and had less concern about their external trappings. But today, in larger numbers than ever, boys seek their self-esteem through appearance. Toned, sleek male models explicitly portray the ideal body. These models often spend five hours a day in the gym and gulp down steroids to achieve their image; not surprisingly, boys fail to measure up in the same way that girls fall short of the ideal defined by supermodels. Males now account for about 10% of reported cases of eating disorders. However, since men and boys conceal their problematic eating behavior and seek help in much smaller numbers than females, current statistics probably fail to capture the full extent of the problem.[21]

Even these distressing statistics on the prevalence of eating disorders grossly underestimate the emerging crisis of dysfunctional eating. Most studies of eating disorders use highly specific, stringent criteria for arriving at diagnoses. For example, to qualify for a diagnosis of bulimia nervosa, a person must binge and consume excessive laxatives, starve, frantically exercise, vomit, or self-administer enemas or diuretics at least twice a week for three consecutive months. If you miss a week, you don't qualify! So, if we look simply at dysfunctional eating, the rates skyrocket. For instance, a full 80% of female college students admit to having binged.[22] One study recently found prevalence for bulimic behaviors, such as vomiting or using laxatives to lose weight, occurring at a rate of 3 to 10 times that of expected rates for a full-blown diagnosis of bulimia.[23] Finally, researchers rarely study certain types of dysfunctional eating, such as that shown by some kids who control their weight by chewing huge amounts of food and then spitting it out.

THE TERRIBLE COSTS OF EATING DISORDERS

Does it really matter if kids seek appearance-based self-esteem through contorted conduct and bizarre diet? Yes, it does matter—a great deal. Eating disorders inflict unimaginable ravages on the body and the soul. People with eating disorders spend close to 90% *of their waking hours* thinking about their weight, food, or hunger. And the obsession never ceases; the fixation even weaves themes of dieting, eating, and food through their dreams.[24]

Food preoccupation produces peculiar eating protocols as well. For example, some kids carefully separate their foods and anxiously guard against allowing one food to make contact with another. Others with eating disorders slowly crumble their food, move their food around in ritualistic fashion, or arrange a plate with one raisin and one Cheerio, each sliced into thirds. These miniscule meals may last for hours.

Ponder for a moment how food preoccupation must interfere with the life of a student. How could students even listen to a lecture on American history with thoughts of eating constantly consuming their attention? And that doesn't even take into account how responding to the press of laxatives or induced vomiting intrudes on study time.

Although bothersome, these effects pale compared to the physical and psychological misery suffered by those with eating disorders. As the example of Michael showed, anorexia nervosa kills. About 10% of those with anorexia eventually die from starvation, cardiac arrest, or suicide. The heart muscles starve and atrophy. Blood pressure drops, blood flow slows, and dangerously slow heart rhythms develop. The starving process depletes certain minerals necessary for maintaining regular electric currents in the heart, such as potassium and calcium. Males have a grimmer prognosis because physicians usually diagnose them later than females.

If anorexics don't die, they may develop hypothermia; that is, their body temperature plunges. Their bodies compensate by growing soft hair known as lanugo on their trunks. The body also tries to protect its major organs such as the brain and heart. It does so by slowing down unessential body processes. For example, females stop menstruating and become sterile, thyroid function diminishes, blood pressure drops, and respiration slows. These in turn result in dry skin, constipation, brittle nails and hair, bone loss, and cold intolerance. Sleep difficulties compound the fatigue caused by starvation. Anorexics can't sleep in part because of discomfort. They lose their natural padding in the form of fat tissue and experience pain when sitting or lying down.

When anorexia afflicts kids and teenagers, the effects magnify and endure. About 90% of adult bone mass forms during puberty. If children and adolescent girls fail to develop strong bones because of reduced estrogen levels and electrolyte imbalances, their bones become porous and easily fractured, hallmarks of osteoporosis. Unfortunately, even after 11 years of recovery, 85% of women who had anorexia as adolescents continue to have low bone density. Among girls who later recover from anorexia, a full quarter of them never regain menstruation and fertility. If menstruation does return, and they succeed in getting pregnant, they have a greater chance of miscarriages. Any offspring they bear are at increased risk for birth defects, low birth weight, and poor health. If the anorexic also purges, health risks proliferate.

Purging, characteristic of both bulimia nervosa and one type of anorexia, kills less often than starvation, but it devastates the body nevertheless. Like starvation, the binge/purge cycle also can upset the balance of electrolytes, causing seizures, fatigue, muscle cramps, and lethal heart rhythms. Gastric acids in vomit slowly eat away tooth enamel and erode gums. These effects do not reverse, and some patients require the extraction of all their teeth. Intemperate vomiting also provokes broken facial blood vessels, rashes, enlarged salivary glands, and swelling around the eyes, feet, and ankles. Some purgers develop calluses on their knuckles from repeated scraping across their teeth as they stick fingers down their throats. When purging continues for years, the tissue in the esophagus, weakened by constant washes of gastric acids, ruptures. And chronic laxative abuse eventually weakens the walls of the rectum to the extent that they protrude through the anus.

Increased eating disorders in children and adolescents raise special concerns because of the chronic nature of these problems. Anorexia nervosa carries a grim prognosis. Overall, studies indicate that three-quarters of *treated* anorexic patients improve over time. However, most continue to struggle with disordered eating, distorted body image, and poor social adjustment. A mere 25% of anorexics manage a full recovery. These results apply only to those who seek treatment; many more fail to do so.[25]

Bulimia has a somewhat more favorable outlook, in that more bulimics recover with treatment. Nevertheless, relapse occurs at a high rate. The first long-term follow-up study of treated bulimics found that 30% of treated patients persisted in binging and purging 10 years later. Further, many bulimics fail to seek treatment.[26]

The costs of eating disorders are enormous due to their chronic nature and wide-ranging physiological and psychological effects. The cost of outpatient treatment and medical monitoring can exceed $100,000 per patient. Inpatient treatment averages more than $30,000 per month, and most patients require repeated inpatient admissions. Families suffer for years, worrying about their loved one's health, emotional stability, and social functioning.[27] The staggering costs and dire consequences of eating disorders should heighten the dismay of anyone who is alarmed at seeing burgeoning numbers of kids taking this path. And the costs to individuals, families, and society make it urgent to understand the forces that compel children to risk their health in the quest to improve their body images.

SELF-ESTEEM AND EATING DISORDERS

Researchers have hypothesized a host of causes for eating disorders. Some evidence, for example, suggests a genetic predisposition for eating disorders. Relatives of patients with anorexia or bulimia are more likely to suffer from an eating disorder. Identical twins are the most likely to share the disorder, followed by fraternal twins, and then other family members, supporting a genetic link. However, what these studies suggest is that genetics may create a heightened vulnerability to eating disorders, not necessarily that genetic inheritance is a direct cause.[28]

Other studies have linked additional biological differences to eating disorders, including hypothalamic-pituitary abnormalities, disordered metabolism, and hormonal abnormalities. However, it is unclear whether these abnormalities help to cause eating disorders or are themselves caused by the disorders. In time, research likely will answer these questions.[29] In any event, genetic and biological factors do not address the question of why eating disorders have been rising.

Aside from biological or genetic factors, some investigators have implicated the interplay of cultural and family influences in the development of eating disorders. Interestingly, eating disorders are not found in countries where food is scarce. Cultures like our own that produce food in abundance also produce an abundance of eating disorders. These cultures usually place more emphasis on thinness and self-esteem through beauty. As we have already noted, the media transmit and reinforce these cultural norms. Still, not everyone in our culture develops an eating disorder, so such influences cannot be singled out as the cause of these disorders.

Family influences provide a more suggestive clue. Families of eating-disordered patients emphasize achievement, looks, social recognition, and weight control more than most families do. In other words, they place great import on obtaining validation from external sources. It's how much money you make and how good you look that counts. At the same time, research has shown that these families place *less* value on intrinsic goals such as being connected to a community and affiliating with others.[30] In short, these families emphasize values that sound a lot like those espoused by the self-esteem movement. They place great importance on looking good, feeling good, and focusing on the *self*.

The self-esteem entrepreneurs have their own explanation of eating disorders. As with countless other problems afflicting youth, they claim that those with eating disorders suffer from low self-esteem. The "cure," therefore, is to improve the self-image of eating disorder victims.

In one sense, the self-esteem movement has a point: Numerous studies support the idea that anorexics and bulimics think quite poorly of themselves. Though a few studies have failed to find a relationship between eating disorders and negative self-evaluation or low self-esteem, the vast majority of research studies do support this connection, and these findings hold up across various racial groups.[31] To take an example, researchers in one study prompted dieting students to feel temporarily worse about themselves. This momentary lowering of self-esteem caused them to increase their focus on and concern about their bodies and weight.[32] These findings would make you think that a critical part of the treatment of patients with eating disorders should include boosting self-esteem.

But before jumping to conclusions, first consider other behavioral, social, and personality risk factors that have been linked to the development of eating disorders. Persons with eating disorders usually have a heightened self-awareness. They spend a lot of time thinking about themselves.[33] Their standards for shape and weight go beyond cultural norms.[34] These attitudes, we maintain, are by-products of the focus on self that is promoted by the self-esteem movement.

In addition, bulimics, in particular, seem to be more impulsive, showing a tendency to act without thinking.[35] Bulimics also smoke, use drugs, and drink more than other people, and they have sex with more partners.[36] Large numbers of those with bulimia have unstable moods and self-images; they often idealize others and then reject them.[37] Girls who binge and purge engage in two to four times more aggressive behavior when compared to girls who do not.[38] As we will argue in later chapters, these tendencies toward sensation seeking, aggression, and instant gratification are more characteristic of those with inflated self-esteem than of those with low self-esteem.

Moreover, researchers have consistently found that those with anorexia are highly perfectionistic. Clinicians describe these patients as having excessive standards. Anorexics push themselves to succeed and show extreme sensitivity to criticism. Perfectionists can't tolerate failure, yet they carry a set of unachievable ideals. Many of these anorexics are terrified of humiliation and strive to obtain approval. In doing so, they rarely make demands on others and overly conform to rules. Those with the most severe eating disorders also have the highest degrees of perfectionism.[39] Once again, these tendencies are characteristic of people with inflated, albeit fragile, self-esteem.

One last risk factor: The chance of getting any type of eating disorder is greater for people born after 1960.[40] Interestingly, the self-esteem movement was also born after 1960. That this may be more than a coincidence is suggested by the fact that the risk factors we've just reviewed all occur more often among those with inflated, overly positive self-esteem.

True, we said a moment ago that a number of studies have associated eating disorders with *low* self-esteem. Yet those with stable, low self-esteem typically do little to try to raise their self-esteem. They not only fail to seek ways of enhancing their views of themselves; they actively *discard* information that would help raise their self-images.[41] They actually fear raising their self-esteem because they know the overblown image could be disconfirmed very easily.

Yet all the behaviors associated with eating disorders involve a striving for higher self-esteem. Some of these people literally kill themselves trying to be something better than they are. People with stable, low self-esteem would not have the energy or the desire to persist in the nightmarish life of those afflicted with anorexia or bulimia. Even perfectionism, found prominently in anorexics, suggests strong strivings to *improve* self-esteem.

We believe we can resolve the apparent paradox in these seemingly conflicting data in terms of the model of self-esteem presented in Chapter 2. Bulimics, for example, *do* have overly low self-esteem. *And* they have narcissistic, inflated self-esteem. It sort of depends on when you catch them. How can that be? Recall how in Chapter 2 we talked about the fact that overly high self-esteem puts a person at risk for developing a deflated sense of self. A puffed up self-esteem, like an over inflated balloon, punctures easily. It's unstable. Thus, people can flip between extremes on the self-esteem continuum. In a matter of moments, they can go from having outrageously positive illusions about themselves to utter despair and negativity.

In the past, researchers, thoughts clouded by the messages of the self-esteem movement, only looked for low self-esteem among those with eating disorders. They found it, but they didn't search for inflated self-esteem. In science, if you don't look for something, you won't find it.

Recall that in our model, self-esteem extremes bend back toward each other in a crucial respect: They both reflect excessive preoccupation with oneself. In particular, excessively high self-esteem shades into narcissism. Narcissists, you remember, demand admiration from others, feel special and superior, and react to criticism with hypersensitivity. Only recently have investigators carefully considered the relationship of narcissism to eating disorders, and what they have found is highly suggestive.

Eating disorder experts wondered whether personality traits such as narcissism could distinguish five groups: (1) anorexics who binge, (2) anorexics who diet only, (3) bulimics, (4) people with other psychiatric diagnoses, and (5) persons with no history of psychiatric or eating disorders ("normal controls"). The experts looked at narcissism, mood stability, sensation seeking, compulsion, and inhibited emotional expression. Not surprisingly, they found that all three eating-disordered groups and those with other psychiatric diagnoses had unstable moods compared to the "normal" group.

Nonpurging anorexics tended to be compulsive and restrained in their expression of emotions. Both bulimics and anorexics who purged demonstrated an increased desire for sensation seeking or excitement. Only one characteristic, however, stood out for all three eating-disordered groups: significantly higher scores on a measure of narcissism when compared to normals or the group of other psychiatric-disordered persons. In other words, no matter which type of eating disorder they had, these people were self-centered and believed in their "specialness." The authors concluded that, although subtypes of eating disorders may differ in interesting ways, *narcissism underlies the basic eating disturbance.*[42]

Of course, it's difficult to trust findings like these until they are replicated in other studies. The same year, a study appeared in the journal *Addictive Behaviors.* Researchers in San Francisco asked 117 women to fill out an eating disorders inventory, a bulimia test, and four different tests measuring narcissism. They found that the most severe eating-disordered women scored the highest on all measures of narcissism. In contradiction to some other studies, the women with eating disorders also demonstrated quite high self-esteem.[43]

Another report, in the *International Journal of Eating Disorders,* described an investigation into emotional and personality characteristics in persons with and without eating disorders. The researchers gathered three groups: women with active bulimic symptoms, women in remission from bulimic symptoms, and a third group with no current or past eating disorders. They found that the active bingers had more anxiety, depression, and suicidal tendencies than either of the other two groups. But the most interesting finding was that the women who had eating disorders, whether past or present, exhibited substantially higher levels of narcissism than the non-eating-disordered group. The authors concluded that *narcissism might be a personality trait that predates the emergence of eating disorders.*[44]

In other words, those who ultimately develop eating disorders probably start out with excessively high self-esteem. As their disorder progresses, it takes control of their lives. Some then collapse into depression and low self-esteem. Yet they *retain* their narcissism.

But if narcissism represents overblown, superior self-esteem, how could someone simultaneously possess a crestfallen sense of self? On the surface, it doesn't seem possible. Actually, it's entirely possible for narcissists with eating disorders to feel like failures, to be ashamed, and to feel incompetent. That's because their eating has gotten out of control and created a failure to achieve overly perfectionistic ideals. Those same people might still crave being the center of attention, enjoy manipulating others, and feel special and entitled, qualities that describe crucial aspects of the narcissist. Importantly, both the narcissist and the person with poor self-esteem engage in considerable self-reflection. They self-consciously obsess about their standing in relation to others. Immersed in hollow self-absorption, like Narcissus, many waste away and die.

Tragically, the self-esteem movement naively tries to administer the same prescription for everyone: Raise self-esteem, and everything will be fine. We contend that this approach causes more problems than it solves. In fact, the practice of raising self-esteem can be dangerous. It encourages vanity and self-absorption, which those with eating disorders already have in

overabundance. Besides, self-esteem puffed up by vacuous messages punctures far too easily.

A study titled "Primary Prevention of Eating Disorders:
Might It Do More Harm Than Good?" has verified and reinforced our concerns. This study tested an eating disorders prevention program for 13- and 14-year-old girls. The program
attempted to deter girls from eating disorders as well as from dieting, which often precedes the emergence of an eating disorder.
The intervention consisted of education about eating, dieting,
consequences of eating disorders, and improving *body image and
self-esteem.* Shockingly, six months later, the group receiving the
prevention program reported increased concern with dieting and
restricting their eating, the complete opposite of what the researchers intended. Consistent with our worries, it appeared that
the emphasis on the self and body image increased the girls' self-
focus and thus their desire to diet.[45] In light of these findings
(which do call for replication) and our analysis, we doubt that it's
a coincidence that the eating disorder epidemic began shortly
after the birth of the self-esteem movement.

BODY FIXATIONS: BODY DYSMORPHIC DISORDER, PLASTIC SURGERY, AND BODY ART

Skipping the recommended warm-up, Nick toweled off the
sweaty bench before he sat down. Inspecting his image in the
mirrored wall, puffing up his chest, he took a loud, deep, pur-
poseful breath. He could see the improvements in his muscle
definition and bulk. Not perfect, but getting there. He deduced
that the two daily workouts, six days a week—along with his
varied dietary supplements—had started to pay off.

Nick turned to his spotter and vowed that his bench press-
ing would reach 250 pounds. The two men began to cuss at
each other and exchange punches. This aggressive choreography
helped Nick build rage and focus. Adrenaline surged through

his body, increasing his strength. He laid back on the bench at a 45-degree angle and started with 15 reps at 185 pounds. Pausing, Nick told himself to have no fear; he could not fail. As he lifted 200 pounds, sweat broke out over his body. The veins on his face bulged as he goaded himself to do 12 reps.

His mind flashed back to one year earlier. Nick had started high school with a swagger. He was confident and popular, and he figured he was better looking than most. He vividly recalled a fall afternoon in the boys' locker room when a sophomore called him a puny, dickless wimp. Other boys snickered. Nick spent a lot of time looking at himself in the mirror that night. His self-esteem bubble burst; he had no "real" muscles. He started to feel disgust looking at his pathetic reflection. From then on, Nick gradually developed an obsession about his body, even though by any reasonable standard, his weight, height, and strength were better than for most young men his age.

Nick's thoughts turned back to his workout as he pressed on with escalating anger and motivation. His spotter upped the weight to 225 and called him a wimp. Nick grunted, straining every muscle, and finished 10 more reps. At 250 pounds, Nick faltered. He failed to complete his second rep. His mind filled with thoughts of self-loathing.

After completing his 90-minute workout, Nick scrutinized his body in the mirror, flexing his muscles. He scanned his reflection for flaws, which he found in abundance. He looked at his pecs and detected unevenness no one else could discern. His abdominal muscles failed to ripple sufficiently. Although Nick's body had no detectable fat and his bulging physique brought admiring gazes, he felt disgusted by his imperfect image. Inflamed, but determined, he decided to add anabolic steroids to his already complex regime of creatine, protein supplements, meal replacements, androstene, and ma huang.

Nick suffered from a growing malady, body dysmorphic disorder. Some call Nick's specific form of the problem "reverse anorexia"; others have used the terms *bigorexia* or *muscle dysmorphia*. The primary characteristic of body dysmorphic disorder, according to the American Psychiatric Association, is an obsessive preoccupation with some imagined flaw in a one's appearance. Sometimes a small defect might exist, but the individual's concern grows until it is completely out of proportion with the reality. The imagined or real disfigurement can take multifarious forms. For example, some obsess over misshapen body parts like noses, eyebrows, lips, ears, or chins. Any part of the body might fall under scrutiny, including hands, feet, legs, breasts, and genitals. Boys often fixate on the perceived inadequacy of their muscularity.[46]

Persons with this disorder use magnifying glasses or bright lights and frequent mirror checking to meticulously inspect their presumed disfigurement. They may try to camouflage it with makeup or hats. Some even stuff socks in underpants to augment a "small" penis. Others resort to multiple surgeries. Plastic surgery may or may not resolve the concern and sometimes leads to the eruption of new preoccupations.

Harvard University psychiatrist Harrison Pope estimates that one million American men suffer from body dysmorphic disorder. Like eating disorders, these problems most often begin in adolescence. Hard facts about the growth of body dysmorphic disorder are difficult to obtain for two reasons: Most people with these problems are too ashamed to admit them or seek help, and researchers have only recently begun to investigate this phenomenon. However, experts universally agree that the occurrence of this disorder, once thought to be rare, has surged in the past 20 years.[47]

While the incidence of body dysmorphic disorder has mushroomed, dissatisfaction with one's body has evolved into a virtual norm.[48] Practically no one these days seems to feel satisfied with the shape, tone, weight, or attractiveness of his or her body. Burgeoning industries have scrambled to supply us with an array of potions, lotions, and remedies for our discontent.

Web sites promise the perfect body in just a few months. They offer information on obtaining legal and illegal substances as well as detailed programs for using them. One site declares, "Have you ever looked closely at the physiques of today's top bodybuilders, models, and athletes and thought that they looked too good to be true? Well, you were right, they are . . . the good news is that with a little chemical wizardry, you too can safely have the perfect body of a top athlete, model, or bodybuilder."[49]

Chemical wizardry. Small wonder the National Institute of Drug Abuse issued an alarm about the increase in the use of anabolic steroids among eighth to twelfth graders in recent years. Most users want to bulk up rather than enhance athletic performance.

Those who are after improved appearance also seek approval from others and higher self-esteem.[50] Once again, the cost is substantial. The side effects of misuse of these drugs are wide-ranging and serious. They include shrinking testicles, reduced sperm production, impotence, damage to the heart, liver, and kidneys, stunted bone growth, and certain types of cancer.[51]

Sales of one popular, though controversial, supplement designed to enhance muscle performance, creatine, skyrocketed over 130% from 1997 to 1999.[52] Another increasingly popular supplement, androstenedione, is a steroid hormone that occurs naturally in the body. Health food stores sell it to anyone who asks for it, as they do other supplements. Nevertheless, no trials have shown that it actually works to improve muscle strength, and it has a number of highly adverse side effects, such as muscle and liver disorders, heart disease, reproductive problems, and behavioral problems.[53]

If you can't improve your looks through chemical wizardry, plastic surgeons will happily take your credit cards—and cheerfully dip into the college funds of minors who clamor for a quick fix. In 1998, 22,000 American teenagers had plastic surgery.

Although statistics vary, the number of children getting cosmetic plastic surgery has increased by at least 85% since 1992, when statistics were first compiled.

In March 2000, the *Washington Times* quoted Dr. Little, a plastic surgeon, as saying, "Now we are seeing teens who are looking for a quick fix to their problems. The girl who says, 'I'm a bit overweight, and why should I exercise or diet when I can just get it sucked out?'"[54] The procedure the plastic surgeon is referring to is one of the most popular cosmetic choices of teens. For removing excess fat, the surgeon makes a small incision and inserts a tube attached to a vacuum. The vacuum sucks the fat, loosened or liquefied by sound waves, through the tube. This surgical procedure may take anywhere from 30 minutes to several hours. It can cause burns to the area of fat removal, and little is known about long-term side effects.[55] Our teenagers choose to have the fat sucked out of them at three and a half times the rate that they did in 1992.[56]

During the same time, the number of teenage girls seeking breast augmentation almost doubled. Some girls receive the procedure as a high school graduation present. Boys in growing numbers also seek the scalpel as a means for improving their appearance. After Leonardo DiCaprio bared his hairless chest in the film *Titanic,* requests for chest hair removal at one plastic surgeon's office shot up by 20%.[57]

Why are teens choosing the scalpel in record numbers? Could it be a preoccupation with self-esteem? The Baron Centers for Body Recontouring and Male Penile Enhancement seem to be in no doubt. They advertise, *"The positive results are the same for virtually every person: Greater self-esteem, a new level of self-confidence, the ability to feel your best."*[58] What an inconsequential, empty way to seek self-esteem.

Plastic surgeons have little motivation to investigate the self-esteem or narcissism of their patients. However, in 1997 a study appeared in the *Annals of Plastic Surgery* comparing women who had cosmetic surgery to a control group of women who had not sought such surgery. Not surprisingly, the study discovered that cosmetic surgical patients were significantly more narcissistic than the controls.[59]

So, the search for self-esteem takes our children to gyms, health food stores, and surgeons. In rapidly escalating numbers, it also takes them to tattoo artists and body piercers.[60] In the United States, piercing used to be limited mostly to women's earlobes. Today, piercing sites for both sexes include eyebrows, nose, navel, lips, tongue, and nipples. Girls pierce the clitoral hood, clitoris, urethra, fourchette, labia minora, and labia majora. Boys sometimes request piercing on various spots on their penises or scrotums.[61]

Similarly, tattoos, which once adorned only bikers and sailors, have gone mainstream. Studies have found that 10 to 16% of high school students sport one or more tattoos. This percentage may grow, as current surveys indicate that more than half of all adolescents have an interest in tattooing. Surprisingly, girls make up over half of all tattooed teens. Even though tattooing under the age of 18 is illegal in many states, most get their tattoos around the ninth grade, and some obtain them as young as age 8.[62]

Of course, every generation has searched for some way to rebel and individuate from their parents. Kids in the past have usually turned to outlandish clothes, wild hairstyles, and music carefully selected to irritate. Body piercing and especially tattooing differ in one important way: permanence. Yet teens express casual indifference to both the permanence and dangers of body art. Tattooing or body piercing usually happens spontaneously when a pack of kids deems it "the thing to do." When asked why they did it, most replied that they "just wanted one," or "for the heck of it."[63]

In spite of the cavalier attitude most teens take toward piercing and tattooing, significant risks exist. The most serious risks are infections, which may hide for up to 10 or 15 years. Both hepatitis and HIV can be transmitted during any procedure that breaks the skin and is not performed under sterile conditions. Since many tattoo and piercing parlors are unregulated, the chance of infection is greater. Gum disease has been found among teens with pierced tongues. Various other infections such as tuberculosis, tetanus, and toxic shock syndrome have been reported as resulting from contaminated piercing or tattooing conditions. Piercing also can cause cyst formation, large scars, infection with purulent drainage, and allergic contact dermatitis.[64] And emergency room doctors have reported more injuries and complications due to body piercing. Shari Welch, an emergency room doctor, witnessed three serious complications, including one death, during a period of 18 months because of body piercing. "One doctor got to the point where he said, if you have to rip her tongue just do it," after finding it impossible to insert a breathing tube past the tongue stud of a dying teenage girl.[65]

What sort of teenager takes these risks in the quest for self-esteem? Is it kids with low self-esteem trying to feel better about themselves? One study strongly suggests otherwise. The investigators examined the personalities of tattooed students, comparing these students to a group of students without tattoos. Overall, tattooed students thought quite highly of themselves. They rated themselves as more adventurous, creative, artistic, and individualistic than did the students without tattoos. The young tattooed girls also reported more body piercings in places other than their ears, more shoplifting, and more drug use. The boys had more body piercings, more sexual partners, and more arrests, and they considered themselves more attractive.[66] Perhaps the tattoos did all that for the kids; but it's more likely they were hollow, narcissistic risk takers beforehand.

Obviously, not every kid with a small tattoo or body piercing is a narcissist. Most are pretty good kids trying to fit in or, paradoxically, attempting to express their individuality, just as kids have done for centuries. However, too many go too far. When they do, the focus on appearance takes their attention away from crucial tasks of youth. Specifically, these kids can fail to learn how to relate to others, discover their life's direction, and contribute to their families and communities.

Hollow narcissism is the thread that connects excessive body piercing, tattooing, plastic surgery, body dysmorphic disorders, and eating disorders. We do not intend to discount the incalculable pain suffered by those with some of the more serious disorders. Nor do we wish to reduce the cause of these behaviors to a single factor. Clearly, biological, genetic, and social forces of various sorts play important roles. Nevertheless, study after study supports our conclusion that narcissism runs through all of these obsessive concerns with the body and appearance.

Yet the self-esteem movement continues to insist that kids should feel good, all the time. It recommends that we raise the self-images of all kids. This approach merely increases self-focus and self-absorption, both hallmarks of narcissism.

The self-esteem movement appears oblivious to the perils of narcissism, but you don't have to be. We invite you to consider whether learning to view beauty as less important would help kids a good deal more than inane "I am beautiful" self-affirmations that only deny reality for many of them. More generally, we ask you to reflect on the excessive concern with self that is promoted by preoccupation with self-esteem. Wouldn't you rather see children taking pleasure in helping others, forming good relationships, participating in the community, and contributing to knowledge?

CHAPTER 4

FEELING TOO GOOD:
SPENDING, SENSATIONS,
AND SUBSTANCES

QUINTON'S PARENTS BROUGHT HIM TO OUR OFFICE FOR AN evaluation because he started to exhibit serious temper tantrums. Quinton threw several fits in his second-grade classroom. His teacher reported that once, during "free time," Quinton had to wait to use a computer. Frustrated at the wait, he tipped his desk over in anger. Quinton's parents were puzzled; they told us he had a much faster, better computer, complete with every imaginable game, at home in his bedroom.

Upon further inquiry, we learned Quinton almost always got what he wanted from his parents. Not surprisingly, his behavior at home wasn't as bad as at school. Not only did Quinton have a state-of-the-art computer, but his room over-flowed with electronic toys, designer furniture with a jungle motif, games, action figures, several CD players, and a mini–motorized scooter. All of Quinton's clothes came from high-end stores. His parents competed with neighbors over who could throw the most elaborate birthday parties for their kids. Quinton's parents certainly had his best interests in mind. Both of them worked long, hard hours to achieve their financial success. They arrived home after work exhausted. They felt guilty for failing to spend a lot of time with Quinton. They wanted him to be happy and have high self-esteem. When Quinton whined for attention, they worried. And they admitted the toys took a little pressure off them by providing Quinton entertainment. But what else did the abundance teach him?

When a child has everything, what is there to look forward to? Quinton's parents escalated birthdays and Christmas into spectacular pageants as the only way to capture his interest. Even then, his appreciation faded quickly. After opening 50 presents, it takes a lot for Quinton to feel excited. Kids like him reach a saturation point. Quinton had everything, and he appreciated nothing. He suffered from neglect—a special kind of neglect. Specifically, Quinton's parents neglected to teach him the crucial tasks of childhood: frustration tolerance, self-control, and persistence. Parents and schools alike have failed to address these skills, in deference to building self-esteem. Quinton's parents resorted to spending money as a quick-fix method of sparing his self-esteem. They succeeded. He did have high self-esteem. Quite high.

The self-esteem movement contains three corrosive messages that seduce kids, like Quinton, into searching for quick fixes and instant gratification. First, it preaches the need to *feel good*. Second, it tells them they can feel good *now*. Third, it diabolically tempts kids into believing that they should *always* feel good and never have to tolerate feeling bad. And parents, like Quinton's, all too often aid in the transmission of these messages.

A popular teacher's guide to building self-esteem highlights the first two messages. One exercise instructs kids to keep a happiness list. It tells them to notice and dwell on what makes them happy, feel the happy feeling, store the happy feeling, and write about what makes them happy. Particularly troubling is the statement, *"Try to do this five times everyday. Weekdays and weekends. School days and holidays. Be happy five times everyday."*[1] Exercises like these keep kids focused on their narcissistic, momentary pleasures. If children need to be happy five times every day, there isn't much call for self-control or sacrifice. Implicit within this exercise is the idea that feeling bad is unexpected as well as unacceptable.

Thus, one of the movement's primary goals is enabling our kids to feel happy, contented, and self-satisfied. In doing so, it pushes our kids to believe they can and should feel good all the time. They should feel good *now,* or apparently at least five times a day.

What happens as a result of these messages? The children of the self-esteem movement live in a world of instant gratification and simplistic solutions. They haven't learned how to tolerate boredom or frustration. They respond to the "torture" of being bored by looking for a quick fix. They try to fill the void with new clothes, new toys, new gadgets. *Quinton had high self-esteem and low self-control.*

More profoundly, the self-esteem movement creates a culture that values feeling good about yourself above all else. What does that culture do to children who haven't learned to accomplish worthy goals with their minds or with their hands or are too impatient to invest the effort to do so? What happens to kids who find their shallow self-esteem waning? They find other ways to get that rush of good feeling. They shower themselves with material possessions that add sheen to the surface of life while the soul withers. They consume alcohol and illicit drugs in record numbers. They indulge in hollow sexual encounters. All of this is in constant search of that momentary high, that feeling of superficial satisfaction that evaporates like water on a hot sidewalk. We're raising a generation of kids who have lost the ability to achieve a sense of exhilaration based on genuine accomplishments and on self-acceptance.

Finally, the self-esteem movement abandons kids by giving them no means for dealing with bad feelings when they occur— and bad feelings are simply a part of life. All too often, kids without coping skills resort to self-destructive means of handling distress. This is another path to the same dreary result: seeking relief from bad feelings through gambling, shoplifting, vandalism, promiscuous sex, or drugs and alcohol. Anything to fill the emptiness of their septic souls.

Problems like reckless spending, thrill seeking, and substance abuse are typically blamed on low self-esteem. We think the truth is more often the opposite. You will see throughout this book that overly high self-esteem creates at least as many problems as overly low self-esteem. Moreover, self-absorption stands out as the greater culprit. Unlike the self-esteem movement's traffickers, we don't claim that self-absorption or extremes of self-esteem are primarily responsible for everything that ails us, but they do contribute to a surprising labyrinth of miseries affecting our youth today.

SENSATION SEEKING AND RISK TAKING

Empty kids seek thrills, excitement, and instant gratification. Very often, they willingly take substantial risks in their quest for fun. The self-esteem movement would tell you these risk-taking, sensation-seeking kids are running very low on self-esteem.[2]

Yet, considerable data have linked high self-esteem to sensation-seeking and risk-taking behaviors. For example, a group of researchers wanted to learn more about adolescents and their risk-taking behavior. They asked a group of 440 teens about their willingness to engage in high-risk sports such as rock climbing, sky diving, mountain climbing, and parasailing. Students who endorsed these activities at a high rate also engaged in other kinds of dangerous risks at a high rate and, in addition, took more drugs. Although the researchers expected the data to come out otherwise, this group of adolescent risk takers reported significantly *higher* self-esteem than those who were low risk takers.[3]

Another study looked at kids in an honor society. The researchers found a positive relationship between alcoholism, sensation seeking, and high self-esteem in the social arena.[4] Still another study discovered that male adolescent drivers who caused two or more automobile accidents in the past two years also took greater risks in general and had higher self-esteem scores. If you think about the aggressive driver who cuts you off, do you think of a mousy, self-deprecating individual or a loud, narcissistic creep?[5]

Although most studies in this arena are correlational in nature, one surprising experimental study demonstrated the deleterious effects of having overly high self-esteem in terms of risk taking. Researchers divided students into two groups: one with high self-esteem and the other with low self-esteem. They then presented identical information about health risks of certain sexual behaviors to both groups. Students with high self-esteem demonstrated a statistically significant greater tendency to deny their personal risks and blocked out the information about health risks.[6]

Furthermore, consider the personality characteristics of people with low or high self-esteem. Studies have found that those with overly high self-esteem generally take greater risks, employ self-enhancing styles, and like to call attention to themselves. They also tend to be self-serving and narcissistic and to see themselves as better than other people see them. On the other hand, those with low self-esteem are more self-protective, unwilling to take risks, reluctant to call attention to themselves, cautious, and conservative than their high-self-esteem counterparts.[7] Remember the guy in the mall with purple hair and pierced tongue and eyebrow, kicking back and smoking pot? Would you predict him to have low or high self-esteem? We would guess high.

But a few studies have found relationships between alcoholism, drug abuse, risk taking, and low self-esteem.[8] Our self-esteem model provides a logical explanation for that otherwise incongruent finding. Once again, it's not that high and low self-esteem are the same; the differences between grandiosity and self-deprecation are obvious. But, a given person can have inflated self-esteem that collapses in the face of negative events.

We suspect our purple-haired fellow, as well as most who gravitate to drugs and alcohol or other risky behaviors, began with high self-esteem. Those who continue taking drugs or alcohol to the point of addiction and beyond often suffer horrible personal and interpersonal consequences for their actions. Similarly, those who frequently engage in risky behaviors often find themselves with serious health, financial, or legal problems. After a time, these consequences puncture their overinflated sense of themselves, and they develop low self-esteem. As you will see later in this chapter, if they recover from their various difficulties, their self-esteem quickly rises once again. The bottom line may be that findings depend on when researchers catch subjects in the cycle of their self-destructive behavior.

The drive to seek abundant pleasurable sensations and take risks in the process underlies a host of specific, troubling behaviors. These behaviors warrant a closer look.

The Spending Fix

The pursuit of self-esteem and feeling good follows divergent paths. Some children search for positive feelings through buying new clothes, others by acquiring the latest video game or electronic gadget. Modeling adults, kids often seek status or esteem through empty materialism. They learn these shallow values from their parents, friends, or the media.

To be sure, for many, more money also means more self-esteem. Money defines social class, status, and position. To have money implies that one has competed and won. Money is seen as a universal problem solver, a symbol of achievement and success. As a result, people often spend money to alleviate negative moods,[9] boost confidence, and prevent loss of self-esteem.[10]

Of course, there is some truth in the idea that we can spend our way into feeling better about ourselves, at least momentarily. Most of us, at one time or another, have purchased a new outfit, or treated ourselves to some small luxury when we felt blue. We somehow knew that spending a bit of money frivolously would cheer us up. And it does, ever so briefly—which is probably all we expect. Those with low self-esteem, however, sometimes find themselves compulsively buying even when they cannot afford to. In fact, some compulsive spenders appear to use money to enhance their relatively low self-esteem.[11] Spending money conveys a sense of power or prestige. After the purchase, people experience an instant rush, a feeling of euphoria. Compulsive spenders who have low self-esteem use money and what it can buy to compare themselves to others. They believe in the symbolic power that one derives from money. Unfortunately, as with most addictions, when the initial high abates, the hangover of depression and shame quickly follows.[12]

So compulsive, extravagant spending comes from low self-esteem, right? Not so fast. Recall that our model of self-esteem predicts that problems also happen when self-esteem goes too

high. In fact, it's well known that hallmarks of an overly positive mood state (known as mania) include inflated self-esteem,
grandiosity, and buying sprees. These people feel good and they
want to feel even better. During manic phases, people sometimes run up huge charges they can ill afford. They seem oblivious to the consequences of their spending sprees. Some have
grand but unrealistic plans for future wealth, but when the debt
piles up too high, they experience depression, just like the compulsive shopper with low self-esteem.[13]

Once again, our point is not that low self-esteem isn't a
problem. It can be. However, the messages of the self-esteem
movement resonate with the symptoms of mania: I am grand, I
am special, I can do anything. I deserve it all. The self-esteem
movement promotes a focus on the self and feeling good as
often as possible. Excessive spending serves up a nice, quick
portion of transitory happiness. Is it a coincidence that our kids
are spending and shopping like never before?

The children born in 1980 and after are known as Generation Y, the echo boomers, or the Millennial generation. Num-
bering about 70 million, they soon will compete with the baby
boomers as the largest consumer market.

Generation Y spent $600 billion in 1999. Children under
the age of 12 accounted for $27 billion of that amount. Gener-
ation Y buys cell phones, pagers, clothes, cosmetics, and electronic toys—not exactly necessities. The baby boomers had
four times the number of toys their parents had, *and the echo
boomers have four times that amount.* That's a bunch of toys.[14]
And not only do these kids spend their own money; they also
influence what cars, orange juice, cereal, and computers their
parents select.

Of course, many parents are complicit in all this. In Manhattan, parents must sign up on a waiting list to rent FAO
Schwartz's toy store for a child's birthday party. For a mere
$17,500 a night, children play video games and watch movies
on a huge screen. They can buy a miniature Range Rover with

leather upholstery for just $18,000. Children of one CEO watch the dining room table in their 65,000-square-foot home disappear into a lower-level kitchen where hired hands clear the plates.[15]

There's something wrong about never having to clean dishes, or at least put them into a dishwasher. And it's not only the superrich who excessively indulge their children. It happens in different ways in 1,500-square-foot homes. Parents there, unwilling to risk conflict, pick up after the kids and sacrifice their own needs beyond reasonable limits.

Many of our young clients show the effects of this shower of materialism. Like Quinton, today's teens have habituated to the frills of a booming economy. Many teens base their self-esteem on acceptance into the right crowd. In-crowds or cliques have always existed in high schools, but never to this degree has conspicuous consumption served as the entry card. Admittance into the club requires the right cell phone, name-brand clothing, and electronic planner. Some kids would rather not date than show up in an out-of-favor car. Parents feel compelled to give their kids the money to pull all of this off. They fear the consequences of their kids not fitting in.

That desire to fit in hits hard when college freshmen arrive on campus. And most of these teens have failed to learn self-control or how to delay gratification and so are ill-prepared for the slew of credit card offers they'll receive soon after they register. Companies lure them with Frisbees and T-shirts for signing up. Easy money; don't put off for tomorrow what you can buy today. Feel good. Credit cards allow students to keep up the same standard of living they were accustomed to at home. Further, they can use credit cards for body piercing, recreation, alcohol, or vacations. Cards also allow students to pursue these activities without their parents' knowledge or permission. Once again, no restraints, no self-control.

One Georgetown University student reported obtaining 16 credit cards with a balance of $10,000 among them. He also had a $10,000 debt consolidation loan and he had run up $30,000 in student loans. He's hoping to graduate and land a job with a paycheck sufficient to bail him out of his debt.[16] A freshman at the University of Central Oklahoma hung herself in her dorm room. She had accumulated $25,000 of debt. Credit card bills and her checkbook covered her bed. A University of Oklahoma junior who killed himself in 1988 had compiled $10,000 in credit card debt.[17]

The credit card companies seduce students with low monthly payments. Students assume they can afford the $30 or $40-a-month minimum payment. As their balances grow, they reach their credit limit and obtain another card. Then another. Most students have no idea how long it takes to pay off debt. Few know it takes six years to pay off a mere $1,000 debt when making a 3% minimum monthly payment.

For all their attention to self-esteem and feeling good, parents and schools have failed to teach the basics of delaying gratification, restraint, and knowledge of finances. Admittedly, hard evidence for indicting the self-esteem movement on charges of causing our kids to develop reckless spending habits does not exist at this time. Nevertheless, should we not at least consider the "feel good now" message of the movement as implicitly aiding and abetting the trend?

Gambling: Everyone Wants to Become a Millionaire

Not long ago, if you wanted to gamble, you purchased an airline ticket to Las Vegas. Today, 48 of the 50 states permit some form of legalized gambling, many in the form of lotteries.[18] Furthermore, the Internet beckons any and all comers, whether legal or not. Anyone with a credit card can claim to be of legal age and gamble to their heart's content, or until the card maxes out. This is a new phenomenon.

Like many cities across the United States, a mere 10 years ago, our hometown of Albuquerque had a few bingo parlors on Indian reservations and in churches. Now casinos encircle the town. Billboards and advertising on radio and television incessantly promote the illusory rewards of gambling. *Thus, today's kids are the first generation ever exposed to widely available, government-sanctioned gambling.* This explosive growth has occurred without careful consideration of its effect on society and our kids' values.

Huge profits have prompted states to minimize the risks and promote the benefits of their lotteries. States market their lottery tickets in gas stations, grocery stores, and vending machines. Some suggest that lotteries don't even constitute gambling. State lottery ad campaigns almost equate supporting lotteries with the fulfillment of a civic duty. The California state lottery, for example, is designed (and highly marketed) as a benefit for the state's educational system.

We realize a debate rages as to whether gambling enhances or harms a community. But there can be no doubt about the harm that it inflicts on a certain percentage of individuals. So-called pathological gamblers destroy their lives and families through their addiction. Sure, these folks existed prior to the proliferation of casinos. They bet on football games, cock fights, and virtually anything you can think of. However, when casinos beckon from billboards strewn across our highways and their message carries the government seal of approval, many more fall prey to the lure.

You might ask what this has to do with self-esteem and, further, how it pertains to children. Plenty. First, consider who is drawn to gambling, especially to a pathological degree. Most people probably think of a gambler as one who has low self-esteem—a down-and-out, seedy loser. Occasionally, that description fits. Some people with desperately low resources gamble what little they have, feeling they have nothing to lose. And a few with horribly deflated self-esteem probably turn to gambling as a means of boosting their self-image with hoped-for winnings.

However, research has shown that those with high self-esteem are drawn to risks such as those posed by gambling and take greater risks when they gamble.[19] Furthermore, studies show that those with low self-esteem don't like to take risks.[20] People with high self-esteem expect good things to happen to them. Those with truly inflated self-esteem can barely imagine anything turning out poorly. When they roll the dice, somehow, some way, they'll win. The published odds just don't apply. They believe their odds are magically better than others'. They inflate their control and ability to predict essentially random events. When they lose, they dismiss the outcome as a temporary setback; the next hand will turn things around. If they lose a significant sum, they feel the need to increase their bets to make up for the losses. When they win, they see themselves as highly skilled and responsible for the outcome. They lose due to bad luck and they win due to talent. Not hard to see why they keep at it, is it?[21]

But gambling remains illegal for children. It's hard to think the self-esteem movement could lead them astray in this arena. Think again. Kids with inflated self-esteem want to feel better than others. Like similar-minded adults, they see themselves as having more control over events than they do. Winning keeps them on top.

Imagine a clever marketing genius wanting to exploit children with this mindset. Say he develops a game with a plethora of cute characters. He publicizes that the object of the game is to collect all the characters. He sells these characters in packets. He prints enormous numbers of most of the characters. He chooses to severely restrict production of a few, knowing from reading Robert Cialdini's book *Influence* that scarcity will substantially increase value for the rare characters.[22] This clever marketer stuffs most of the packets with readily obtainable characters. He randomly inserts rare characters into a small percentage of the packets. Yet, all packets cost the same—just as every pull on a 25-cent slot machine costs the same. And, like slot machines, most packets fail to "pay off" with a valuable, rare character. The consumer must buy lots of packets to have any chance of winning. Clever marketing.

Do you recognize the scheme just described? It's Pokemon. More than a few parents have voiced concerns about Pokemon. In fact, some filed a lawsuit alleging that collecting and trading Pokemon cards boils down to illegal gambling. Children buy these packets with the hope of getting a winner. Some kids use their lunch money to buy more cards. In more than a few cases, trading these cards on the schoolyard has led to violence and stealing. One 11-year-old boy craved a powerful card so badly that he agreed to allow a sick 33-year-old man to burn his arm with a cigarette in exchange for the desired card.[23]

We'll let the courts decide whether Pokemon constitutes gambling. What we *will* say is that it's based on the same principles and could lead to addictive behavior in children.[24]

Obviously, most kids manage to play with Pokemon cards without becoming intensely addicted. Just like most adults, kids usually manage to gamble without becoming pathological gamblers. It's possible that some kids with low self-esteem may see winning at Pokemon as a way of enhancing their deflated status. But recall that sensation seeking and risk taking are more prevalent among those with high self-esteem. Thus, it seems likely that the most vulnerable kids are those with inflated self-esteem who desperately seek thrills and excitement and take high risks to get them. And they risk puncturing their high, albeit fragile, self-esteem should they gamble and lose.

Gambling among our kids goes well beyond Pokemon. A study of adolescents in New York asked about specific gambling behavior. Almost a quarter reported they engaged in illegal betting on casino games. About half acknowledged betting on sports or a lottery. Two-thirds bet on card games, and three-quarters gambled on scratch-off games.[25] In Atlantic City, 200,000 teenagers were chased out of casinos in a single year. The director of the nonprofit Council on Compulsive Gambling called gambling the teenage addiction of the 1990s.[26]

Gambling has a seductive allure for teens, more so than for adults. After all, teenagers take more risks than adults. Experts have hypothesized that hormonal production during this time increases the need for arousal and stimulation. Adolescents appear to meet those needs through sensation seeking, thrills, and risky behavior. And these behaviors drop off during adulthood.[27]

So, the message of getting rich quick and having it all may have special allure for our teens. These messages envelope kids through television shows, sweepstakes, and publicity about Internet wonder kids. These schemes for wealth appear thrilling and instantaneous, as well as consistent with the self-esteem movement that encourages our kids to meet their every desire.

We find it particularly alarming that the gambling addiction rate for teens exceeds the rate for adults by 400 to 800%.[28] Jeffrey Derevensky, co-director of the Youth Gambling Research and Treatment Center at McGill University in Montreal, recently warned that children with gambling addictions steal money from family members, shoplift, and even consider suicide when their gambling spirals out of control.[29]

Remember, those with excessively high self-esteem take more risks than others. They chalk up losses to bad luck and credit their own skill when they win. Yet the self-esteem movement continues to promote high self-esteem without considering the potential consequences of overselling its message. Although a direct cause-and-effect relationship has not been established between gambling and the unrestrained promotion of high self-esteem, once again circumstantial evidence concerning the characteristics of gamblers and the high rate of gambling addiction among teens makes us worry. How many overly optimistic teens, pumped up with self-esteem, believe they can beat the odds?

Shoplifting: A Self-Destructive Shortcut to Thrills and Excitement

Teens who shoplift also believe they can beat the odds. Dr. Smith interviewed a half dozen residents of a juvenile detention center about shoplifting. Although none of them were in the detention center for shoplifting, *all* of them had done it. Most started at a very young age. A couple of them reported learning how to shoplift at the age of 6 or 7, in the company of older siblings. Two common themes emerged. First, the teens considered shoplifting a crime that hurts no one. They scoffed at the idea that shoplifting costs anyone anything, believing storeowners' huge profits easily absorb the losses. More important than the denial of cost was the obvious excitement they took in relating their adventures. Robin Hood–like, they delighted in getting away with something.

What they are getting away with constitutes a significant portion of about $16 billion worth of merchandise shoplifted every year in the United States. Five to 10 cents of every dollar we spend in stores goes to cover the costs of shoplifting. A survey by the Better Business Bureau recently reported shoplifting makes up 30% of all reported crime. A shoplifting theft occurs once every five seconds of every day. Furthermore, adolescents account for almost half of all shoplifters.[30]

You might think people shoplift due to necessity. Not so. Most of what people shoplift ends up hanging in the back of a closet or being tossed away. So why do teens shoplift? It seems that values have a lot to do with it. When teens value thrills, fun, and enjoyment over other values, their likelihood of shoplifting increases. Kids who shoplift report a combination of excitement, fear, and adventure.[31] For many, like the teens from the juvenile detention center, shoplifting is a game of skill and daring with the prime objective of getting away without being caught. In other words, shoplifting juveniles appear to be sensation seekers, whom we've previously noted more often have high self-esteem, as opposed to low.

Certain values appear to inhibit kids from shoplifting. Specifically, if teens value empathy and belonging, they are much less likely to shoplift.[32] Empathy involves concern for the well-being and feelings of others. People with empathy are able to put themselves in other people's shoes. Belongingness refers to the desire to relate. Interestingly, consistent with our argument, people with inflated self-esteem tend to have little empathy and poorer relationships with others. They value their own pleasure and importance far more than any concern for what their actions cost others.[33] They just want to feel good and have fun.

Drugs and Alcohol: Another Unhealthy Route to Thrills and Excitement

Drugs and alcohol induce a host of transitory good feelings and sensations. And adolescence has always been a time of experimentation. Therefore, it's not surprising that many teens dabble with drugs. However, children who have been urged to expect to feel good all the time and have failed to learn how to tolerate bad feelings, as well as those devoid of values, connections with others, self-control, and meaningful goals, are at grave risk for abusing substances. The thrills and excitement of drugs and alcohol deliver a shoddy alternative to a well-grounded existence.

You may have heard that substance abuse has declined among our youth. Actually, the statistical records of drug abuse among young people paint a mixed picture. Overall, lifetime use of any illicit drug peaked in the early 1980s and then declined somewhat into the early 1990s. Nevertheless, lifetime prevalence of drug use has shown virtually no net change from 1975, the earliest date for which comprehensive comparison data are available. The lack of long-term change can be attributed to the fact that the modest decline in drug use during the 1980s evaporated during the 1990s. The data on eighth graders is especially appalling. From 1991 to 2000, the reported illegal drug use by eighth graders increased by 43%.[34]

Other statistics present a more frightening picture. For example, between 1980 and 1996, deaths from drug overdoses climbed by over 540%. Furthermore, emergency room drug episodes from 1978 until 1994 rose from about 315,000 to just over 500,000. This is a time when many drug users actually stew in jail cells. Total incarcerations for drug use and sales are up from 25,000 in 1980 to about 275,000 in 1998.[35] One can only assume that if the extra quarter million inmates were out on the streets, they would push up the overall drug use statistics.

Each year, the University of Michigan Institute for Social Research surveys a nationally representative group of students about their drug usage. In the class of 2000, over half (54%) of students reported having used some type of illicit drug.[36] This figure likely underestimates overall drug usage for two reasons. First, some students, even with the promise of confidentiality, will not admit to drug usage on surveys. The other problem with this survey is that it only reaches students attending school. It is well known that high school dropouts and students expelled or suspended have higher rates of drug use.

Television news shows and magazine articles have sensationalized the popularity of new "designer drugs." However, statisticians have only compiled data on designer drugs since 1996. From 1996 to 2000, use of MDMA or Ecstasy increased by 50% among eighth through twelfth graders. Since chemists constantly concoct new drugs, even this extensive survey fails to capture everything teenagers use to get high.[37]

Completely untracked and very disconcerting is the abuse of so-called herbal alternatives. These are legal, unregulated, and available all over the Internet and in many health food stores. Direct e-mail "spam" advertises alternatives to marijuana and hallucinogens. For example, it promotes Kathmandu Temple Kiff for improving creativity, sex, and dreaming. Salvia Divinorun is a legal substance and supposedly a hallucinogen that gives a short-acting, intense high. Other herbal blends include products labeled Spirit Walk, Merlin's Blend, Dream Smoke, and Vision Quest.

Health food stores sell diet aids and energy boosters containing the ingredient ma huang, an ephedrine-like compound that has been used as a stimulant in China for decades. Producing effects similar to amphetamine, when abused ma huang can cause significant health problems due to its action on the heart and nervous system. Reportedly, it can cause high blood pressure, psychosis, and mood disorders. Not only is ma huang an ingredient in such benign-sounding remedies as Metabolife; it also is an active ingredient in products appealing to the drug culture, such as Nature's Sunshine and Herbal Ecstasy. Anecdotal evidence suggests that these herbal alternatives are becoming drugs of choice for many, especially young middle-class students. It makes sense that middle-class students might prefer an Internet search or a visit to the health food store over a back alley for obtaining their high.[38]

Official statistics combined with the explosive growth in herbal products argue strongly that we have *not* won the so-called war on drugs. In fact, an argument could be made that drug use among teenagers has actually increased if the recent abuse of herbal alternatives is factored into the equation. This dismal picture exists in spite of an enormous expenditure of dollars for the development and implementation of various drug "prevention" programs.

As you probably suspect, the self-esteem movement proclaims that the answer to drug prevention lies in raising self-esteem. The National Association of Self-Esteem (NASE) complains that many drug prevention programs concentrate solely on education about drugs, explanations concerning the influence of advertising, social pressures, and the practice of resistance and refusal skills. According to NASE, *a failure to address self-esteem* explains the failure of many of these traditional programs. *The association identifies low self-esteem as the strongest risk factor leading to drug and alcohol use.* And, not surprisingly, it recommends including self-esteem building as an integral part of all drug prevention programs.[39]

Sounds like good advice. Certainly the association's idea is intuitively appealing. But does it hold water? Let's look at a highly prominent prevention program that includes self-esteem building in its curriculum. The Drug Abuse Resistance Education program, commonly known as DARE, is the world's largest drug prevention endeavor. Started in 1983, it is a $230 million project with programs in all 50 states and 44 other countries. This cooperative venture between law enforcement and education is being taught in 80% of American schools.[40]

The DARE program includes two major components, information dissemination and affective education. DARE teaches information on drug use, misuse, and effects, as well as the influence of media and alternatives to drugs. The affective education includes a curriculum of self-esteem building, stress management, and decision making. DARE thus follows the advice provided by the National Association of Self-Esteem by including the boosting of self-esteem as an integral part of its program.

How effective is DARE in preventing drug use? Researchers randomly assigned 18 elementary schools to receive the DARE program and 18 others to not receive it. The study employed sound scientific principles in using an experimental group (schools with the DARE program) and a control group (schools without the program). The findings indicated that although DARE had shown some early, short-term effects, these disappeared for all groups by the six-year follow-up. Alarmingly, this study also found evidence for what the researchers called a boomerang effect: Suburban DARE graduates obtained higher scores on all four drug use measures than suburban students not taking the DARE program. Specifically, suburban DARE graduates reported *more alcohol use and drug use both during the past 30 days and over their lifetime.*

The investigators also looked at whether receiving booster sessions or more drug education might improve these disappointing outcomes. They naturally thought that giving the students more drug prevention activities would help. The results were stunning. The more drug education, the worse things got. They discovered that additional drug education produced more negative attitudes about police; more positive attitudes about alcohol, drugs, and cigarettes; and increased delinquency.[41]

Well, the DARE proponents argued, that was just one study. And there might be a sleeper effect—just wait until these kids are adults, and then the positive effects will emerge. Another research team took the "dare." This study followed over a thousand students for 10 years after either the DARE program or no prevention program. After 10 years, the students who had completed the DARE program used cigarettes, alcohol, marijuana, or other drugs at the same rate as those who had not received DARE. The investigators concluded that DARE failed to produce any lasting changes of value.[42]

In light of these findings, how the National Association for Self-Esteem continues to think drug education plus self-esteem boosting will reduce drug usage escapes us. It's also curious how these programs maintain such high popularity. Perhaps just the apparent "common sense" of teaching kids to stay away from drugs and feel better about themselves explains part of it. And the kids get T-shirts, bumper stickers, coloring books, pennants, florescent pens, and fancy graduation certificates with the DARE logo affixed. As researcher Donald Lynam and his colleagues concluded, "these 'feel-good' programs are ones that everyone can support, and critical examination of their effectiveness may not be perceived as necessary."[43]

Perhaps we should question the "common sense" that underlies the advice of the National Association for Self-Esteem. Is it really true, as we all "know," that drug addicts and alcoholics universally have low self-esteem? Recall the book commissioned by the California Task Force on Self-Esteem, the same group that spawned the National Association for Self-Esteem. The commission hired experts to review all available research and document the relationship of self-esteem to alcohol and drug abuse. What did their own experts find? Not much. In fact, they concluded, "Empirical studies concerning the relationship between alcohol and drug abuse and self-esteem show mixed results."[44] They were unable to definitively establish low self-esteem as a causative agent of drug or alcohol abuse.[45]

It's only fair to report that the researchers did find that people entering treatment programs suffered lower self-esteem and that their self-esteem goes up after recovery.[46] But we can't conclude these subjects had low self-esteem when they started to drink. It's hardly surprising if a person hitting rock bottom and deciding to go into treatment feels bad and suffers from low self-esteem. Nor is it surprising that self-esteem improves once the individual successfully finishes treatment.

Furthermore, given the relationship between sensation seeking, risk taking, and high self-esteem, we have additional cause for worry. As we reviewed earlier, sensation seekers more often turn to drugs and alcohol for momentary pleasures.[47] So, will raising self-esteem increase drug abuse? We can't make such a definitive statement based on existing data.

However, given what we do know, would you really want to run the risk of pumping our kids up on self-esteem messages? Recall that alcoholics are more self-absorbed than others.[48] Do you think it's a good idea to focus our kids' attention so much on their "specialness"?

SEX: A HAZARDOUS ROUTE TO THRILLS AND EXCITEMENT

Another grand idea promulgated by the self-esteem movement proposes that children or young adolescents who engage in promiscuous sex suffer from low self-esteem. First, let us consider whether the current sexual practices of adolescents represent a problem. Then let's look at the proposed cause of the problem and the associated "cure."

How much of a problem is sexual promiscuity among our young people? In one respect, the news is good. Although teenage pregnancies have varied over the decades, the rate of births declined about 25% from 1970 to the late 1990s. However, the rate of unmarried teenage mothers increased by over 80% during that same time period. So there are fewer babies overall, but of those born, many more are born to single mothers. Teens' contraception use likely accounts for the overall decrease in the birth rate.[49]

Although teens' use of contraception is increasing, the sexual activity of teens also climbed through the '70s and '80s. Surveys suggest stabilization or even a slight decrease in a few behaviors over the decade of the '90s.[50] Nevertheless, other data suggest that sexual activity among teens under the age of 15, as well as among middle-class and white teenagers, was starting to increase by the mid 1990s.[51] In fact, in 1999, 8.3% of students admitted to having intercourse prior to the age of 13. Furthermore, in that same year, about half of all teens admitted to having had sex, whereas in 1970, only 29% did so.[52]

These statistics may actually convey an overly positive picture because of changes in teenagers' sexual activities. Almost all surveys of teenage sexual behavior in the past several decades have focused on whether or not teens have engaged in sexual intercourse. This line of inquiry may be too narrow. You wouldn't be surprised to see a box of condoms available for students in a high school nurse's office. But you might not expect to see a second box of condoms, flavored, without spermicide, labeled "for oral sex only." That's exactly what a reporter found when she visited a high school in New York.[53] Recent trends indicate that growing numbers of adolescents, fearful of AIDS, sexually transmitted diseases, and pregnancy, may be turning to oral sex for what they wrongly perceive as a safe alternative to intercourse.

One study discovered that about 20% of *virgin* high school students acknowledged they'd engaged in either mutual masturbation with a partner or oral sex.[54] Another report on urban adolescents found about a third of the virgins had engaged in heterosexual masturbation, and many of those had also engaged in oral sex. In addition, many professionals in the field have opined that oral sex is increasing rapidly among our youth, particularly in the middle school years.[55] Dr. Marsha Levy-Warren, a psychologist for preteens and adolescents, has stated, "I see girls, seventh and eighth graders, even sixth graders, who tell me they're virgins, and they're going to wait to have intercourse until they meet the man they'll marry. But then they've had oral sex fifty or sixty times. It's like a good night kiss to them, how they say goodbye after a date."[56] Hard data are difficult to find because studies have only recently begun tracking this aspect of adolescent sexual behavior.

If, as many contend, teenage oral sex occurs more frequently today, then overall sexual behavior on the part of teenagers is also increasing. In either case, it remains well above 1970 levels and has only recently stabilized or declined slightly.

So sexual activity should remain an area of concern for parents and others concerned about kids. How about the cause of sexual promiscuity? The self-esteem advocates would tell you that low self-esteem underlies early sexual behavior.

Let's return to *The Social Importance of Self-Esteem,* the book written by the movement's own experts, and see what they found. One chapter reported on four studies that specifically looked at the relationship between self-esteem and sexual intercourse. The first of these did find a connection between low self-esteem and premarital sex. However, the researchers found this connection only among a group of Mormon teenagers who attended church regularly. The finding did not apply to the rest of the sample.

Two other studies reported that *high* self-esteem was associated with early sexual activity. The fourth study found higher self-esteem in *non*-virgin males and no relationship between self-esteem and the sexual activity of girls. The authors concluded that the evidence failed to support an association between self-esteem and sexual intercourse. That's interesting. We think the findings actually supported a modest relationship between self-esteem and sexual intercourse, but the relationship was the opposite of what the researchers were looking for.[57]

Two other studies conducted after the book appeared also supported this connection between high self-esteem and sexual intercourse. The first looked at a sample of 308 students. It found that students with *high* self-esteem had more sexual partners than students with low self-esteem. Those with high self-esteem also demonstrated higher sensation seeking.[58] In the second study, the investigator started out with the belief that people with high self-esteem would engage in fewer risky sexual behaviors. He found the opposite; those with high self-esteem took *greater* risks, such as a great number of partners and more sexual activity overall.[59] When researchers report findings opposite to what they're looking for, you can usually figure the results are robust and valid. Nevertheless, the self-esteem message has so permeated the minds of professionals that many still call for programs to increase self-esteem as a way of *reducing* adolescent sexual behavior.

For example, an article in a recent nursing journal discussed the problem of early sexual behavior and unprotected sex. The authors proffered that "successful intervention measures include promoting increased self-esteem."[60] This advice, if successfully carried out, very well might result in increased risky sexual activity.

Our model of self-esteem predicts problems from having an excessively high self-esteem. Although less research supports this contention, we believe that a deflated self-esteem doesn't help either. For example, we have little doubt that some, especially girls, start having sex to boost a flagging self-esteem. The research has tended to look at that data as a composite average rather than teasing apart possibilities such as whether a group of girls, both overly high and low in self-esteem, are drawn into sexual activities.

FEELING *TOO* GOOD: A SYNTHESIS

Too much. Too much conspicuous consumption. Too much gambling, drug taking, and promiscuous sex. Too much narcissism and focus on the self. How do we measure up? How do we compare to others? How can we feel good all the time? Unfortunately, none of us can feel good all the time, nor can we be better than others all the time. In fact, trying to feel good all the time may be dangerous. Most of the research we've reviewed supports a conclusion contrary to the message of the self-esteem movement. Those with inflated self-esteem tend to take more risks and seek more sensations and thrills.

Furthermore, the cure to the excesses we've reviewed surely does not exist in efforts to raise kids' self-esteem. No convincing evidence exists that supports the value of raising self-esteem in order to reduce substance abuse, pathological gambling, promiscuity, or compulsive spending. Knowing that self-absorption poses a risk for most forms of mental disorders, how can we justify the continued drive to promote self-esteem?[61] Although we can't say so with certainty, this promotion very well may exacerbate the very problems it's trying to solve.

Obviously, most kids do okay in school, aren't alcoholics or drug addicts, and haven't gotten pregnant. Our concern is that the thinking encouraged by the self-esteem movement seduces the vulnerable kids into a quest to feel too good, all the time. If kids can't find good feelings through genuine accomplishments, they feel driven to seek good feelings from empty sources such as drugs, alcohol, spending, or sex. Moreover, if we allow ourselves to focus too much on our kids' self-esteem, we're likely to be part of the problem instead of part of the solution.

CHAPTER 5

VIOLENCE: THE DARKEST SIDE OF SELF-ESTEEM

SATURDAY NIGHT. THREE BOYS, TWO 15 YEARS OLD AND ONE 16, left a party, promising to return with more beer. Confident of success, they pulled into the convenience store parking lot and waited until the lone customer drove off. Laughing and excited, they planned their next moves. The oldest would act as decoy by asking the cashier for directions. The other two would grab the beer and run.

"Can you tell me how to get to Highway 528 from here?" the 16-year-old decoy asked. The cashier pointed out the window to indicate the direction, but then he spied the two other boys reflected in the glass. He shouted, "Stop now and drop the beer!" The kids dashed for the exit; the clerk reached below the counter and pulled out a gun. As the clerk leveled his gun at the escaping kids, the decoy pulled out his own gun. He fired four shots, slamming the cashier to the floor. The cashier wailed, "My God, I'm shot. Help me." The 16-year-old stood over him and coldly aimed his gun. "Don't shoot, don't shoot! I'll give you whatever you want!" The next sound was of one final shot being fired.

The kids, with beer in hand, returned to the party. After slamming down a few beers, they bragged to friends about their adventure. Video cameras had caught their heinous act in its entirety, and police arrested all three perpetrators. The others at the party corroborated the videotape. When asked why they didn't come forward earlier, the corroborators declared they could never snitch on a friend.

The community responded with shock and outrage, partly because all the kids came from middle-class families. When interviewed, the juveniles blamed everyone but themselves. They blamed the cashier for pulling out his gun. The 16-year-old said he wished he'd never gone to that party, as if that were the cause of his actions. The attorney for one of the 15-year-olds blamed his client's attention deficit disorder for his participation in the robbery and murder. None of the kids showed remorse, only regret for getting caught.[1]

Stories like this one have become so common that they are losing their capacity to shock. What is striking about the violence we observe among our youth is less its prevalence than the nature of the crimes being committed: cold, pointless, unfeeling, brutal. Once again, self-esteem promoters think they have the answer: Violence and aggression result from low self-esteem. If we're concerned about raising peaceable, law-abiding kids, we should work to raise kids' self-esteem.

The fact is that there is little evidence to support this interpretation of the cause of violence and aggression, which means that the purported "cure" is, at best, unsupported by data. Worse, there is a great deal of evidence that suggests that violence and aggression are far more common among those with excessively *high* self-esteem, particularly the self-absorbed individuals we have called narcissists. The evidence we review in this chapter suggests that, once again, focusing on kids' self-esteem is not only the wrong answer to a serious problem but could very well make the problem much worse.

VIOLENCE AMONG OUR YOUTH

How common is violent crime among our youth? FBI crime reports track arrests for murder, manslaughter, forcible rape, robbery, and aggravated assault. These statistics form what is known as the Violent Offenses Index. In 1970, the index recorded 20,416 children under the age of 14, and 44,570 15- to 17-year-olds arrested for a violent crime. In 1999, the corresponding numbers were 33,703 and 68,677. These represent increases of 61% and 64% respectively when adjusted for differences in populations of the two time periods.[2]

These increases occurred despite declining juvenile crime rates between 1994 and 1999. During this period the arrest rate for children under 14 declined by about 29% and the rate for those between 15 and 17 declined by about 40%. Even with these "improvements," today's arrest rate remains considerably higher than the rate in 1970 and represents more than a threefold increase since 1960.[3]

Headlines across the country have celebrated the downward trend in juvenile crime since 1993. Unfortunately, the shrinking arrest rates have done nothing to quell the concerns of our surgeon general with respect to youth violence in general. The surgeon general's 2001 report on youth violence stated, "the propensity for and actual involvement of youths in serious violence have not declined with arrest rates. Rather, they have remained at the peak rates of 1993, a troublesome finding. In January 2001, as this report goes to press, the first indications of a long-awaited downturn in self-reported violent behavior are being countered by signs from the FBI's Uniform Crime Reports database that the decline in arrests of youths for violent crimes has bottomed out, and for some index crimes, has begun to climb again."[4]

The extensive report by the surgeon general attributes much of the decrease in arrest rates to the reduced use of lethal weapons by our youth. However, confidential surveys indicated that close to 15% of seniors in high school have acknowledged committing a serious violent act. *"These acts typically do not come to the attention of police, in part because they are less likely than in years past to involve firearms. Over the past two decades, the number of violent acts by high school seniors increased nearly 50 percent . . . neither this incident rate, nor the proportion of high school seniors involved in violence has declined in the years since 1993 . . . the best available evidence from multiple sources indicates that youth violence is an ongoing national problem, albeit one that is largely hidden from public view"* (emphasis added).[5] In other words, the surgeon general's survey revealed that youth today are engaging in as many violent acts as ever recorded.

Furthermore, the so-called improvement in juvenile arrest rates applies mostly to males. Female juvenile crime rates increased substantially more than rates for males up until 1994 and since then show a mixed pattern rather than an overall decline, as seen with males. In particular, assaults by females rose 57% from 1990 to 1999. Girls are committing more crimes and more violent crimes than ever before.[6]

Nevertheless, juvenile violent crime arrests have indeed decreased in the second half of the '90s. It would be comforting if we could attribute the decline to improving moral standards and decreasing hostility on the part of our youth—or, perhaps, to higher self-esteem. However, this modest improvement more likely results from a variety of other factors. Unfortunately,

these factors involve externally imposed controls and constraints rather than a strengthening of the inner character of
our children.

To begin with, we've witnessed an intense fortification of
many American homes, cars, and businesses. Today we protect
ourselves behind peepholes, security doors, and wrought
iron–clad windows. Alarms blare through neighborhoods and
parking lots, even inside briefcases. Retailers for vehicle security
systems sold $161 million of equipment in 1993. By 1998, they
racked up sales of $330 million.[7] Approximately 13,000 alarm
companies operated in the United States in 1990. The number of
alarm companies in 2000 was almost double that.[8] Furthermore, we have vastly increased the number of local, state, and
federal police officers as well as private security guards.

School security, which began as a trivial afterthought, in recent years has exploded into a dynamic business. Public schools
in this country spent close to $800 million in the year 2000 on
security. That's about $20 for every student in the United States.
Today, closed-circuit television cameras watch over doorways,
hallways, and cafeterias. Students enter hallowed halls of learning through metal detectors designed to intercept guns, knives,
and other weapons. Many schools require transparent book
bags. School administrators once considered lockers a place for
coats, books, and love notes. Now steel rods block access to
long rows of lockers, which principals fear conceal contraband.
High-tech solutions to school violence include fingerprint-coded
ID cards and other biometric identification systems.[9]

In the 1950s and 1960s we feared nuclear war. Students shud-
dered under desks and in basements during mock nuclear attacks.
Today, we fear crazed schoolchildren with guns. Students huddle
in closets, bathrooms, and locked classrooms during drills designed to protect them from assaults by their classmates.

In addition, schools and campuses routinely provide escort
services for teachers and students who must attend late func-
tions. Twenty years ago, police rarely frequented schools. Now,

most high schools and many middle schools have a regular police presence. Armed and unarmed police officers patrol the halls, parking lots, and athletic fields. Police dogs complement officers' efforts by sniffing out drugs and explosives. Furthermore, police attend after-school events such as football games and proms to deter problems.[10] Small wonder schoolyard crime has recently declined. But if the reason for this improvement is the improved character and self-control of our kids, *what are all those police doing in the schools?*

Many experts also consider the overall decreases in crime in the latter half of the 1990s as likely due to more community policing, intense efforts to reduce gun trafficking, heightened vigilance on the part of the public, and the improved economy.[11] And we'd rather not speculate on what the juvenile crime rate might be if we emptied out the detention centers and jails. We lock up more of our citizens, both young and old, than any other country in the world. For adults, the incarceration rate increased by 280% from 1960 to 1997.[12] The population of juveniles detained in public facilities rose 47% from 1983 to 1995, which you would expect given the increase in crime rates during that time. However, the juvenile incarceration rate continued to climb by 16% from 1995 to 1997, even as juvenile arrest rates declined. Not only did the population of children in jail grow, but the population changed. Juveniles who committed such acts as vandalizing, running away, or minor shoplifting were released or given probation. The percentage of kids in jail accused of murder, rape, robbery, or aggravated assault more than doubled. Given that about 7% of delinquent youths commit 80% of the violent crime, locking up increased numbers of kids (especially the violent ones) logically should have a significant impact on the juvenile crime rate.[13]

No doubt the efforts of law-enforcement personnel and of those who work with our troubled youth have helped decrease juvenile crime. But that's not the same thing as youth becoming honest, upright citizens who know right from wrong. Developmental psychologist Lawrence Kohlberg explored how children learn to distinguish right from wrong. His now classic theory described a sequence of stages of moral development. During the earliest, most primitive, stage, children act to avoid punishment rather than using ethics or principles to guide their behavior. Kohlberg's studies indicated that this stage applied largely to children under the age of 10.[14]

Today we apply the fear of being caught and punished—consistent with this earliest stage of moral development—to curb youth crime. These measures have apparently worked for some of our kids, as indicated by the recent reductions in the rate of juvenile arrests. However, the factors just cited—the shadows cast by overcrowded jails and detention centers; the fortification of homes, businesses, and schools; the proliferation of security systems; mushrooming police forces—suggest that we have less crime because *we've made it more difficult to commit and get away with it.* We don't nurture the moral fiber of our children; we either scare them into compliance or lock them up so they can't commit crimes.

And we continually up the ante in terms of punishment. More children than ever get sent to adult prisons, especially those who kill. We are the only country in the civilized world that tosses troubled children into the embrace of hardened criminals, pedophiles, and murderers. Yet even that horror has failed to deter our youngest murderers. The United States towers over the rest of the industrial world in terms of homicides by juveniles under the age of 15. The homicide rate for kids 14 years or younger in the United States is five times higher than the rate for the other 25 industrialized countries *combined.*[15]

In 1999, 4 children between the ages of *5 and 8* and 19 children between the ages of *9 and 12* committed murder. Killing by kids escalates rapidly from there, with 496 13- to 16-year-olds having committed a murder that year. Overall, juveniles commit about 16% of all murders in this country.[16]

In light of facts like these, we should take small comfort in the modest declines in juvenile arrests, especially for violent crime. Furthermore, recall that the surgeon general reported that overall juvenile violence has remained at peak levels, but merely out of public view. Therefore, we desperately need to come to grips with the sources of violence and aggression in our youth.

ANGER, AGGRESSION, AND SELF-ESTEEM

Many clinical psychologists and academicians continue to believe that low self-esteem causes anger, aggression, and violence. This assumption has been ubiquitous for decades. It has gone virtually unchallenged, uncritically accepted—at least until recently.

For many years Dr. Smith served as an educational diagnostician responsible for evaluating young students with behavior problems. She saw students referred for acting out, fighting on the playground, arguing with teachers, refusing to do work, vandalizing, committing theft, and behaving disrespectfully. A measure of self-esteem formed part of the assessment. Again and again she discovered that the most aggressive students exhibited high, not low, self-esteem on these standardized measures. They denied feelings of inadequacy or low self-worth and endorsed items like "I feel good about myself most of the time." The majority of these referred students blamed their troubles on unfair teachers, classmates who provoked them, or principals out to get them.

Dr. Smith found herself mystified by the inconsistency between her own observations and what the experts and prevailing theories were saying about self-esteem and aggression. Her interest in this area received another boost from her work in the juvenile detention center, a reservoir of aggressive juveniles, many of whom exhibited overly high self-esteem. Dr. Smith wondered whether these kids in some way actually suffered from a disguised form of low self-esteem, as the experts kept saying.

Further scrutiny indicated that Dr. Smith's aggressive kids indeed suffered from overly high self-esteem. However, they had some similarities to those with very low self-esteem. The kids were brittle, lacked resilience, and had high emotional volatility. Nevertheless, they thought of themselves as better and stronger than and superior to others, not the other way around. At the same time, they occasionally flipped to low self-esteem when their defenses and anger no longer worked for them. In other words, when utterly defeated, these juveniles got depressed and suffered from low self-esteem.

During the time Dr. Smith made her observations, Dr. Charles Elliott and a colleague developed a model challenging prevailing notions about self-esteem.[17] As we described in Chapter 2, the model demonstrated striking similarities between overly high and low self-views. The model helped Dr. Smith understand the inconsistency between her observations and the experts' contentions. It clarified why experts have consistently labeled those with a sense of grandiosity and narcissism as suffering from low self-esteem. Overly high self-esteem is easily punctured. So, when something or someone threatens the fragile facades of those with inflated egos, they mount a vigorous defense.[18] If their protective efforts fail, they may sink into a deflated state, that is, low self-esteem.

Consistent with this model, psychologist Dr. Martin Seligman recently indicted what he calls the "I-we" imbalance for causing both depression and inflated self-esteem. Seligman believes that Americans have a big "I" and a small "we." If big "I" people believe they are extremely important and that whether they succeed or fail is of earth-shaking importance, any failure can bring on depression. Moreover, small "we" people can no longer find solace in extended families, close communities, religion, or patriotism. Seligman contends that depression has increased tenfold over the past 50 years and that the average age of onset is now early adolescence, making what used to be an adult disorder into a childhood illness.[19]

Like us, Seligman implicates the self-esteem movement and the big "I" as a contributor to violence. He believes we have a generation of kids we've taught to feel good about themselves independent of how well they're doing. When these self-aggrandizing kids run into someone who tells them they aren't as good as they think they are, they have two choices. They can blame someone else, or they can defend their self-esteem with anger. Here is Seligman's recipe for schoolyard murders:

> *You've got a kid with a mean streak. You've got a kid that has an unwarranted sense of self-worth. When this boy comes across a world that tells him that he's not as worthy as he sees himself, and he further sees that he's a victim of that person, this will fester into seething anger. If this candidate has easy availability of guns, if he's got minimal parental supervision, this can explode as murder.*[20]

Our contention that overly high self-esteem actually connects to violence more than low self-esteem holds enormous implications. Well-meaning teachers and parents who carelessly puff up children's egos may inadvertently create little monsters. Yet parents and professionals who have worked prodigiously to raise self-esteem for decades won't change course without a lot of convincing evidence. For that reason, we will review a broad swath of research implicating high self-esteem as a prime ingredient in anger and aggression among both children and adults.

The California Task Force

First, what did the group charged with the task of demonstrating the importance of self-esteem discover about the relationship between aggression and self-esteem? The authors commissioned by the California Task Force looked at the relationship between self-esteem and violence. Dr. Thomas Scheff and colleagues reviewed studies that tested the hypothesis that low self-esteem caused crime or violence. They found essentially *nothing* and concluded, "Even reviewers who are completely sympathetic to the intentions of the quantitative studies acknowledge that these studies have produced no results. Several thousand quantitative studies later, there are still no results that are both strong and replicated."[21]

So, after finding little to support their cause, these authors redefined the meaning of self-esteem. They depicted self-esteem as the "ratio of pride to shame." Thus, Scheff and colleagues viewed hostility as a reaction to threats that could lower the ratio—in other words, that would cause a loss of pride and an increase in shame. They managed to associate this process with *low* self-esteem because they viewed aggressors as feeling shame and humiliation. Yet pride is associated with quite *positive* self-views. Indeed, in their desire to support the role of low self-esteem in causing aggression, these authors ended up proposing a model that in reality is more consistent with our view that high self-esteem, rather than low, more often leads to aggression.

Aggressive Children

Do aggressive children demonstrate high or low self-esteem? Several recent studies have addressed this question. In one study, researchers asked mothers, teachers, and classmates to rate two groups of second and third graders (62 aggressive and 53 nonaggressive children) on measures of competence and social acceptance. They also asked the two groups of children to rate themselves. Interestingly, the aggressive kids more often rated their competence in a perfect, idealized way, giving themselves higher ratings than their mothers, teachers, and friends gave them. In contrast, nonaggressive children tended to rate themselves *lower* than their mothers, teachers, or friends did. In fact, the most aggressive students had the greatest inconsistency between their own ratings and the ratings made by others.[22]

A much larger study of 859 third, fourth, and fifth graders found similar results. All students were asked to indicate how they thought other kids in their classrooms would rate their "likeability" on a five-point scale. Then all students actually made ratings of each other in terms of likability and, in addition, how aggressive they viewed their peers. Researchers discovered that children who overestimated the likability ratings they would receive were seen as significantly more aggressive than those with more accurate perceptions. Even quite modest degrees of inflated self-perception were associated with higher levels of aggression.[23] Collectively, these findings match Dr. Smith's earlier observations that behavior-disordered and delinquent kids seemed to have an inflated self-esteem, even though others did not think highly of them.

A third study refined the analysis of aggressive children and discovered several interesting subgroups. The first group consisted of kids like the aggressive children in the previous study; that is, they thought highly of themselves, whereas teachers, mothers, and peers thought more negatively of them. The second group of aggressive kids also .thought positively of themselves, but so did the other raters. The third group held negative self-views and were rated similarly by others. Although this last group of aggressive kids held a negative self-view, keep in mind that our self-esteem model predicts similarities between those with excessively low and those with excessively high self-esteem. More important, consistent with our model, the *most* aggressive and delinquent group was made up of the kids who viewed themselves positively while others viewed them negatively. In other words, they think better of themselves than they really are and aggressively defend that view.[24]

Similarly, a fourth study found aggressive kids to view themselves in more extreme, rigid, and polarized ways than nonaggressive kids. Their self-perceptions were either all good or all bad. Once again, however, the most dangerous children were the ones who saw themselves as all good.[25] This finding also conforms strikingly well to our model of self-esteem.

Bullies

Research into bullying provides additional evidence concerning the relationship between self-esteem and aggression. Bullies terrorize millions of kids every day in our schools. Bullies use fear and intimidation to bludgeon their victims. Bullies not only tease but harass, threaten, and physically harm their innocent victims. The victims frequently develop a phobia of going to school or other problems such as depression and anxiety. These emotional problems can cause inability to concentrate and diminished interest in academics, resulting in poor grades. A recent survey indicated that about 40% of children in grades six through twelve had threatened another student at school in the past year. These threats included hitting, slapping, and kicking. Twenty-five percent of students reported fear of a bully and almost 20% claimed to have been hit, slapped, or kicked at school.[26] And bullies continue to aggress as adults, having four times the rate of serious crimes of non-bullies.[27]

Sometimes bullying exacts a fearful price. Kelly Yeoman was overweight, wore glasses, and was not good at sports. For years, bullies at her school stabbed her with pencils, called her names, and beat her up. Her glasses were broken and eggs were thrown at her house. She was terrified to walk home from school and rarely went outside. When Kelly complained to her teachers, they told her not to be a tattletale. Kelly's parents approached the tormenters, who hurled obscenities at them. The parents begged the school for help and even sent a letter from a lawyer demanding action. It was all to no avail. Kelly Yeoman was 13 years old when she killed herself.[28]

Popular stereotypes characterize bullies as socially inept, oafish, and dense. Recent findings have overturned that description. Bullies know what they are doing. Specifically, bullies are manipulative experts in social situations, using cold, sophisticated methods in carrying out their terror.[29] Bullies like to show off and perform. They enjoy dominating others. They maintain their one-up status by putting others down. When threatened, they react with rage. Researchers have confirmed this picture of the bully by finding links between exhibitionism, dominance, grandiosity, hostility, and aggression.[30]

In short, bullies are not just losers with low self-esteem looking for attention. Bullies feel good about themselves. They feel more secure and anxiety-free than their victims. Bullies are narcissistic, hostile kids who constantly try to self-aggrandize. They dominate and put themselves above others. Why? Highly acclaimed social psychologist Dr. Roy Baumeister reviewed evidence supporting the idea that bullies have a highly favorable view of themselves. He concluded, "The bully has a chip on his shoulder because he thinks you might want to deflate his favorable self-image."[31]

Low self-esteem is not typically one of the bully's problems. What is a problem for bullies is inflated self-esteem, especially when it is threatened.

Juvenile Gangs and Delinquency

More evidence for the positive relationship between high self-esteem and violence lies in the literature on juvenile gangs and delinquency. Not surprisingly, delinquents, like bullies, have a puffed-up sense of themselves. In their own eyes, they are the elite. But that elitism rests on a precarious pedestal. They find the slightest assault on their self-respect abhorrent. You can't maintain a sense of superiority and incorporate any significant degree of negative qualities into your self-concept.

Sociologist Elijah Anderson analyzed gangs and found that so-called respect forms a central part of the code of the street. He determined that gang members believe themselves to be special, superior to others. At the same time, they maintain constant vigilance, watching for any event that could challenge their superiority or even indicate a failure to recognize it.[32]

Dr. Smith recently interviewed a group of gang members in the Albuquerque Juvenile Detention Center. The six young men uniformly agreed that respect stands above all else. They maintained respect by defending the status of the gang against any and all threats. She asked the boys what constituted a threat to the gang's respect. Several boys cited the idea of being "dogged" as especially insulting. Being "dogged" referred to a disagreeable look displayed by a member of another gang. That's it, just a bad look. This bad look could result in a show of force between gang members ranging from mere shoving to beatings and even killing. Gangs mock humility and admire victory in combat. Devoted and obedient, gang members willingly sacrifice their lives, or the lives of their family members. Like soldiers in battle, they defend a noble cause: respect. Or should we say self-esteem?

Gangs believe in their own group's superiority over other gangs. Sociologist Jack Katz even argues that gangs have a peculiar investment in keeping the cycle of community violence going because such violence justifies their existence as a way of defending against a dangerous world.[33] When gangs insult other gangs, it seems to represent their way of establishing superiority and maintaining their overly high self-esteem. Once gangs receive an insult, they feel a driven need to retaliate in order to maintain their facade of power and mystique of dread.

Dr. Roy Baumeister (1996) critically reviewed the literature on delinquency and gangs and also concluded that gang members are egotistical: "Gang members apparently think, talk, and act like people with high self-esteem, and there is little to support the view that they are humble or self-deprecating or even that they are privately full of insecurities and self-doubts."[34] Oddly, many experts continue to blame delinquency and violence on low self-esteem despite the lack of evidence to support their position.[35]

Additional evidence contradicting such experts can be seen in a study of 129 adolescent boys taken from a juvenile detention center and a high school. Researcher Dr. Leslie Pearlman found that narcissism, the antithesis of low self-esteem, predicted the amount of self-reported violence and aggression in both groups.[36] Once again contradicting popular notions, another study found that low self-esteem did not increase delinquency in a sample of 830 urban students from New York.[37]

Finally, Dr. Smith conducted a pilot study of delinquents in the context of her position as a psychologist working at a juvenile detention center. At first glance, this study appeared unrelated to self-esteem. Dr. Smith implemented a well-researched aggression replacement and social skills curriculum[38] for incarcerated students during a six-week summer program. She assessed students' self-reported social skills at the beginning and at the completion of the program.

The first surprise came when Dr. Smith found students rating themselves within the average range on social skills, in obvious contradiction to reality. The social skills measure looked at qualities such as cooperation, getting along with others, conflict resolution skills, and empathy. Many of the students had been diagnosed as having behavior disorders, which means that they were oppositional, aggressive, and lacking in the social skills needed to get along with others. All were repeat offenders; many had committed assaults, domestic violence, and even murder. One would have to look far and wide for a group of students who were less socially skilled, yet they appeared to consider themselves equal to most others. Clearly, they had bloated self-perceptions.

The second surprise came at the end of the six-week program, when the students rated themselves somewhat lower on social skills. This finding came after three hours per day of direct instruction in communication, empathy, conflict resolution, and character education. The only reasonable explanation of these findings is that these delinquents had slightly lowered the ratings of their skills to come closer to reality because they had gained awareness of what constitutes social skills. On the face of it, one would think that the program had failed: Students should have learned some skills and should have felt more competent. But if we recall that these students started out with an unrealistically high notion of their social skills, the results make a lot of sense. It would appear that these students started with overblown perceptions of their skills. If anything, the program may have deflated those self-perceptions— arguably a good thing to do. These students needed more humility, not more pride.[39]

Wife Batterers and Rapists

Up to this point, we have considered aggressive children, bullies, and delinquents. We can strengthen our confidence in the relationship between inflated self-esteem and aggression by reviewing data from other populations. Indeed, widely discrepant populations show identical patterns. For example, one researcher assumed that abusive husbands suffered from low self-esteem. He gathered a sample of 50 abusive husbands and 50 non-abusive husbands. Though he predicted the opposite, abusive husbands demonstrated higher self-esteem than the non-abusive husbands.[40] By now, you might predict this result. Wife batterers often abuse their wives when they feel their dominant, superior role has been called into question. In other words, overly favorable views of the self are all too easily threatened. This threat leads to violence.

Men who rape also seem to believe in their superiority. Sixteen-year-old Jake saw a therapist because of a court mandate. He had attempted to rape a cheerleader. His attorney successfully struck a plea bargain because the plaintiff didn't want to testify. After several months of therapy, Jake's therapist encouraged him to start dating. They worked on the issue and the needed skills for a number of sessions. Jake worked up the courage and asked a popular girl to go to a school dance with him. She laughed, "Are you kidding? I have to wash my socks."

Jake felt humiliated. Rage rapidly surged through him. He stormed home and stole a bottle of vodka from his parents' liquor cabinet. As he quickly downed half a bottle, images of her mocking laughter and thoughts about how to get even engulfed him. He fantasized omnipotent sexual prowess and control over women. Feeling intense restlessness, he left his home looking for a way to assuage the demons inside him. Jake plunged into predator mode. He drove slowly around several parks, scanning for prey. At the third one, he spotted a lone, attractive 13-year-old girl. He craved dominance and felt an overwhelming urge to conquer. He pulled over to the side of the road and called to her. Hours later, the hysterical girl's mother drove her to the emergency room. Jake had brutally beaten and raped her.

Rape apparently restores positive views of the self. Most rapists do not commit their heinous acts for sexual pleasure, but to feel superior and enjoy the helplessness of the victim. Rape is all about power. Rapists often feel they have been wronged, hurt, or mistreated, usually by a woman. In other words, someone has threatened their self-esteem.[41] The so-called threat often represents a misconstrual or misinterpretation of the woman's intent.[42] For example, if Jake had been politely turned down, he still may have felt the same rage, believing that his manhood had been diminished. Often, as in Jake's case, the victim is someone other than the one who challenged the rapist's superiority.

When author Diana Scully interviewed convicted rapists, many boasted of their sexual prowess. Some even believed their victim likely thought highly of them. Some of these men considered themselves highly talented achievers. Since Scully interviewed these men in prison, one has to assume these self-views represented rather serious distortions in an overly positive direction.[43] Once again, inflated views of the self, when threatened, seek ways to restore their original exalted position. Unfortunately, that restoration all too often occurs at considerable expense to others.

Psychopaths

Nowhere does the role of inflated self-esteem or narcissism play out more prominently than in psychopaths. Psychopaths are dispassionately violent monsters who callously rape and rob vulnerable victims and kill without remorse. Social predators waiting for the next opportunity to score, they manipulate, charm, and intimidate their victims. And psychopaths are busy people. When not in jail, they commit an estimated 50% of serious crimes. Many of our serial killers, drug dealers, perpetrators of domestic violence, and gangsters are psychopaths.[44]

Do psychopaths suffer from low self-esteem? Quite the contrary. Psychopaths possess self-confidence to the point of arrogance. They feel superior, more intelligent, and more special than the rest of us. Dr. Aaron T. Beck, renowned psychiatrist, described the psychopath. "Their lack of empathy for the people they hurt is a major component of their congeniality with violent crimes . . . quite adept at reading other people's minds, they use this skill only to dominate and control others and not to identify with the people they hurt."[45]

Unlike other criminals, psychopaths don't need an excuse to harm, kill, rape, or victimize. They love to brag about their conquests and exploits. They view themselves narcissistically, existing at the center of the universe.

Psychologists J. Reid Meloy and Carl Gacono visited the inner world of the psychopath through the use of the well-known Rorschach inkblot test, which allows skilled interpreters to assess aspects of personality and thinking styles that sometimes can't be discerned from other types of psychological testing. In a large sample, they found that psychopaths exhibited a particularly malignant, sadistic, and aggressive form of narcissism. They were grandiose and self-focused, and their relationships with others were generally defined by dominance rather than warmth.[46]

The grandiosity of psychopaths is so extreme that they manage to escape guilt. Why don't they feel guilt? Guilt would bring down their superiority and self-esteem and thus can't be tolerated. Psychopaths do no wrong.

A psychopath can torture and murder while blaming the victim. Like the teenage robbers at the beginning of this chapter, a psychopath would say the cashier shouldn't have pulled the gun. That's why he died. They've even been known to say their victims *benefited* from their hideous deeds. After killing an elderly woman in a wheelchair for her money, a psychopath might very well declare that he helped end the poor woman's pain.

Of course, not all narcissists are psychopaths. A wide array of influences contribute to the development of psychopaths, including genetics, learning experiences, brain dysfunction, and so on. Still, the extraordinary self-absorption and superiority of psychopaths show what narcissism is like at its absolute extreme. And it doesn't look anything like low self-esteem.

Child Killers and School Shooters

We now see psychopaths blooming at disturbingly early ages. When you think about the declines in juvenile arrests, also consider the fact that we're seeing a type of crime virtually unheard of among children before.

Examples are all too familiar. Nathaniel Abraham announced one fall day that he was going to shoot someone. He practiced with a stolen gun on targets and then shot and killed 18-year-old Ronnie Greene Jr. Nathaniel bragged to friends about the shooting the next day. Police arrested him on Halloween Day, in costume. Nathaniel was 11 years old.[47]

A pair of boys aged 10 and 11 were convicted of dropping a 5-year-old boy from a fourteenth-story window. Why? The 5-year-old had refused to steal candy for them. The boys, at ages 12 and 13, became the youngest inmates in the Illinois correctional system.[48]

Another young criminal's own mother turned him in to authorities. He celebrated his twelfth birthday two days after committing his crime. He and his fellow gang members tortured and raped a 13-year-old girl in an abandoned house. In order to eliminate the evidence and the victim, who might identify them, the gang set the site of the crime ablaze. A neighbor, Dumar Stokes, scrambled to investigate and found a flock of boys fleeing the scene. He demanded that they put the fire out. The soon to be 12-year-old boy allegedly shot at him but missed. Instead, he killed 82-year-old Viola McClain, who was innocently standing on her porch.[49]

How early in a child's life can we find the seeds of violence? Authorities charged a 6-year-old boy with the attempted murder of an infant. He callously tossed the baby out of its crib and kicked and beat the infant with a stick. The baby, only one month old at the time, will likely suffer permanent brain damage. The kindergartner was believed to be the youngest child in the nation ever charged with attempted murder.[50]

Recent years have witnessed an alarming new trend: school shootings. These tragic episodes are taking place in high schools, middle schools, even elementary schools. Often the precipitating event seems absurdly trivial—to us. School officials sent one honor roll student home from school for throwing water balloons. The 13-year-old boy went home and found a handgun in his grandfather's dresser. He returned to school, but his teacher refused to let him in. He proceeded to shoot and kill the teacher.[51]

The sense of being wronged seems to be a common theme in these frightening crimes. Fourteen-year-old honor student Barry Loukaitis, dressed in black and armed with three loaded guns, sauntered into his algebra class. He shot his teacher in the back and two classmates in the chest. "This sure beats algebra, doesn't it," Barry coolly remarked as he towered over the body of a dying boy gasping for breath while choking on his blood. Barry admitted he had a victim in mind when he strode into the classroom, specifically a boy who had teased him at one time—who had the misfortune of having challenged Barry's self-esteem.[52] "He loved what he did. This was his moment of glory," said Renee Erb, prosecuting attorney.

Evan Ramsey warned several friends to go to the safety of the second-floor balcony because he planned to bring a gun to school. He reportedly said, "You'll see who's better then." He walked in, shot an athlete in the stomach, and killed him. The athlete had ridiculed him previously. Evan then roamed the hallways, tracking the principal, whom he found and killed. Students knew the principal as a strict disciplinarian. He had placed Evan Ramsey on the detention list. The friends Ramsey warned heeded his advice and watched from the balcony. They'd told no one. Ramsey thought it would be cool to shoot up the school.[53]

"I am not insane. I am angry. I do this to show society, push us and we will push back," wrote 16-year-old Luke Woodham. On the morning of October 1, 1997, Luke, wearing a baggy overcoat, approached a 16-year-old sophomore whom he had briefly dated. The year before, she had broken off the relationship, telling him she wanted to see other boys. Luke pulled a hunting rifle from beneath his coat and shot Christina Menefee fatally in the neck. For 11 minutes, he methodically fired and reloaded his gun, killing another student and wounding seven others. Later, police found his mother dead at home. When asked why, he replied, "The world has wronged me."[54]

Who are the school shooters? Are they neglected children suffering from inadequate self-esteem? Were they abused by their parents? More often than not, the answer is to the contrary. Like other school shooters, 15-year-old Kip Kinkle blamed his problems on others, not himself. Yet his parents—both popular, respected teachers—did their very best to make him happy. They spent time with him, took him on vacations, made few demands, and sought professional help early and often. They weren't completely oblivious to signs of trouble.

They worried about their son's temper and his interest in guns and bombs. He idolized the Oklahoma City bomber and the Unabomber, Ted Kaczynski. They also had concerns when young Kip put lit firecrackers into the mouths of squirrels and chipmunks. Yet, according to family friends, his parents were unable to say no or set limits. After some hesitation, they agreed to buy him a gun. They debated over buying him a single-loading bolt-action gun or something capable of more rapid fire. Acceding to his wishes, they decided on the more lethal gun.

Kip proceeded to kill his parents. Then he used his .22-caliber semiautomatic Ruger rifle to fire off 50 rounds at Thurston High School, killing 2 and wounding 25.[55]

Hitler's birthday, April 20. Eric Harris and Dylan Klebold laughed and whooped it up while killing 12 classmates and a teacher at Columbine High School in Colorado in 1999. One of the shooters said, "Oh, look at this guy's brains and the blood." The gunmen targeted minority students and popular athletes. Fortunately, several bombs they had planted failed to detonate. At the conclusion of the killing extravaganza, Eric and Dylan killed themselves. They had planned this massacre for over a year. Two months before the slaughter, Dylan wrote an essay. In it, he described an assault on jocks by a man in a black trench coat. He wrote that the blood from the first nine victims reflected in the light of a street lamp. Police retrieved the 11-and-a-half-page story from Klebold's BMW. Comments by the teacher on the essay included "Great details" and "Quite an ending."

By now the nation knows these children did not grow up in poverty. In fact, Eric's house was valued at close to $200,000, and Dylan's at close to $400,000. Neighbors described parents of both sons as solid, sensitive, and normal. Both sets of parents had taken their kids in for counseling. Dylan's father even prided himself on being his son's soul mate.

Investigators worked diligently to understand these two young killers. They reviewed diaries and interviewed friends and classmates. In some writings, both Dylan and Eric complained about their lack of self-esteem. At the same time, their feelings of superiority surfaced in other works. In a videotape, they talked of how evolved they were, how they considered themselves superhuman. One of Eric's writings stated, "I am God." Both wrote of disdain and hate for others—not exactly the writings of kids with low self-esteem.[56]

We could go on, but anyone who reads the newspapers or sees the news on television can supply any number of similar stories. The question is, why this epidemic of murderous violence? Many of the kids who have perpetrated these crimes were considered nerds, not part of the in-crowd. Certainly they were teased and harassed. Surely, then, they suffered from low self-esteem.

Perhaps a few did have low self-esteem. But more of these child killers appear to be full-blown narcissists, if not psychopaths. Even those with low self-esteem clearly harbored delusions of grandeur and the need to feel powerful and dominant. These are not characteristics typical of low self-esteem. In fact, research suggests that most of those with low self-esteem have a significantly lower risk of aggression and violence than those with high self-esteem.[57]

What we observe in youthful killers is not an inward-looking disparagement of self, but rather grandiosity, a pronounced tendency to blame others, and hostile feelings directed outward in murderous ways. These are kids whose universe is centered on one thing: themselves. They are kids who believe they should feel good, all the time, and who become enraged when life doesn't cooperate.

IS EXCESSIVE SELF-ESTEEM THE CAUSE OF IT ALL?

Incredibly, for decades traditional views of delinquents, aggressive kids, murderers, rapists, and psychopaths implicated low self-esteem as the major cause of their antisocial acts. This perspective hypothesized that people who feel inferior strike out at others in an attempt to make themselves feel better. As you have seen, however, the evidence runs to the contrary. If anything, aggression and violence are much more closely linked to excessively high self-esteem and narcissism. It's one thing to say that the self-esteem movement's diagnosis is both unsupported and wrongheaded. But does that mean that we should draw the opposite conclusion? Is excessive self-esteem the cause of all this senseless violence? Let's consider some evidence on this point.

Psychopaths, rapists, aggressive kids, bullies, delinquents, and school shooters. What image usually comes to mind when you think about these sorts of characters? We suspect you usually think of men and boys. Not that you believe most men are aggressive or violent, but that they commit a disproportionate share of these acts. And that is, in fact, the case. The males of our species do engage in more violence and aggression than females. Many believe this phenomenon has a genetic base. Still, it's worth asking whether males or females have higher self-esteem. You guessed it. Almost every study on this issue has found that males typically have higher self-esteem than females. One report analyzed 216 of these studies and found that the self-esteem of young males consistently exceeded that of young females. This finding was especially true for adolescents.[58]

Admittedly, the size of this difference was relatively small, and in any case an association between higher self-esteem and aggression would not, of itself, establish a causal link. Nevertheless, there is other suggestive evidence to consider. Recall, for example, that the rates of female violent crime and aggression have risen in recent years. Huge increases in arrests have taxed states to find more room for girls in their locked facilities. Interestingly, physical assaults by female juveniles have increased at the same time that arrests for assaults by male juveniles have decreased. Between 1981 and 1997, the rate of violence against persons committed by girls increased by 235%.[59] Why would the rate for female violence be growing at such a staggering level? Does this increase have anything to do with self-esteem? Again, the evidence is suggestive: One renowned expert contends that female self-esteem appears to be rising relative to that of men in recent decades.[60] While hardly conclusive, this trend does suggest an avenue of exploration: whether the increasing self-esteem in females has some relationship to the increase in violent female juveniles.

We need to be cautious here, lest we commit the error we have charged self-esteem promoters with—namely, drawing conclusions about causes and effects from correlational data. Of necessity, most of the studies we've cited in this chapter and others have reviewed relationships such as the one just noted about how female self-esteem and female violence have risen in tandem. We cannot definitively assert a cause-and-effect relationship based on such data. *However, the impressive number of these studies across widely divergent populations and problems increases their credibility and the likelihood that at the bottom of these associations is some causal relationship.* Furthermore, in some areas, such as aggression, researchers are beginning to compile the kind of experimental data that permit us to draw stronger conclusions.

In one particularly clever experiment, researchers identified a group of highly narcissistic students and a group of students who scored low on a measure of narcissism. They told these students they were going to be administered two newly developed IQ tests. What the students didn't know was that the purpose of the experiment had nothing to do with IQ tests. The researchers wanted to know how they would react to positive or negative feedback.

When narcissists received positive feedback on their IQ performance, they enthusiastically chalked up their success to their own ability. However, when researchers told them they did not do so well, the narcissists got mad; they couldn't stand the negative information. Those low in narcissism also attributed successful feedback to their own ability, but to a lesser degree than the narcissists. In contrast to those with high narcissism, they did not show anger in response to negative feedback.[61]

Other researchers extended that finding by determining that narcissists not only feel anger but also express it. In their study, 540 students filled out a questionnaire measuring narcissism. The investigators asked the students to write a short essay. Regardless of the quality of the essay, half of the students were told that their essays stunk. The other half received glowing feedback on their writing. Of course, the person giving the feedback was in cahoots with the experimenters. Next, the subjects performed a competitive task with the person who had evaluated their writing. The task allowed the students to zap the evaluator with an obnoxious, loud noise. Not surprisingly, narcissists who had received negative feedback on their writing chose to inflict the loudest noises, while the narcissists who had received praise administered milder noises. And the non-narcissists inflicted mild-mannered noises regardless of the feedback they received.[62] Once again, narcissism was the crucial difference between more and less aggressive subjects.

Finally, like the California Task Force, Dr. Baumeister and colleagues comprehensively reviewed evidence from a wide range of authors who contend that low self-esteem causes anger and aggression.[63] Baumeister repeatedly found that these authors' own evidence failed miserably in supporting their view that low self-esteem leads to aggression. In fact, Dr. Baumeister concluded from his exhaustive critique that the single major cause of aggression and violence appears to be *overly high self-esteem that is threatened by others*. He firmly asserted that when someone contradicts, challenges, or impugns those with inflated self-esteem, they react with aggression. Of course, he notes, everyone finds a decrease in self-esteem unpleasant. However, those with swollen self-esteem respond with far more intense hostility.

Dr. Baumeister's conclusion may sound similar to the ideas we cited earlier from the California Task Force. As you may remember, the task force proffered that when challenged, those with pride suffer humiliation and become aggressive. Similarly, Dr. Baumeister found that those with high self-esteem (and presumably pride) react with aggression when impugned. There's one important difference, however. Dr. Baumeister did not suggest—nor did he see any reason to assume—that these high-self-esteem people actually felt humiliated. Rather, he contended that those with overly high self-esteem will aggressively defend their turf. In any event, both the California Task Force and Dr. Baumeister ended up supporting the idea that what starts the ball of aggression rolling is overly high self-esteem.

All this is not to say that everyone with high self-esteem engages in violence and aggression. Some people feel pretty good about themselves, and they have pretty good reasons. They have good values, have worked hard, and have accomplished much. Their self-esteem stands solid as a rock, and it rarely varies. When these people experience failure or criticism, they shrug it off or feel bad for a brief time. Like everyone, they can feel angry, but their anger doesn't boil over and consume them. The overriding question is how to figure out which people with high self-esteem will resort to rage and which ones won't. No doubt, some people with low self-esteem also get angry and violent at times. Once again, which of them will and which of them won't?

Some experts believe that the *stability* of self-esteem, rather than simply the level of self-esteem, accounts for some of the difference between those who become violent and those who do not. Stability of self-esteem refers to the fact that some people's self-esteem remains constant. For example, those with stable low self-esteem fail to appreciate themselves even when others do. And some with stable high self-esteem always value themselves regardless of life's vicissitudes. Another group of people fluctuate between high and low self-esteem, depending on momentary circumstances.

One researcher addressed the issue of self-esteem stability in a novel way. He evaluated both the stability and the level of his subjects' self-esteem. He did this by asking students to carry beepers for a week. Each time they received a page, they completed a feelings coding sheet that asked whether they were feeling happy, proud, frustrated, useless, or angry. Also, on each day, a different page alerted them to fill out a self-esteem rating. The results? Those with high but unstable (variable) self-esteem reported more hostility, anger, and aggressiveness than any other group. In contrast, those with high, stable self-esteem reported the least hostility. Those with unstable low self-esteem fell in the middle on anger and hostility.[64]

We should note that this experiment dealt with normal college students and used a measure of self-esteem that did not tap extremes of self-esteem such as narcissism. The model we have presented in this book would predict that the more extreme ends of self-esteem, whether high or low, would likely produce greater amounts of instability and aggression. However, the tendency toward aggression is likely to be worst for those with overly inflated self-esteem because the self-centered narcissist is involved in a constant struggle to maintain a fragile, grandiose self-image.

We don't want to give the impression that all aggression results from overly high self-esteem or even overly high, unstable self-esteem. Obviously crime, delinquency, bullying, aggression, and murder have many complex causes. Some evidence supports the idea that genetics play an important role. Furthermore, environment, culture, and early childhood events also contribute to the incubation of anger and violence.

We do maintain two things, however. First, despite substantial evidence to the contrary, low self-esteem has been unjustly singled out as a cause of violence and aggression, a fallacious idea that has led to completely mistaken ideas for "cures" for these social ills. Second, a far more plausible contributor—overly high-esteem—has been left hidden in the shadows.

The emphasis on raising self-esteem and focusing on what Seligman calls the big "I" only keeps the lights out. It allows inflated self-esteem to stand as something to strive for and admire. In light of the evidence that suggests a link between inflated self-esteem and aggression, we can only wonder how much we are contributing to violence among our youth when we encourage a flimsy self-esteem and a vigilant preoccupation with defending the almighty self.

CHAPTER 6

"YOU'RE SO SPECIAL!" SELF-ESTEEM IN THE SCHOOLS

FIFTH GRADERS NOISILY PUSH INTO THE CLASSROOM AFTER LUNCH recess. Mr. Harrison quickly settles them down with his loud, serious commands. He reminds the class that this is Thursday, the day when Ms. Berger, the school counselor, visits for affective education. The class erupts with groans and snickers. Mr. Harrison secretly approves of his class's reaction, but he proceeds to tell the students to form a circle with their desks. Ms. Berger always insists that a circle allows students to communicate more effectively and as equals. Mr. Harrison needs to remain in the room when Ms. Berger conducts affective lessons because the students seem to spiral out of control in her presence.

139

Ms. Berger announces today's lesson: "What I like about you." She tells popular Sandra to stand in the middle of the circle. Each member of the class must say something nice about Sandra. Sandra giggles as the students recite various glowing compliments such as "You're really smart," "You're pretty," "You're funny," "You care about people," and so on. Sandra beams when they finish, clearly relishing the attention.

Ms. Berger hopes the lesson will boost the self-esteem of all the recipients, including the less popular students. Accordingly, she calls on Richard, a quiet student with few friends, to take his place in the circle. Richard's face turns red, but he complies with the request. Ms. Berger instructs the class to tell Richard something nice. Silence falls over the classroom, followed by stifled laughter. Ms. Berger tells the class they aren't being nice. She says everyone is full of wonderful qualities. For example, Richard is exceptionally well behaved. Richard blinks back tears.

Self-esteem in the classroom. If you feel that you haven't personally seen the self-esteem movement in action, drop by a school sometime and ask to see their self-esteem curriculum. Competing with reading, writing, and arithmetic, lessons for improving self-esteem consume precious instructional time.

Although it takes away from academics, affective education at least looks relatively harmless. But is it? Careless self-esteem boosting corrodes kids' inner core. Look at the example of Sandra. Already popular, with a fine opinion of herself, does she really need to hear a bombardment of flattery? Sandra soaks up the glory, filling her self-esteem balloon with self-adoring messages. As she experiences these exercises over her next seven years in school, she learns to value self-love, self-centeredness—in a word, narcissism. On the other hand, Richard may remember his moment of humiliation for the rest of his life. False affirmations can't fool children with deflated balloons. Richard heard the dreadful silence of his classmates. Ms. Berger's feeble attempt to rescue him only made things worse. When you fabricate positive messages, those with low self-esteem suffer. They're painfully aware of the gulf between reality and illusion.

Look closely at most self-esteem curriculums, and you'll see efforts to puff kids up with cheap gimmicks, inane slogans, and narcissistic games. These activities start in kindergarten and continue year after year through high school.

Consider what goes on in some of these curriculums. Jack Canfield, author of the mega-selling Chicken Soup series of books, wrote a self-esteem handbook for teachers in 1976; it went through 30 printings prior to its second edition, which appeared in 1994. He tells teachers to spend *several days* of precious school time having students make advertisements and commercials to *sell themselves to the world*. After they complete their projects, students share with one another. Adds Canfield, "We suggest that contests, judging, and prizes be avoided; they only create unnecessary competition that can lead to feelings of inadequacy and resentment among those who do not win."[1]

Another of Canfield's ideas is the magic box. The teacher begins the activity by asking the class, "Who do you think is the most special person in the world?" After the children respond, the teacher continues, "Well, I have a magic box with me today and each of you will have a chance to look inside and discover the most important person in the world."[2] The teacher places a mirror in the box and takes it around to each child. She asks, "Who is the most important person in the world?" The child responds, "Me!"

Perhaps you think this exercise looks like a waste of classroom time. But at least it appears benign. Is it? Recall our discussion from Chapter 2 about experiments on self-absorption. Some of these studies increased participants' self-focus by using exercises quite similar to Canfield's magic box. They found that doing so caused negative feelings to intensify and lowered problem-solving ability.[3] Although these experiments have not been replicated with children, wouldn't you want to exercise considerable caution in using exercises such as these?

Another of Canfield's early inspirations is called "mirror bragging." Students are instructed to brag for two minutes about themselves. Then teachers tell the students to *exaggerate* their performances by "standing up proudly, throwing chests out, talking enthusiastically, etc."[4] Canfield boasts of the exercise's ability to make students feel more comfortable bragging.

These mindless exercises are a blatant misuse of academic time and have the potential for causing harm. They steal from our children's education and have the potential to create a gaggle of little narcissists. Do you really want your kids thinking they're the most special beings in the world?

Project Self-Esteem is a curriculum for children in kindergarten through sixth grade. It promises improved self-esteem and prevention of drug and alcohol abuse. Here's an example of how the project works. Students play a game of Simon Says, except no one sits down so that no one feels bad for making a mistake. The directions tell the children to stand up and shout, "I am special," again and again.[5]

The Best Self-Esteem Activities for the Elementary Grades contains a cornucopia of similar exercises. In one of these, students sit in a circle and close their eyes. They try to remember times when people said nice things to them. Students are asked to report what they come up with to the group and are asked, "Why is liking yourself so very important?"[6] Frankly, we'd like to ask the same question.

Barbara Sher, in *Self-Esteem Games,* suggests having children stand in front of a mirror while saying self-admiring affirmations. Another exercise exhorts children to fantasize about *things* they want—anything from spaceships to eighteen-speed bikes. The exercise is called "Even Happier,"[7] yet another flagrant example of promoting self-esteem through materialism and self-admiration. Titles of self-esteem curriculum books published throughout the '90s provide further understanding of the way that the self-esteem movement continues to engage in a spirited, superficial coronation of the self. For example, *101 Ways to Make Your Child Feel Special*, *I Believe in Me: A Book of Affirmations*, and *I Am a Star: My Building High Self-Esteem Book*. Finally, our nomination for the title most illustrative of self-focused narcissism: *Building Self-Esteem Through the Museum of I: 25 Original Projects That Explore and Celebrate the Self*.

These titles represent merely a few out of hundreds of self-esteem curriculums hawked to schools and parents. They all have the same look and feel. They all use simplistic strategies to wipe out any negative thoughts and feelings and replace them with positive thoughts and feelings.

Self-esteem invades more than specific curriculums. It colors the climate of the classroom and the home. For example, in the book *Building Self-Esteem in Children*, authors Patricia Berne and Louis Savary tell parents and teachers never to embarrass children because it can damage their self-esteem. How far does this advice go? "I took Tommy, one of my tutoring students, to the library and I let him take out a book, but I never asked him if he had read it. I did not want to put him in the embarrassing position of perhaps having to admit he hadn't read it or didn't like it."[8]

Why on earth wouldn't you ask Tommy if he'd read the book? It's like not asking Tommy if he's done his homework for fear of embarrassing him and damaging his self-esteem. How can you get most kids to do their schoolwork if you're afraid to ask them whether they've done it or not? Advice like this and the self-esteem curriculums share an obsessive concern with the self: "I am special." "Feel good; be happy." If only it were that simple.

If it were so simple, we would see improved academic performance and reductions in all the other social ills that have been blamed on low self-esteem. At the very least, we would see data indicating the value of such activities for helping to prevent bad outcomes or to promote good ones. Of course, we see neither. In the absence of evidence that these programs accomplish the goals they purport to accomplish, shouldn't we be concerned about the time taken away from academics—especially since such academic time appears to be in short supply in our schools today?

Don't think so? Research conducted by psychology professors Harold Stevenson and James Stigler found that by the fifth grade, American students sitting in academic classes engage in learning only about 65% of the time. They spend 35% of classroom time sharpening pencils, finding books or materials, or quieting down![9] Drs. Stevenson and Stigler also looked at the total amount of time that teachers directed activities (whether academic or not) in the classroom. They found teachers took the lead in the students' activities less than half of total class time in both the first and fifth grades. In other words, *nobody* took charge of the classroom 51% of the time in the U.S. schools studied. By contrast, in countries where school achievement far exceeds that in the United States (for example, Taiwan and Japan), teachers led children's activities up to 90% of the time.[10] Making matters even worse, a significant portion of the 49% of teacher-led instructional time in U.S. schools gets expended on raising kids' self-esteem. Scary thought.

STUDENT-CENTERED VERSUS
TEACHER-DIRECTED LEARNING

When you open the door to Mrs. Greene's third-grade classroom, you see colorful paper butterflies hanging from the ceiling and hear the buzz of 22 children. A group of four sits at a small round table with Mrs. Greene, reading from a beautifully illustrated picture book. As one boy struggles with a word, she gently corrects him. This particular group reads from a pre-first-grade reader, or primer, and if you listen more closely, it sounds as if the children know the story by heart.

In a brightly carpeted corner of the room, a sign designates THE SCIENCE CENTER. Under the sign, a girl is standing on a chair while three other students sit on beanbags watching her. One student holds a stopwatch, another a clipboard, and the third an apple, a feather, a pencil, and a piece of paper. This group will learn about gravity by having the girl drop the objects, timing their descent, and charting the times.

At another round table, a small group of students work addition and subtraction problems by counting tiny rubber bears. In one area, a couple of children draw designs on computers, while another builds a tower with blocks. Finally, an educational assistant helps a boy trace his body on a huge sheet of paper. Others in this group cut out their own shapes or color them. The kids hang their body cutouts with clothespins on a line stretching across the back of the room. A huge banner above it declares: "SPECIAL SUPER STARS OF THE THIRD GRADE!"

The recess bell rings. Mrs. Greene tells the children to clean up their areas. One student leaps up and runs to the door, ignoring Mrs. Greene's request to stop. Another pushes her chair in, accidentally knocking it over. She leaves it and runs to the door. Children trample on crayons, scissors, and paper as they pile out of the room. Mrs. Greene laughs, shakes her head, and, with the help of her aide, cleans up the mess.

Parents and administrators consider Mrs. Greene a master teacher. Student teachers from the university regularly visit to learn about her "student-centered" teaching methods. A student-centered classroom emphasizes thinking skills over content. Indeed, Mrs. Greene calls herself a learning coach. She remains in the background while her students explore. She tries to facilitate discovery rather than direct her students to subject material that might not interest them. So, for example, students participate in "hands-on science," a method of teaching based on the notion of discovery through exploration and experiencing. This is the rationale for teaching the concept of gravity by having students drop and time the fall of different objects. Similarly, Mrs. Greene's kids learn about math concepts through experiential manipulation rather than rote memorization of math facts.

Because Mrs. Greene believes that students learn best when they work independently, with minimal direction, she chooses easily mastered materials. She prefers to teach reading by a "whole language" approach; she knows it appeals to children more than drill and practice with phonics. Whole-language advocates believe children will learn to read naturally, just as they learned to talk. They believe that reading to children and exposing them to the written language will inspire students. So Mrs. Greene sits and reads with the kids—even if they do know the story by heart.

In this kind of classroom, students' interest and motivation drive the learning. Rather than all working on the same assigned task, students choose from a variety of engaging activities. Committees and group projects are intended to enable the children who need extra help to receive it from their classmates.

Above all, Mrs. Greene "knows" that good self-esteem forms the foundation for all learning. That's why the children work on projects, like the portrait cutouts exercise, designed to make them feel special and cared about. Mrs. Greene celebrates success in her classroom. She does not believe in grades because no child should experience failure. She works hard to minimize her students' frustration, believing that doing so will reduce the need for discipline. Like most teachers in her school, she does not retain a student who fails to master grade-level material. She worries about the harm retention would inflict on a child's self-esteem. She believes if a child does not succeed in her classroom, most likely it is due to a learning disability.

Mrs. Greene, like so many dedicated teachers, works long hours to provide the best educational opportunities for her lucky students. She has received the teacher-of-the-year award several times. Parents and children feel good about her classroom.

What an idyllic atmosphere for learning and emotional development! We guess that if you'd read the description of Mrs. Greene at the beginning of this book, you'd rush to enroll your own children in her classroom. But by now you know that the seductive slogans generated by the self-esteem movement may not accomplish what they promise. As a basis for exploring the effects of the self-esteem movement in education, let's briefly look at the history of the so-called student-centered classroom and how it contrasts with teacher-directed education.

The roots of student-centered education lie in progressive education and humanistic psychology. Progressive education began in the early 1900s and called for having students learn relevant material through experiences with the environment rather than serving as receptacles for information provided in a textbook or lecture. Progressive educators considered that children sitting quietly in rows working on the same material was unnatural, likely to cause frustration and interfere with learning. Believers in progressive education had a modest impact on our schools in the early years.

Humanistic psychology, and in particular Carl Rogers, provided a major impetus to progressive education. Rogers viewed education as therapy and called for unconditional positive regard for all students, consistent with his approach to therapeutic clients. He implored public schools to unleash students' potentials by eliminating inhibitions and constraints. Rogers valued the development of confidence and self-esteem over the learning of facts or specific content. Thanks in large part to his teachings, self-esteem became an accepted prerequisite for learning. Various popular books promoted the idea of childhood as a magical time, a time of creativity and imaginative play. The adult world should not pressure, stifle, or stress children.[11]

The self-esteem movement and student-centered education thus go hand in hand. They both focus on ensuring that kids always feel good about themselves and feel good in general. The movement considers bad feelings anathema to childhood, something to avoid as much as possible.

Teacher-directed education presents a strikingly different picture. The teacher-directed classroom depends more on traditional textbooks than on fun, experiential learning. The approach teaches basic skills through repetitive drill and often boring practice. Children sit in an orderly fashion and listen more than they talk. The approach uses materials that are more difficult because the teacher takes responsibility for helping the students master the concepts. Grades and competition are assumed to help motivate students and provide them and their parents with accurate feedback about their performance. Clear rules for behavior are provided, and compliance is demanded. The teacher takes charge, establishes the curriculum, and presents it in a logical, sequential manner. Reading education begins with phonics. The goal of mastery of the material is held above that of self-esteem, and students who fail to progress are retained.

Throughout most of their history, American classrooms were highly teacher directed. In tandem with the rise of the self-esteem movement from the 1960s on student-centered education gradually infiltrated and eventually overwhelmed public education in the United States. Only in the past few years, fueled by concerns about academic performance, have significant voices challenged the child-centered approach. Recent attempts to return to a more teacher-directed strategy have increased, but they have encountered substantial resistance on the part of both parents and teachers.

So, which method does a better job of educating our children? We believe that reason and research, not ideological dogma, should dictate choice of educational methods. America's longest, most expensive, and largest study of educational practices began in 1968 and ended in 1994. After 26 years of study, independent research labs analyzed the conclusions. Teacher-directed education was pitted against a wide variety of child-centered teaching methods. The results were replicated over and over, year after year. Students in the teacher-directed classrooms consistently performed higher on measures of cognitive ability and academic achievement. Other studies on this same issue have also replicated this result.[12]

Now, let's look at what research has disclosed about a couple of the components of self-esteem–inspired, student-centered education.

JOHNNY CAN'T READ, BUT HE FEELS GOOD

Reading has received more attention than virtually any other aspect of education, and the controversy over how to teach kids to read has captured the attention of classroom teachers, school administrators, and even state and national legislators. The battleground in reading education pits the whole-language approach against arduous training in phonics and alphabetic principles. Advocates of whole language correctly claim young children naturally learn to speak. Babies hear language that initially sounds like gibberish. Slowly, but surely, infants make sense of it all through natural, playful practice. No one sits down and methodically reviews sounds and their meanings. Nor does anyone teach preschoolers how to make use of verbs, nouns, and sentence structure. Yet almost all children learn to speak in complex sentences before formal schooling begins. Proponents of whole language claim kids can learn reading in the same natural way.

Furthermore, they contend that whole language captures kids' interest more effectively than boring repetition of reading mechanics. Thus, whole-language teachers read interesting stories to children and assume they will gradually grasp the meanings of words. They use many beautiful books. If a child does not understand certain words, teachers encourage them to try to "figure the word out" by looking at the pictures and the context. Advocates believe this approach, also called "literature based," causes less frustration for beginning readers. Essentially, their position comes from the feel-good aspect of the self-esteem movement. Maureen Stout, author of *The Feel-Good Curriculum*, put it this way: "Whole language learning is the icon of what self-esteem is about: making education a therapeutic and caring experience rather than a deliberately demanding intellectual one."[13] In other words, whole language isn't just a theory about how kids learn to read. It's also rooted in self-esteem, always-feel-good dogma.

In contrast, phonics teaches that letters have sounds and they relate to speech and reading in a systematic way. Children learn to attack each word and sound it out. Drill and repetition of these skills eventually lead to fluent reading. Advocates say phonics enables children to sound out words they have never seen before. They additionally claim that the method develops spelling skills. Critics call it dull and say it takes too much work.

It should not surprise you that the same legislature and governor that passed a bill calling for the enhancement of self-esteem throughout its state schools also adopted whole language on a wholesale basis around the same time. In 1987, even though the reading scores of California students had risen throughout the 1980s, the state declared that its children would henceforth learn to read the so-called natural way—that is, via the whole-language approach. Education officials worried that the old phonics-based textbooks bored their kids. So the state bought new textbooks and eliminated most phonics instruction. Incredibly, administrators in some schools even confiscated the old phonics textbooks. A few renegade teachers clandestinely taught phonics behind closed doors. These experienced teachers knew through experience that many students need direct instruction in the sounds and symbols of our language.

An early sign of trouble came in 1989, when California reading scores dropped for the first time in a decade. *The state responded by eliminating the reading achievement test.* Officials couldn't bury their heads in the sand for too long, however, as the United States Congress ordered the National Assessment of Educational Progress to test children throughout the United

States in 1993 and to rank the states for the first time. Prosperous California managed to beat out only Guam and Mississippi. In 1995, Mississippi improved and California hit dead bottom. In 1996, the state's new governor mandated the use of reading textbooks emphasizing phonics. By 1998, California students began to show substantial improvements in their reading test scores.[14] In fairness, it is possible that some of California's reading woes stemmed from an influx of non-English-speaking students. However, the strikingly prompt turnaround following mandated phonics is suggestive.

How sad that even as the new millennium unfolds, the reading wars go on. Each side argues with fanaticized passion. Hoping to bring reason to the battle, Congress finally stepped in and formed the National Reading Panel to review the more than 100,000 studies on reading completed since 1966. These experts found phonics skills essential for learning to read.[15] And yet, in the face of inspired pressure from whole-language advocates, the panel waffled and failed to make a definitive statement, even though research unequivocally supports the superiority of intensive, systematic phonics over whole language. Kenneth Anderson, a law professor at American University, reviewed the report and lamented, "The report gives the impression of having been written one paragraph by one political faction, the next by another, with each sentence negotiated phrase by phrase; a corporate lawyer would instantly recognize the genre. . . . Everything, seemingly, is a pretty good method of teaching if it has a powerful constituency behind it."[16]

Current well-designed research continues to support the effectiveness of phonics over the whole-language approach. In 1998 the prestigious *Journal of Educational Psychology* reviewed the evidence and conducted a rigorous experimental test of reading teaching strategies. Children provided with direct instruction in alphabetic sounds and their corresponding letters (that is, phonics) improved significantly more than children who read for the same amount of time out of equivalent textbooks with no direct instruction (the whole-language approach).[17]

Pitifully, politics obscures the message of meticulously collected, sound data. The reading wars fail to abate simply because many in the field of education capitulate to political ideology rather than basing their stand on scientific findings. Whole-language enthusiasts tenaciously cling to their doctrine and attack any and all disconfirming data. They counter the fact that time and again children read better with phonics instruction with the argument that children exposed to whole language *like* reading better. In other words, they change the goal from teaching kids to *read* better to hoping they'll *feel* better about it. Incredibly, whole-language subscribers have also stopped using standardized measures of reading and substituted measures of— you guessed it—*self-esteem*. Attitude, enjoyment, self-esteem, and feeling good rule over reading achievement.[18]

We need to point out that many bright students can indeed learn to read quite well with almost no instruction. However, more than a few kids require training in the relationship between sounds and symbols in order to learn to read. This training appears especially important for children who have little exposure to reading materials in their homes, as well as children whose first language is not English. Furthermore, once skilled in the foundation of phonics, children can continue to improve their reading skills by reading a variety of great literature.[19] But if we try to make reading fun and easy using only whole language and interesting stories, many kids will end up functionally illiterate.

In fact, in 1983, the National Commission on Excellence in Education labeled the United States a "nation at risk" and proposed massive reform to ameliorate the mediocrity of American education.[20] In the years since that disquieting appeal, an entire generation has passed through our schools; unfortunately, by 1998, 10 million students still managed to reach twelfth grade without developing basic reading skills. The Nation's Report

Card, a government-funded educational assessment, has tracked students for close to three decades, routinely testing samples of fourth-, eighth-, and twelfth-grade students. You could mistake the charts of these scores for an EEG of a patient who died during surgery: flat. And that's disturbing because two-thirds of fourth and eighth graders fail to achieve reading proficiency for their grade level. At first glance, twelfth graders perform slightly better, with a mere 60% failing to achieve reading proficiency.[21] But even this improvement evaporates when you consider the fact that about 15% of students drop out prior to the twelfth grade and thus never take the test.[22] Furthermore, private school children, who outperform public school kids on average at all grade levels, and in every subject area, bring up the overall statistics and thus soften our alarm. Although only by a few points, among public school students, 9-year-olds read more poorly today than they did in 1980. "Educational progress" is starting to sound like an oxymoron in this country.[23] But at least the kids feel good.

JANE CAN'T ADD AND SUBTRACT, BUT SHE FEELS GOOD, TOO

Math in 1950: A shirt sells for $9.50. The store puts the shirt on sale for 30% off. What is the sale price of the shirt?

"New math" in 1970: A set S of shirts is priced at set M of money. The set M of money consists of 950 units. Make 950 dots representing the elements of set M. Represent set SP (for sale price) which contains .30 fewer units than set M.

The new, new math in 2000: A shirt sells for $29.95. The e-store puts it on sale for 30% off. Take your calculator to someone to help you calculate the sale price. Or draw a picture of a shirt and tell a friend how you feel about the fact it was manufactured by exploited children in a sweatshop. Finally, would your self-esteem suffer if you bought such a cheap, no-name shirt? Discuss your feelings in your focus group.

These examples, although whimsical, nevertheless capture the essence of how the feel-good philosophy underlying the self-esteem movement has mucked up the way students are taught math. How could the feel-good folks influence this logical, straightforward subject? Well, according to the National Council of Teachers of Mathematics in 1989, math should be *joyful, fun, and engaging.*[24] Hence the new new math. This approach posits that drill and repetition of math facts and rules lead to boredom and lack of motivation. As with whole-language reading, advocates believe that if students are simply exposed to mathematical material, they will discover and learn naturally. Discussions of why numbers are manipulated the way they are supplement pictures and concrete materials. The learning of calculations and formulas is de-emphasized, and kids are encouraged to use calculators and computers to take the drudgery out of computations.

These people fear confusing children and making them uncomfortable when challenged. Kids may even develop a recently discovered psychological disorder: math anxiety. Therefore, math educators must move away from an emphasis on right and wrong answers. Children's emotions need to be protected.

Admittedly, many of these ideas, on the surface, sound pretty good. What better way to learn about fractions than cutting up cakes and pies? Kids can learn about height and weight by measuring each other. Surely the experience of hands-on math is more meaningful than robot-like repetition and drill. Compare a group of children eagerly constructing bridges out of paper straws to 40 kids sitting in straight rows chanting multiplication tables.

Yet almost immediately there were warning signs. Once again California stood in the forefront of educational innovation. In 1985, about the same time the state adopted the self-esteem movement and whole language, California turned to a more creative approach for mathematics. Teachers were advised to spend less time on memorization of basic math facts and to facilitate mathematical communication and creativity. When tests results in 1991 indicated that just 8% of eighth-grade Californians could add fractions, and the state had dropped to the bottom third of the nation on math tests, state education officials ignored the data.

California's experience is suggestive, but direct comparisons of the new new math with earlier math teaching styles are difficult to come by because the strategies in most American classrooms represent a potpourri of philosophies, lessons, and areas of emphasis, both old and new. Visit classrooms in today's schools, and you'll see that most teachers actually employ a mix of math teaching methods. Thus, we need to look to international comparison studies to see how kids in this country are faring. In 1980 and again in 1987, a group of international researchers looked at math and science proficiency among elementary school children in three cultures: American, Japanese, and Chinese. Previous studies indicated that Asian high school students outperformed American high school students in science and math. The researchers studied elementary school students to see how early the discrepancy occurred. They also looked at differences in teaching techniques. With a lot of help from scholars around the world, these researchers designed tests that could fairly measure skills in all three cultures.

The full results can be found in the book *The Learning Gap,* but a brief summary is enlightening. When children enter school for the first time in China, Japan, and the United States, Japanese children perform better than U.S. or Chinese children on mathematics tests. By the end of first grade, both the Chinese and Japanese students surpass the Americans. By the fifth grade, the highest-performing American school falls below the lowest-performing Asian school. These authors worried about the widening gap between the students. Shockingly, they discovered that, unlike kids in any other country, *the longer American students remain in school, the worse they do in comparison.*[25]

How embarrassing. It would be too obvious for the United States to ignore such findings and abandon the research. How could international comparisons be made without producing such humiliating findings? Including students from a bunch of countries unlikely to score as high as U.S. kids would make a nice start—countries like Morocco, Turkey, Moldova, and South Africa, for example.

The United States government did exactly that by comparing math and science performance of students in 38 countries. The National Center for Education Statistics published the results of the Third International Mathematics and Science Study-Repeat (TIMSS-R) and unabashedly boasted in the lead summary statement, "In 1999, U.S. eighth-graders exceeded the international average of 38 nations in mathematics and science."[26]

Sounds pretty good. We exceed the average of 38 nations. Let's look at the statistics behind this bold claim. You could easily interpret that statement to mean we beat out 38 nations. The truth is, the average score obtained in the United States barely exceeded the *average* score of all 38 nations combined. In terms of math scores, the United States fell in the middle of the heap (19th out of 38), losing out to China (Taipei) and Japan, and also Singapore, Republic of Korea, Hungary, Slovenia, the Czech Republic, and Bulgaria, among others. In science, we climbed up one rank to 18th out of 38, behind most of the same nations that outperformed us in mathematics. The large magnitude of the difference between the highest-scoring countries and our scores was highly significant.

Obviously, a slightly different mix of countries easily could have resulted in the United States performing below the combined average of 38 nations. Prominent nations from the industrialized world such as France, Germany, Switzerland, Norway, and Sweden represent interesting omissions from the study.[27] Perhaps next time we'll see more Third World countries included—that is, if we want to ensure landing in the top half of the pile while remaining committed to feel-good philosophies that include self-esteem curriculums, grade inflation, and shorter school days and years.

Some readers might argue that in the United States, we attempt to educate all of our children, rich and poor, bright and disabled. Therefore, these comparisons are unfair. Surely our brightest students outperform those in other countries. Not so. Our high school students who qualified to take the advanced math test in the international comparisons came in next to last, beating only Austria. Those high school students qualified to take the advanced physics test did slightly better, besting three other countries. Even at that, only a handful of American students were advanced enough to take this exam. On the standard physics exam, the United States placed *last* among the 16 nations that participated in the test.[28]

Many of the countries, whose students outperform ours, do so with worn-out textbooks, basic curriculums, and so-called unsophisticated teaching methods. Too often, American schools choose teaching methods based on what entertains and feels good, ignoring what works based on scientific data. This is not to say that learning can't or shouldn't be fun. And integrating some strategies from both whole language and new math *may* have value in engaging kids' attention. Nevertheless, considerable caution should be exercised prior to adopting so-called integrative or balanced approaches.

Although the idea sounds like the perfect way to end educational wars, to date, research has not demonstrated increased effectiveness for balanced approaches in reading or math. Unless or until it does, existing research tells us we need to *emphasize* basic foundational skills in reading, writing, and arithmetic and have less concern for feeling good.

FEELING GOOD IN SPECIAL EDUCATION

Darrel, Jasper, and Juan all attend the same regular education first-grade classroom. The classroom teacher, Mrs. Walker, works with the three boys in reading. She is frustrated by their lack of progress but is sympathetic because each boy has a problem. Darrel comes from a disadvantaged home. He began first grade without knowing all of his letters and appears more interested in recess and physical education than learning. Jasper whirls around the classroom, oblivious to what he is supposed to be doing. At the first conference, Mrs. Walker plans to suggest to Jasper's parents that he get evaluated for attention deficit disorder. Juan comes from a family who speaks only Spanish. He attends a special bilingual class in the afternoon but just doesn't catch on to reading. By the end of first grade, the three boys still can't read even basic words. They have memorized several simple books, but fail to recognize words out of context. The boys have similar report cards, with many comments like "needs improvement" and "works hard," though no grades appear.

Of course, the school passes them on to second grade with the hope things will get better. As in most elementary schools, holding students back when they don't master the grade-level material occurs very rarely, if at all. By the third grade, each boy still reads at a beginning first-grade level. Jasper's behavior spirals out of control. Constantly in trouble for not listening, not finishing his work, and not following directions, he spends many days out of his classroom, working on handouts in the school detention room.

Juan sits in quiet despair. Not understanding much of what goes on in the classroom, he hopes the teacher will just ignore him. She does. He languishes in the back of the classroom, falling further behind every day.

Darrel still likes physical education and recess but, like Jasper, can't seem to control his behavior. Darrel bullies others, gets into fights on the playground, and shows disrespect to his teachers. The staff believes that he acts this way because of low self-esteem and searches for ways to bolster his self-image.

For three years, kind teachers, aware of these poor children's difficulties, valiantly attempted to protect the boys' self-esteem. They maintained meager expectations. Teachers shortened the boys' assignments, gave them extra time, paired them with more able partners in committees, and praised every effort. Even with all of the extra help, by the spring of their third-grade year, the boys were referred to the special education department for testing.

A bilingual school psychologist evaluated Juan. Regular and special education teachers, the principal, the director of special education, and Juan's parents crowded into a small office to hear the results and decide what to do. Juan's mother told the psychologist that her son was always cheerful at home and helped his parents with their successful landscaping business. The psychologist said Juan was smart. But Juan had a *disability*, a learning disability. The school psychologist knew this because Juan couldn't read in Spanish or English. The nine professionals nodded in agreement. Juan's mother felt sad that her son was sick; she wondered if it was her fault.

Jasper and Darrel also were tested, and similar meetings were held. It turned out that they both had disabilities, too. Jasper earned the label "other health impaired" because of his newly diagnosed attention deficit hyperactivity disorder. As for Darrel, the committee believed that his poor behavior interfered with his education, so they pronounced him "seriously emotionally disturbed." The committee whisked all three boys off to special education.

Disabled? Maybe. It's also possible the boys needed a different approach to reading instruction. Or that the classroom was too distracting. Or that, once the boys were identified as belonging in the low reading group, teachers stopped expecting them to learn much. And it's possible that the boys simply didn't try hard enough.

The diagnosis of a learning disability is not a simple task. When evaluating for these problems, a highly skilled diagnostician usually can discern whether or not a child has a real learning disability or is simply discouraged, poorly taught, or indulged. Simple scores on tests do not answer the most important questions, yet too often test scores are used to label our children disabled.

Unlike some critics, we understand that learning disabilities and attention deficits are very real. We appreciate the difficulties these disabilities cause for children, parents, and teachers. However, too many children end up with the label "learning disabled" when they shouldn't. Because of the realities of school systems today, most evaluators face mounting moral and ethical dilemmas. What should we do when Johnny can't read? Educational diagnosticians feel intense pressure from regular education teachers to solve the problem of student underachievement by issuing a one-way ticket to the special education classroom. Calling a child disabled lets everyone off the hook. No one is at fault—not the child, the teachers, or the parents. *Everyone can go on feeling good.*

During the school year 1998–1999, *one out of every eight* public school children received special education services. In other words, educators identified more than 12% of our schoolchildren as disabled! And the rate of disabilities continues to climb. In just the past 10 years, the identification of learning disabilities (LD) increased by 38%.[29] As one group of experts recently stated, "LD has served as a sociologic sponge that attempts to wipe up general education's spills and cleanse its ills."[30]

What's the problem with calling students disabled if it gets them extra help and prevents the experience of failure? When these students get stamped as disabled, teachers and parents drop their expectations. With lowered expectations comes easier material in the classroom, which guarantees slower progress.

Over 30 years of research confirms the power of expectations. In a classic study, children took a test supposedly designed to predict "blooming." The researchers told the teachers that certain children in their classrooms were about to take off intellectually. In reality, the researchers were interested in the effects of teachers' expectations; the "bloomers" were actually just picked out of a hat.

At the end of the school year, "bloomers" indeed bloomed. Tests indicated much higher achievement than that shown by their "ordinary" classmates.[31] Keep in mind that the only difference between the kids was the teachers' expectations.

Expectations may especially influence students with learning disabilities. In one preliminary study, researchers told a group of dyslexic readers that a new treatment would greatly improve their reading. They informed another group that the treatment probably wouldn't help. The treatment was actually the same for both groups, and it doesn't work. Yet those with hope made great strides in reading; in fact, most gained more than two academic years. Not surprisingly, those in the group who didn't expect much improvement made meager gains. Astonishingly, after the sham intervention that provided a hopeful message, 40% of the dyslexic students no longer fulfilled the criteria for dyslexia.[32]

The message from such research? Expect more; get more. That's why it's so important if expectations in special education fall short of what students can really achieve. And once children are put in special education, most of them stay there. Despite more money spent, smaller class sizes, and intensified help, students only make slight gains in these programs. In fact, the more special education they receive, the further behind the "regular" student population they fall.[33]

Along with the disability label comes a pronouncement of a child's intelligence or potential. Unfortunately, our culture views intelligence as a consistent, stable trait. When we tell parents and teachers a child has low intelligence and a learning disability, we have sentenced this child to a lifetime of low expectations and underachievement. In attempting to prevent the bad feelings associated with failure, we doom our kids to thinking like helpless victims.

Contrast our cultural beliefs with those of Asians, who view effort rather than innate ability as pivotal to accomplishment. Expectations for excellence rule in Asian schools. All students must master basic skills. When some children don't catch on as fast as others, they are not labeled disabled, but are prodded to try harder, study more, and persist.[34] Asian cultures celebrate effort over ability, and the results speak for themselves.

Special education rose to prominence in a culture that shuns the idea of assigning blame and responsibility. A culture of narcissism and self-absorption. If Johnny can't read because he has a disability, no one is at fault. But, if he can't read because he watches six hours of television every day or because his teacher fails to use the right reading method, either Johnny, his parents, or his teacher must shoulder a portion of blame, responsibility, and bad feelings.

FEELING GOOD THROUGH COUNTERFEIT ACHIEVEMENT

College admissions staffs consider many factors when deciding which students to admit. High school grades and SAT scores stood paramount among the various criteria in the past. That's because grades represent the way schools certify student performance. Having an A or 4.0 grade point average virtually ensured a ticket into almost any desired college. However, just as the dollar loses purchasing power due to inflation, grades have lost much of their value. Evidence for grade inflation is particularly striking when juxtaposed with SAT scores. As the table on page 163 depicts, the percentage of students obtaining an A average increased over the past decade, while the SAT scores of these top students declined.

One reason grades rise every year may be that students complain more than they ever did before. They have been

A COMPARISON OF HIGH SCHOOL GRADES AND SAT SCORES
FOR A STUDENTS IN 1990 AND 2000

High School Grade Avg.	1990 Percentage	2000 Percentage	SAT Total Scores 1990	SAT Total Scores 2000
A+	4%	7%	1253	1238
A	11%	16%	1162	1149
A–	13%	17%	1105	1093
Total	28%	40%	1173*	1160*

*Average SAT score for A students

SOURCE: *The College Board, 2001*[35]

taught that they deserve the very best grade, and they demand it. "Twenty years ago students grumbled, then lived with the grades they were given. Today, colleges of every stature permit them to appeal low grades through deans or permanent boards of inquiry. In the *Chronicle of Higher Education,* Prof. Paul Korshin of the University of Pennsylvania recently described his grievance panel as the 'rhinoplasty committee,' because it does 'cosmetic surgery' on up to 500 transcripts a year."[36]

Good grades supposedly result from hard work. But our students work less on homework than ever before. Many teachers fail to assign homework because students don't bring it back or parents complain. If too many students who don't do their work flunk, intense pressure and sometimes disciplinary actions are brought to bear on their teachers. So it shouldn't be surprising that a third of American 17-year-olds reported that their teachers did not assign any daily homework whatsoever.[37] This state of affairs should at least give our students plenty of time to sleep. Nevertheless, more than 36% of college freshmen oversleep and miss classes today, as opposed to 19% who did so in 1968.[38]

Apparently, our students work less today than before, yet they "achieve" far higher grade averages. Why? Good grades create warm, cozy feelings for teachers, students, and their parents. Furthermore, administrators, parents, and students make fewer complaints about teachers when the A's and B's flow like beer from the tap at the local college brewery.

Most important, no one wants to harm our kids' self-esteem by awarding realistic grades. Dr. Smith's son, Trevor, attends a local public high school and receives special services as a "gifted" student. This year, he enrolled in a mentorship program. A teacher matches students with professionals in the community so that the students get first-hand experience in the working world. Trevor wanted to work with an attorney or judge. Unfortunately, the teacher responsible for setting up the mentorship at the beginning of the school year failed to do so. Ostensibly, the teacher made multiple phone contacts and claimed he could not find an appropriate mentor. The semester ended and Trevor happily brought his grade home. He was pleased. Why shouldn't he be? He received an A.

His mother did not feel pleased. She interpreted the message to her son as getting away with something. In fact, the A was a fraudulent representation of his performance. Furthermore, in her view, the teacher demonstrated negligence by not at least providing alternative work if indeed he was unable to find a mentor.

Dr. Smith decided to approach the school administration with her concerns. Upon investigation, she found that Trevor was not the only student without a mentor and that all of the students without mentors received A's. When confronted, the teacher rationalized that his students should not suffer; after all, it was not their fault. And in all of his years of teaching, Dr. Smith was the first parent to ever complain about an A.

Outrageous as it may seem, this is probably not an isolated incident. However, many teachers and parents are clamoring for a change in the practice of grade inflation. Demands are increasing for our schools to prove that they produce a quality product. Fed up with schools focused on making students feel good with diluted standards, politicians and the public they represent are calling for yearly statewide and national testing. Many states have taken up the call. Unfortunately, dishonesty invades and degrades our statewide testing programs. Too many school systems deceive the public with smoke and mirrors. A recent review of standardized testing practices revealed numerous vices ranging from peccadilloes to chicanery and outright fraud. For example, some schools directly or indirectly encourage below-average students to stay at home on the day of standardized test administrations. Most schools exclude students with disabilities from the tests or give them "accommodations"—in other words, extra help. The fact that more students are labeled "disabled" every year thus provides an instant boost to statewide test scores. Other schools hang on to outdated tests with which their students and teachers have become familiar in past years.

Furthermore, administrators often encourage teachers to teach the test.[39] In one survey, over 8% of teachers believed using actual test items to practice on was acceptable. Close to a quarter professed that rewording and rephrasing test items and using them for practice was okay. Over a third believed that practicing alternate test forms was also appropriate.[40] Yet publishers of tests do not consider any of these practices acceptable.

Worse, numerous examples of outright cheating have been cited over the years. Perhaps the most outrageous occurred in Fairfield, Connecticut, in 1996. A highly respected elementary school, which had received two blue ribbon awards from the National Department of Education, obtained incredibly high scores on standardized tests. When officials examined answer sheets, they discovered what became known as Erasergate. That's because five times the number of erasures were found as compared to other schools. Not only that, but 89% of the erasures involved changing a wrong answer to a correct one. When the students were retested, they received significantly lower scores.[41]

Reflecting this sad state of affairs, John Cannell published a study called "The Lake Wobegon Report."[42] (Children in Lake

Wobegon, a mythical town made famous on public radio's *Prairie Home Companion,* starring Garrison Keillor, are "all above average.") Similarly, in 1988 Cannell found that *all 50 states* obtained scores on standardized tests that exceeded the published averages. All over the country, newspapers proclaimed that students in "our" state performed above the national average. But how can all states possibly exceed the national average? They can't. Various deceptive practices contributed to this phenomenon.

Are we being too harsh? After all, haven't scores on the nation's college entrance exam, the Scholastic Aptitude Test (SAT), recently increased? Indeed, scores on the SAT have changed. The College Board and educators received a barrage of demands for an explanation as to why the SAT scores had plunged over the past few decades. Everyone felt bad. So the board simply changed the scoring. If Johnny scored a 450 on the verbal portion of the test in 1990, that same performance would give him a 530 on the test in 2000. And if Jane scored 620 on the math portion in 1990, her score, with the same number of correct answers, would now be 640. Talk about fuzzy math.[43] But if the scores are adjusted to account for this change, overall combined verbal and math test scores in the year 2000 languish 40 points below those for the class of 1967.

We should note that math scores improved at the end of the '90s. The modest improvement may have resulted partly from a decision by the College Board in 1994 to allow, and even encourage students to bring in their calculators. We have no objection to calculators, which may enable students to tackle especially complex problems. However, their use may explain some of the increases in SAT math scores since 1994. In fact, the SAT board supported this possibility when they stated:

Research shows that students who use calculators on the SAT 1 do slightly better than students who do not. That's

because the use of a calculator tends to ensure that stu-
dents who apply sound math reasoning will not miss a
question because of computational errors.[44]

By no means are we suggesting that the various deceptive testing practices have occurred due to the self-esteem movement and the desire to have our kids feel good. But we are saying that the self-esteem movement, with its emphasis on feeling good, contributed to declining educational standards. The only way to uproot the self-esteem movement and improve on other ineffective educational practices is to hold schools accountable.

EXCUSES AND EXPLANATIONS

Some reformers scream for more money to improve our schools. Yet, in today's dollars we spend almost 75% more money per student now than we did in 1970. In spite of billions more dollars and every imaginable innovative reform and remedy, our students stagnate in mediocrity, below 1970 achievement levels.

In fact, with calculators and spell checkers in hand, when our students begin college, many face the realities of poor, inadequate preparation. Almost a third of our nation's college freshmen require some type of remedial coursework. And in the state that values self-esteem more than any other—California—over half of all freshmen serve time in remedial classes.[45]

The self-esteem movement preached that boosting our children's confidence would improve their academic achievement. But American kids already feel good about themselves. They consistently demonstrate greater optimism about reading and math skills than do children in Beijing, Taipei, or Sendai, even though they do more poorly on math and reading achievement tests. Fifty-eight percent of American students in one study expected to perform in the above-average or best student group in the following year in mathematics; just over 25% of the Chinese and Japanese students rated themselves that highly.[46]

Four recent studies compiled evidence on a rather paradoxical phenomenon: the relationship of *actual* competence to *perceived* competence. Researchers found that students who were especially incompetent in areas such as reasoning, humor, and grammar consistently rated themselves as above average in skill. Whereas their test scores placed them in the *bottom* 12%, their self-ratings placed them in the *top* 40%. In contrast, highly competent performers tended to slightly *underestimate* their skills.[47] This set of studies demonstrates a striking similarity to the results obtained with American and Asian students. Less competent Americans rate themselves highly; more competent Asian students have more humility. *Not allowing our students to experience failure and frustration, while pumping up their self-esteem, does them no favor.*

Studies concerning "self-image disparities" have found similarly paradoxical results. These studies have looked at the difference between a person's "ideal" self-image (how I would like to see myself, for example as an A– tennis player) and "real" self-image (how I actually see myself, as a C– tennis player). At the dawn of the self-esteem movement, Carl Rogers suggested that we're all better off we if perceive little difference between our ideal and real self-images.[48] Although the idea has intuitive appeal, various studies have found that higher discrepancies between ideal and real self-images appear to result in higher intelligence, higher levels of development, and improved ability to portray roles that require the ability to take other people's perspective.[49]

Sadly, misguided concerns about fluffing up self-esteem, regardless of actual facts, continue to prevail. We believe the time has come to squash the feel-good movement. Our children deserve to be educated for excellence. Our democracy requires an educated public. The rapid advances in technology and science threaten to leave our students unable to compete with the better-educated workforces in other countries.

Fortunately, there is a rising clamor to do something different in our schools. As parents, teachers, and citizens, this is an issue in which all of us have a stake, and a voice. One thing we can do is insist that reforms address issues by looking at research rather than self-esteem dogma or the latest educational fad. We can demand that students learn to appreciate high expectations, hard work, and the satisfaction of caring for others. We insist that the time is ripe for abandoning the well-intentioned emphasis on self-esteem and feeling good in our schools—a recipe that has inadvertently inculcated a culture of narcissism.

CHAPTER 7

THE PERFECTION
PARADOX

CAROLYN NOTICES THE TIME AND HURRIES HER SON THROUGH breakfast. She practically pushes him out the door and into a waiting taxi. He whines and complains about wanting to stay home. As usual, they're running late.

The tutor, Ms. Kenney, works just a few blocks away, but through city traffic, it takes almost 15 minutes to get there. Ms. Kenney charges $150 an hour, and Carolyn is annoyed that Travis will lose out on several minutes of his session. When the cab pulls over, Carolyn throws a $20 bill at the driver and grabs Travis by the hand, pulling him out of the cab into the office. With only a few weeks left before the entrance exam, Carolyn begs Ms. Kenney to schedule more sessions.

Ms. Kenney reassures Carolyn that Travis has made great progress over the past six months in his twice-weekly sessions. She is certain Travis will do well on the test and the subsequent interview. But Carolyn remains adamant and increases the sessions to four times a week, just to make sure. More than 600 of the city's brightest apply each year for the 16 available slots, and she isn't about to take chances.

The week before the test, Travis works on how to make appropriate small talk with the examiner and practices relaxation strategies designed to manage his anxiety. Ms. Kenney feels proud of her work with Travis and compliments both him and his mother on their commitment to excellence. She encourages Travis to get a good night's sleep before the test and to eat a nutritious breakfast. She gives him a hug and again promises success.

Ms. Kenney quietly tells Carolyn that Travis knows the material necessary to make the first cut. The only problem she foresees is his test anxiety. He needs to keep his fears under control or he might freeze. She turns to Travis and reminds him to use the visualization and deep-breathing techniques they have worked on when the morning of the test arrives.

Travis sleeps poorly the night before and wakes up crabby. Carolyn's hands tremble as she pours coffee for Travis. She read that caffeine could help boost memory and attention. Travis, feeling nauseous, announces that he doesn't want to take the test. At her wits' end, Carolyn explodes. Travis takes the test.

Three weeks later, the good news arrives. Travis has made the first cut. School personnel interview and observe Travis and ultimately admit him. Thousands of dollars of tutoring and hard work have paid off. Three-year-old Travis will enter the prestigious Greenfield preschool in the fall.[1]

Little Travis is certainly not a child who faces few expectations. In the previous chapter, we lamented the declining standards in our schools. When teachers and parents preach the value of self-esteem and feeling good above all else, they often fail to instill a viable set of expectations, standards, and objectives in kids. "Feel-good" kids devoid of these aspirations concern themselves with their own comfort and therefore accomplish little, wallowing in mediocrity or much less.

Indeed, we have taken the self-esteem movement to task for encouraging kids to have puffed-up views of their own "specialness" without any foundation for that exalted view of themselves. Ironically, however, it's possible to arrive at an equally problematic result by a quite different route. We feel compelled to note that *the answer to a lack of standards is not found in pursuing the opposite extreme, specifically, excessive standards.* Extremes inevitably lead to problems, as you've seen throughout this book.

Nevertheless, some parents go to that opposite extreme and pressure their kids to a state of overachieving perfectionism. From early on in life, they push the message that their kids should obtain top grades, succeed in sports, and strive for all possible honors. No goal is too high for their children. And these parents justify any means of getting there.

Regrettably, their children also evolve into hollow, self-absorbed beings, but of a different type. The kids develop excessive, unrealistic standards of excellence and intolerance for any failure. Like their feel-good cohorts, perfectionistic kids become self-absorbed. Psychologist Sydney Blatt, who has constructed a career studying perfectionism, has concluded that those who excessively focus on developing their sense of self, autonomy, and self-worth often turn into narcissistic perfectionists.[2]

What does research say about the connection between perfectionism and self-esteem? Similar to the data on eating disorders and substance abuse, some studies indicate low self-esteem occurs more often in those with a high degree of perfectionism,[3] while other studies indicate narcissism shows up more frequently among perfectionists.[4] However, the range and quality of these studies do not equal those of most of what we've reviewed on other topics. In any event, we do not directly blame the self-esteem movement for causing perfectionism in our kids.

Rather, we believe children become perfectionists due more to their parents' influence than to anything else.

Carolyn began training Travis early in the fine art of self-absorption. She analyzed each new behavior, each accomplishment, and pressed for more. In addition, she started teaching him to read with special videos designed for 1-year-olds. As he grew, she signed him up for violin lessons, gymnastics, and accelerated math classes. She believed those activities would look good on his application for a private grade school and, later, a prestigious college. She considered success more important than anything else in life for her son. Occasionally, Carolyn worried about her son's anxious nature, but she continued to push him. When he did well, she told him he could do better. When he failed to live up to his potential, she resorted to harsh criticism, reasoning that criticism would motivate her son. Carolyn often bragged about her son's accomplishments to her friends and felt content in the knowledge that his achievements would ultimately give him confidence and high self-esteem.

Carolyn didn't teach her son to read so he would develop a joy of reading. Nor did she sign him up for violin lessons, gymnastics, and accelerated math because of her love of music, sports, or mathematics. She did these things to enhance his résumé. Carolyn obsessed over her son's triumphs.

Do such high expectations and degree of pressure hurt kids? What's so awful about perfectionism? After all, wasn't it the absence of expectations that we criticized in earlier chapters? By comparison with kids who have no standards, doesn't Travis appear destined for a successful life? And don't you want your kids to go as far in life as they possibly can?

THE PERFECTION PARADOX: TRAVIS GROWS UP

Perfectionism might be wonderful if it led to, well, a perfect life. Unfortunately, the truth is just the opposite. Consider what happens to Travis.

Travis thrives in the challenging preschool program. Once he graduates from preschool, he continues in Greenfield's accelerated elementary program. Travis starts his day early; after school, he rushes to various demanding extracurricular activities. Following a late dinner, he puts in two hours or more on homework. Weekends consist of more practice, homework, tutoring, and lessons. Travis does not object to this regimen; his friends all have similar lives. However, anxious by nature, he worries about every assignment and project.

Exams cause particular panic. Travis measures his worth entirely on the basis of his performance. The night before a test, he compulsively engages in a ritual of sharpening exactly six pencils. He sharpens and re-sharpens them in order to achieve a perfect point. Sometimes the pencils get too small in the process of re-sharpening, and he feels compelled to start over with a new pencil. He also spends a lot of time selecting the right shirt; it must be a certain shade of blue, and the fabric must have just the right feel for good luck.

Travis enters middle school at the top of his class. But his anxiety doesn't abate. Instead, his fear of failure mounts, and his rituals proliferate. It takes him twice as long as other children to complete assignments because he dwells on his handwriting, the right shade of ink, and any imperfections on his paper. The emotional turmoil associated with doing his schoolwork causes so much pain that he starts to procrastinate. When a teacher assigns a paper, Travis puts it off until the night before the due date. Then he struggles over each word, never feeling satisfied with what he produces. Tired and disgusted with his work, he leaves the unfinished paper in his computer.

Perfectionism paralyzes Travis. He prefers to accept a failing grade for not turning anything in to submitting his work to the teacher's judgment. He dreads the possibility of not measuring up to his own standards, which mirror those of his parents. Procrastination only delays the ultimate judgment. For the first time in his life, his grades plummet. His mother increases the pressure, but it does no good. She sends Travis to a therapist and hires more tutors. Eventually, she is forced to take him out of Greenfield and enroll him in a less demanding school. Unfortunately, he never regains an interest in academics. He graduates from high school and goes through a series of mundane jobs well beneath his potential.

Travis fell victim to the *perfection paradox*. The harder he tried to attain perfection, the less perfect he became. *The more he wanted, the less he got.* He procrastinated because of his fear of mistakes and failure. He believed that his own worth depended on a perfect performance. Like many perfectionists, he also became obsessive. Extensive research has documented that procrastination and obsessive-compulsive behaviors often plague the perfectionist.[5]

In addition, when perfectionistic children or adolescents fail, they are at great risk for depression. Much as for those with overly high self-esteem, when the balloon bursts, perfectionists collapse. Dr. Blatt noted, "Perfectionistic individuals experience depression that is focused primarily on issues of self-worth and self-criticism; they berate, criticize, and attack themselves, and experience intense feelings of guilt, shame, failure, and worthlessness."[6]

Other researchers have found numerous links between perfectionism, hopelessness, and suicide. Psychiatrists interviewed and evaluated over a hundred teens between the ages of 12 and 17 who arrived at an emergency room after attempting suicide. About half of the adolescents said they truly wanted to die. Others were looking for relief or escape. Some viewed their attempt as a cry for help, a way to get back at family members, a way to frighten someone, make people feel sorry, show someone how much they loved them, or make people understand how unhappy they were. All these children obviously felt depressed, hopeless, and angry. However, one personality factor, more than any other, differentiated kids who wanted to die from those who didn't. Perfectionism. Kids most serious about killing themselves desperately sought *perfection*.[7]

In fact, the lethality of perfectionism reaches a peak in adolescence. All of us remember the horror of looking in the mirror and finding a new, swollen red blemish just before school. And you knew that upon arrival at school, no one would see anything except that volcanic eruption on your face. Concern about others' opinions couldn't be much higher than it is during these years. Some psychologists have coined the term "imaginary audience" to capture the perception many teens have that everyone's looking at them. And professionals hypothesize that the normal self-focus of adolescents, when combined with perfectionism, makes any failure or short-coming intolerable.[8]

Still, most perfectionists manage to struggle through adolescence, and many achieve great success. Let's assume Travis graduates at the top of his law school class and, becomes a partner in a major firm. His perfectionism seemingly has served him quite well. He alone accounts for over a third of his law firm's income. He has written numerous articles for law journals and acquired a national reputation in his specialty. His mornings begin with a workout in his home gym followed by a light breakfast. At 6:30 A.M., Travis settles into a posh leather seat and dictates notes for the day as he drives to work. He leaves work at 7:00 P.M. on a good day. Travis has it made. Respected by friends and colleagues, living in luxury, and surrounded by his wife and three children—what else could he want?

Research on perfectionism tells us that Travis likely suffers more than you would think. His children feel resentful of his frequent criticism, unyielding standards, and lack of warmth. They feel they're never good enough to get his approval. And his relationship with his wife looks even worse. She also feels resentful, unappreciated, and criticized. She contemplates divorce or an affair. Travis himself feels a chronic malaise and alienation from others. He isn't quite depressed, yet he is perpetually unsatisfied. He yearns for something more but doesn't know what. His "drivenness" leads to high blood pressure, headaches, and chronic back pain. His doctor tells him to slow down, but Travis dismisses the advice without hesitation.

ACCELERATED KIDS: THE HIGH COSTS OF PERFECTIONISM

Perfectionists usually acquire a variety of twisted beliefs that subvert their emotional well-being. By definition, they feel a compulsion to achieve perfection. With perfection, they fantasize, they will finally receive love and acceptance or they will stop feeling so intensely anxious. Many believe that if they fail to achieve perfection, something horrible will happen. They will be worthless, stupid, failures. They will endure endless humiliation and shame. With these beliefs, no wonder perfectionists suffer.

Indeed, perfectionism lies in bed with a host of maladies in addition to reduced motivation, malaise, alienation, and suicide. Perfectionism creates pressure and stress.[9] Children striving for 100% each and every time are doomed to frustration and stress when they inevitably fail. According to counselor Bettie Youngs, Ph.D., more than one in three children demonstrates worrisome signs of stress, including dizziness, aches and pains, and wheezing.[10]

Scientists have long known that stress exerts a wide range of deleterious influences on the body. In fact, stress has been implicated as important in 50 to 70% of all physical illnesses. When a person is stressed, the central nervous system reacts and causes the adrenal cortex to spill out epinephrine, which leads to rising glucose levels and accelerated heart rate. If stress persists, the body becomes less resistant to infection and disease. With prolonged stress, immunosuppression occurs.[11]

Mental stress plays a significant role in triggering heart attacks; stress increases pumping action, heart rate, and constriction of arteries, and it elevates the risk of rhythm disturbances.[12] Furthermore, perfectionism is a common trait in those with heart disease.[13] Perfectionism also shows up more often among those who report a wide variety of other physical complaints, such as severe headaches, stomachaches, and shortness of breath.[14] Due to the stress it causes, perfectionism likely heightens risk of concentration problems, chronic fatigue syndrome, stroke, digestive problems, weight problems, and even diabetes.[15]

The ravages of stress resulting from perfectionism start early in life. Even babies can show signs of stress. Some parents cart their 6-week-old babies off to music and movement programs designed to enrich and increase neurodevelopment. In the process, they disrupt naptimes, which vary day to day for most babies. These babies become irritable, fussy, and difficult to soothe. They may lose sleep and develop irregular eating patterns. Cranky babies turn into temperamental toddlers. As they grow, the pressure continues.

Just a few decades ago, only rare parents sent their little tykes to preschool. In fact, fewer than 5% of 3-year-olds attended preschool in 1965. By 1997, the enrollment had skyrocketed to 40%.[16] Many of these preschools have accelerated academic programs. There's nothing wrong with that, if you don't take it too far. But extreme emphasis on early academic mastery arguably runs the risk of diminishing the development of crucial social and behavioral skills. Children between the ages of 3 and 4 need to learn self-control, how to take turns, how to get along with others, and how to tolerate frustration. They also need to learn how to pay attention, how to think logically, and how to use their senses in learning.[17] Instead, 3-year-old children at the Mendham Country Day School, an accelerated preschool, learn the full upper- and lowercase alphabet. The 4-year-olds add, subtract, learn sound/symbol relationships, and get homework two nights a week.[18]

Children enjoy and learn in good preschool programs. Research has documented that for disadvantaged children, these programs have the potential to ameliorate deficiencies. But you should know that research has largely failed to support the value of pushing reading and writing on 3-year-olds.[19] In the absence of research showing that these programs provide long-term gains in academic achievement, it's prudent to consider whether these programs could cause harm. We believe they could, in at least two important ways. First, by emphasizing academic rigor so early, they may rob kids of the chance to develop the foundations of social development. Second, these efforts run a real risk of instilling perfectionistic, overachieving, self-absorbed values. Such drivenness may cause preschoolers to show serious signs of stress. Some may regress and wet their beds again, act with uncharacteristic immaturity, throw temper tantrums, or suffer sleep difficulties.

Elementary students whirl between lessons, games, practices, and academic enrichment. A University of Michigan survey discovered that children's free time decreased by well over a third from 1981 to 1997. Math and reading enrichment centers, unheard of in the 1980s, have sprouted up in strip malls throughout the country. The same Michigan study reported that from 1981 to 1997, preschool and elementary kids doubled their participation in sports.[20]

Many families hyper-schedule grade school children in the hopes their kids will have every conceivable opportunity. Kids need adult-sized Day Timers to track all of their frenetic activities. In our practice, we see children with anxiety disorders caused by weekly schedules with dance, drama, soccer, homework, and piano lessons. Family meals consist of fast-food drive-thru caught on the fly. The mini-van has replaced the family dinner table. Even the family vacation often gives way to summer sports camps, computer camps, academic enrichment camps, and weight-loss camps for the pudgy prepubescent. Well-intentioned parents want absolutely the best for their kids.

The "best" includes the best college. Panicked parents, reacting to the lack of standards in schools today, increasingly seek out quick fixes. They know grades alone won't work anymore. That's because college admissions officers have awakened to the pervasive grade inflation running rampant throughout our nation's high schools. In response, they've turned increasingly to SAT scores for helping them screen applicants. Because of this increased emphasis, the college test prep industry has profited enormously. One company, Kaplan Educational Centers, racked up $70 million in profits in 1992, which soared to $300 million in 1999.[21] Programs range from $395 to $795 for a basic group course. Worried parents send their kids for individual tutoring. In Manhattan, the hourly rate for private SAT tutors often runs from $100 to $300. Well-known tutors command over $500 per hour. Imagine the stress felt by these kids when their parents shell out this kind of money and expect a perfect performance.[22] (As an aside, we can't resist noting that this intensified coaching has occurred at the same time that SAT scores have been advancing at an anemic rate.)

Too many parents expect perfection on the playing field as well. The newspapers are filled with sports rage stories from Little League, hockey, and soccer games, including an incident in our hometown of Albuquerque that epitomizes the absurd lengths to which some parents will go in order to see their kids win. The date is October 12, and Albuquerque Academy high school is playing a football game against St. Pius X. During the first quarter, several Academy players return to the sidelines bleeding from cuts on their hands and arms. One student sustains wounds requiring 10 stitches. Referees check the St. Pius equipment and discover two defective chinstrap buckles on the helmet of junior Mike Cito. These buckles have a razor edge that slashes the flesh of any player making contact with Cito.

Mike Cito's father, Stephen, is a successful *pediatric* dentist who felt upset about another team's treatment of his son during a previous game. He volunteered to work the sideline chains but was so vocal at one game that officials demanded he leave. Prior to the Academy game, he had his son, Mike, bring home his helmet. There, he ground the chinstrap buckles to a fine edge, apparently hoping to give his son's team an "edge."[23]

Success and winning at any cost. Dr. Cito served 48 hours in jail, and the judge ordered him to perform 400 hours of community service. St. Pius expelled Mike, who was also given probation for one year by the court.[24]

The list of miseries associated with perfectionism goes on. Our story about Travis noted that he could act rather compulsively at times and would often spend inordinate amounts of effort sharpening pencils. Other perfectionistic kids acquire full-blown obsessive-compulsive disorder, known as OCD.[25] OCD can take control of an afflicted person's entire life. Some kids with OCD spend hours each day washing their hands; others develop bizarre compulsive rituals such as folding and refolding their clothes; still others check and recheck their homework even if it means going to bed much later than they should. To be honest, we can't be sure if perfectionism causes OCD or vice versa. However, perfectionism's elongated string of loathsome associations certainly implicates it as an unwelcome companion to most kids' lives.

As the Travis story illustrated, anxiety is yet another of these associations. Perfectionistic kids worry about their performance. They dwell on how others see them and agonize over schoolwork, popularity, and perceived status. These kids have higher levels of test anxiety and are less likely to ask for help.[26] Perfectionistic kids more often develop panic disorder, which is a form of anxiety. Kids with panic disorder may have intense fears and discomfort that often includes physical sensations like palpitations, sweats, shakes, and disquieting chest pain. It also can involve a fear of going crazy, losing control, or dying. These symptoms frighten and sometimes disable their victims. Perfectionistic children are also more likely to develop social phobias and other types of specific fears.[27]

Thus, perfectionism contributes to physical ailments, depression, anxiety, obsessive-compulsive disorder, procrastination, and suicide. And, as noted in an earlier chapter, perfectionism often accompanies eating disorders like bulimia and anorexia. You might have noticed that the plagues of perfectionism sound rather like the afflictions associated with self-absorption. In previous chapters, we have discussed how self-absorption can lead to narcissism, depression, alcohol and drug abuse, eating disorders, anxiety, vulnerability to emotional distress, delinquency, violence, and a lack of direction or goals.[28] Why should perfectionism and self-absorption result in such similar outcomes? If you think about it, extreme perfectionists ruminate about their number one concern: themselves. Perfectionists focus intensely on the self; perfectionism is one type of self-absorption.

THE ROLE OF PARENTS IN PERFECTIONISM

If you're a parent, you probably don't want your children to turn into perfectionists. So, what causes kids to become perfectionists? As with other complex traits and behaviors, genetics or temperament undoubtedly may predispose a child to perfectionism. Nevertheless, research has documented that parenting matters when it comes to developing perfectionism.

In particular, studies reveal that two parenting styles produce very different outcomes in children. Carolyn, Travis's mother, epitomizes the kind of parent who produces a perfectionistic kid. She practiced law in a prestigious firm. She never allowed her son to see her own mistakes, worries, or problems. She wanted her life to stand as a shining example for her son. She wanted him to believe she was perfect so that he could strive for perfection.

Carolyn felt her son's achievements reflected on her worth as a mother. She was enmeshed with her son; his successes were hers. When he floundered, she lashed out with anger to motivate him to work harder. He was her trophy.

When Travis shared his accomplishments with her, she praised him. Yet, at the same moment she also took pains to point out how he could further improve on his performance. If Travis brought home a report card with four A's and two B's,

Carolyn would immediately tell him he needed to bring up those B's next time. If he won a race, she'd say that was nice, but the competition wasn't very stiff. In effect she would tell him, "Nice job, but not good enough." This pattern of praise fused with criticism cruelly established the belief in Travis that he could never quite measure up.

Parents such as Carolyn hold back emotional approval. Their kids strive mightily to obtain it, but they constantly hear they haven't quite reached the standard. After years of trying to please their parents, these kids internalize their parents' unobtainable goals and never feel satisfied with much of anything they do.

Parents like Carolyn obsess about their children's accomplishments in terms of awards, grades, prestigious schools, and earning potential. These parents have what's known as a *performance orientation*. They usually respond harshly when their children make mistakes and possess equally lofty standards for themselves. Children of parents with a performance orientation gravitate toward extreme perfectionism. These kids brood over their mistakes. Sky-high expectations, accompanied by nagging doubts about their ability to achieve their goals, produce unrelenting tension. These kids feel incessant pressure from their parents and they learn to create their own pressures from within.

Sally exemplifies a contrasting parenting style that leads to a very different outcome. Like Carolyn, Sally spends a lot of time reading with her son, Jesse, and provides him with various enriched opportunities. However, her values differ from Carolyn's. Sally loves art and literature, and she hopes to pass these interests on to her son. She has less concern with his ultimate outcome in terms of success and achievement. She encourages Jesse to seek understanding, to enjoy challenges, and to develop his own interests. She views Jesse's happiness as something that will evolve from hard work and the satisfaction of learning and pursuing his own dreams. She firmly guides him to develop good work habits, curiosity, and self-control.

Parents like Sally focus on seeing their children enjoy mastery, learning, and challenge. They relish watching their children develop understanding of concepts and skills more than earning external sources of validation such as trophies and grades. This parenting style is called a *learning goal orientation*. These parents don't intertwine their lives with those of their children. They accept their kids and tolerate imperfections. In essence, they foster *acceptance* in their children. At the same time, they don't dismiss high standards. Children of parents with a learning goal orientation exhibit less perfectionism, less concern about mistakes, and increased confidence in their actions as compared to children of parents who have a performance orientation.[29]

We should mention a third style of parenting that looks quite different from the two just described and that often leads to perfectionism in kids. These parents live in chaos. They may have a series of unstable relationships, financial problems, health concerns, and various other adversities. They live unorganized lives and fail to provide stability. Their children may learn to live as chaotically as their parents do. However, not infrequently, one child will seek control and structure through perfectionism. This child may excel in schoolwork and keep his or her room meticulously organized and clean as a defense against the disheveled lives of the parents.[30]

How can you tell if your child is developing into a driven perfectionist or simply embraces reasonably high standards? It is an important distinction to make. On the one hand, you don't want to discourage your child from striving to succeed; on the other, the costs of perfectionism are too great to ignore. The following descriptions may help identify perfectionistic tendencies:

Perfectionistic kids may:

- Need to be the best in everything and become extremely upset when they aren't.

- Refuse to participate in activities they are not very good at; for example, they may avoid playing certain sports or participating in dance or music if they cannot be one of the best.

- Throw temper tantrums or become excessively agitated when they make mistakes.

- Seem motivated more by the fear of failure than by a striving for success.

- Get lost in details; such kids might spend inordinate amounts of time searching for errors, perfecting every assignment, or grooming in front of a mirror.

- Very much want to succeed but badly lack confidence.

- Struggle to make even the simplest decisions.

- Overreact to any criticism.

- Think in extremes; for example, something is either wonderful or horrible, good or bad, with no shades of gray.

- Hate being interrupted during their routine and have problems adapting to new situations.

- Recheck everything they do.

This checklist is not a scientifically validated test of perfectionism. It merely represents common characteristics of perfectionistic kids. If you worry that your child has a few of these symptoms, it is not a bad idea to review your own parenting style. Consider trying to soften your criticisms and adapt some of the characteristics of the learning goal orientation.

"HEALTHY" PERFECTIONISM?

At this point you might be wondering whether there isn't an alternative to both underachievement and perfectionistic over-achievement. After all, perfect performance produces many advantages: outstanding grades, honors, financial rewards, praise from others, pride. In school, perfectionists conscientiously tend to details. Perfectionists take pride in organization and neatness. They work hard and can accomplish great feats. Classmates often feel in awe of perfectionists. Giving up perfectionism runs the risk of abandoning excellence.

Surely there's a healthy perfectionism, a perfectionism that retains all of the advantages with none of the costs. Interestingly, studies of perfectionism across cultures have shown that Asian Americans can have higher levels of perfectionism with fewer of its associated problems than Caucasian Americans. This result may be due to the fact that this group shows less focus on the self. Asian American perfectionists seek accomplishment only partly for themselves and have a greater concern for their families and community than other American groups. This heightened concern for others may protect them from the pernicious effects of self-absorbed perfectionism.[31]

This line of thought suggests that it's all a matter of balance, the balance between focus on one's self versus concern for others and a balance between excessive as opposed to slipshod standards. With a healthy regard for personal accomplishment balanced with commitment to others, one can tolerate higher levels of perfectionism. This idea explains why some healthy individuals accomplish great feats without suffering the exorbitant costs of unbalanced perfectionism. By the same token, the lack of such balance accounts for the enormous pain and anguish too many perfectionists endure.

As you will see, it is this kind of balance that we believe is promoted by the acceptance alternative. And it is to that alternative that we now turn.

CHAPTER 8

THE ACCEPTANCE
ALTERNATIVE

SWIMMERS, FRIENDS, AND FAMILIES PACK THE HOT, NOISY natatorium for the high school state finals. The 200-yard freestyle relay event is about to begin. Team members Mario, Russell, Brett, and Michael huddle together in a corner. The boys realize that the results of this race will determine which school wins the championship. Brett, the lead swimmer, and Michael, the anchor, are the team's strongest swimmers, frequently alternating best times. Mario is quick and reliable, while Russell swims equally fast, but with more ups and downs. At the last meet, Russell disqualified the team by missing a turn.

When the announcer calls for the swimmers, the boys line up behind the starting block. Brett desperately wants to swim his best time. Even more than winning the race, he craves beating Michael. He hopes his picture will be in the paper tomorrow so he can boast to his friends. He appears agitated as he stretches and scans the crowd. He turns to Russell and hisses that he'd better not screw up this race like the last one. Anguish registers visibly on Russell's face. Michael puts his hand on Russell's shoulder and reassures him that it's only a race; he just needs to do the best he can.

Brett takes his position on the block and flies into the air simultaneously with the sound of the starting gun. The boys scream as Brett shoots into the lead by a body length. But at the turn, Brett's feet make poor contact with the wall and he lags behind. Obviously shaken, he loses his rhythm and falls into third place. He climbs out of the pool and slams his goggles on the concrete. Furious, he turns from his teammates and heads for the locker room.

Meanwhile, Mario manages to pull into second place. As Russell dives into the lane, he continues to ruminate over Brett's words. He falls well short of his best time and slips back into third. While Russell swims, Michael feels compassion mixed with a little annoyance toward Brett, for whom this race is so very important. And he particularly feels touched by Russell's despair. Michael knows he's had more than his share of victories, so losing this event won't affect him the way it will Russell. Still, he feels inspired to pull it out for his teammates.

As Russell's hand touches the wall, Michael bursts off the block into the water. The noise from the crowd swells as he slices through the water. Furiously reaching, stretching, and kicking, he propels into second place. By the turn, he moves into striking distance of first. Hearing the noise from the locker room, Brett looks out in time to see Michael capture first place by a tenth of a second. Michael grins with satisfaction as Mario jumps up and down in delight. Russell looks relieved but still disconsolate, thinking more about his own performance than the team's victory. As for Brett, his initial surge of joy gives way almost immediately to chagrin as he realizes that Michael will be hailed as the hero who pulled out the race. "That damned Russell," he thinks, already forgetting that he himself had put the team in third. Instead of going out to celebrate with his teammates, he turns disgustedly into the locker room, filled with anger toward Russell, Michael, and the stupid fans.

Four boys, all champion swimmers. Yet they respond to the same event very differently. Mario and Michael don't see the race as having a lot to do with their personal worth. They enjoy the swim team and the camaraderie. They strive diligently to improve, but failures don't shatter them. Their emotions are less volatile than those of their teammates. In contrast, Russell lacks confidence and takes failure to heart. His emotions vacillate from normal to despair. When Brett criticizes him, he falls apart. He focuses far more on himself than on the team. So does Brett, but for a different reason. Brett is rather full of himself. In fact, he is something of a narcissist. He looks down on others and quickly disparages anyone who fails to measure up. At the same time, he feels crushed by any personal failure. His emotions vacillate from elation to despair. Russell suffers from low self-esteem, while Brett illustrates the dark side of overly high self-esteem. Yet they are alike in that both are self-absorbed. Neither knows the joy in living that Mario and Michael experience, because neither has learned acceptance, the alternative to excessive preoccupation with the self.

SELF-ABSORPTION AND THE DARK SIDE OF SELF-ESTEEM

For years, self-esteem traffickers have sold us the message that increasing kids' self-esteem will cure most of their ills. They have preached the sermon that you can and should feel good, that everyone deserves to have it all. Don't deny your impulses.

You should not have to tolerate pain. You should want the most and the best of everything.

Unfortunately, the self-esteem peddlers are like the Sirens from Greek mythology, sea nymphs whose beautiful songs seductively lured sailors to their demise on the rocks surrounding their island. The self-esteem traffickers miss the point that the root of the problems they identify isn't low self-esteem, but *self-absorption*. And because they misdiagnose the problem, the traffickers prescribe exactly the wrong solution. They recklessly promote the kind of concern with self that leads straight to narcissism. They might intend for kids like Russell to turn out more like Mario and Michael—happier, more fulfilled, feeling better about themselves. But, in fact, their prescription would turn Russell into Brett.

Previous chapters have laid out the argument that excessively high self-esteem exacerbates the very problems identified by the self-esteem movement. Paradoxically, promoting self-esteem as a way to make kids happier and better adjusted can lead to discontent, distress, and, sometimes, even low self-esteem. In this section, we briefly review why this is so and present a few other observations that pull together the threads of the argument. With this understanding firmly in mind, you'll be well prepared to understand—and defend—the acceptance alternative to preoccupation with self-esteem.

The Effects of Promoting Narcissism in Our Kids

As you recall from Chapter 2, low self-esteem and excessively high self-esteem converge in the sense that at the root of both is the consuming concern with oneself that we have called self-absorption. At the high end of the spectrum, self-esteem blends into narcissism. It is in failing to understand the risk of promoting narcissism that the self-esteem movement ends up exacerbating the very problems it tries to solve.

Self-absorbed narcissists can't tolerate negative feelings such as anxiety, frustration, or depression. Instead of accepting that bad feelings are an inevitable part of life, narcissists usually seek to quickly quell such emotions by resorting to substance abuse, sensation seeking, buying sprees, or eating frenzies. Their misguided goals lure narcissists into a trap. They frantically pursue happiness through money, success, and status. Yet, upon obtaining wealth and achievements, they discover that happiness remains out of reach. So they renew the search for yet more money, more success, and more status, convinced that eventually, more will translate into euphoric well-being. Success instead of happiness, status instead of joy. And when their exalted view of themselves is frustrated or threatened, they lash out with anger and aggression in order to destroy the menace.[1]

People with such inflated self-esteem also suffer from distorted perceptions of both themselves and others. Because they can't stand to think poorly of themselves, they defensively reject any negative feedback or information about who they are, while at the same time perceiving their own negative traits in others. For example, 14-year-old Cynthia treats people rudely. She speaks abruptly and demands immediate attention from waiters, waitresses, sales clerks, and bank tellers. When she went to the mall to buy a CD, she vigorously complained about the long wait. The clerk wearily explained that the problem was due to some sales staff calling in sick. Nevertheless, she tried to empathize with Cynthia. "Don't patronize me," Cynthia snapped, and she stomped over to the store manager to accuse the clerk of deliberate insolence.

Researchers have verified that those who cannot accept negative thoughts about themselves often see these identical traits in others.[2] Psychologists refer to this phenomenon as "defensive projection." Cynthia acts rudely, but she cannot see that quality in herself. Rather, she sees rudeness in others, even when it isn't there. Like most narcissists, she ends up failing to get the universal approval she so desperately seeks. People don't like her very much.

Another distortion produced by inflated self-esteem lies in the need, not only to rate oneself compared to others, but also to feel positively superior. Narcissists therefore look down on friends and peers, and they let them know it. This tendency explains why they utterly fail to achieve true intimacy. And those with such distant attachment to other people suffer from a host of psychological maladies, even though their views of themselves are filled with positive illusions.[3]

Narcissists feel driven to protect these positive illusions. This self-absorbed hypervigilance creates tension and wariness about fluctuations in their rating on some mythical hierarchy. No doubt, this constant surveillance accounts for the finding that self-absorption underlies anxiety, depression, and most other forms of psychopathology.[4] Obsessing about ranking prevents narcissists from asking what they really want, or what is really important in life. As psychologist Dr. Albert Ellis has remarked, "you largely focus on your own navel and the pseudo-problem of proving yourself instead of finding yourself."[5]

The Fallacy of Global Evaluations of Self

Narcissists' obsession with rating themselves leads to another distortion that is also exacerbated by promoting self-esteem. How do you rate a person *in toto?* The same person may be honest, loyal, generous, trustworthy, irritable, occasionally violent, hardworking, and dedicated to the community. And even those traits vary over time. How can you possibly add up these characteristics in a global rating of worth? And isn't that the very tendency we observe in people with low self-esteem, who confuse one failure or "defect" with an all-encompassing abjectness of being?

The fallacy of this kind of thinking should be obvious. Consider Joseph, a hardworking senior in high school. He plays on the varsity football team, earns excellent grades, and works part-time at a nursing home. Joseph attends church with his family every week and often visits the nursing home on his own time after services. He loves old people, small children, and animals. Joseph is popular with his friends and respected by his teachers. His family is very close.

When Joseph receives a full scholarship to an Ivy League school, his friends invite him out to celebrate at one of their houses. Joseph realizes that there is alcoholism in his family so he has made it a point not to drink. On this evening, though, his friends hound him into breaking his promise to himself, saying that this special occasion demands that he cut loose a little and celebrate. Reluctantly, he drinks a combination of vodka and lemonade. The concoction goes down easily and Joseph doesn't have any idea how potent the drink really is. After a second drink, he is flying.

Later in the evening, a group of students from another high school shows up. They have been drinking too. One of them starts to harass a girl that Joseph has known for years. Joseph intervenes, telling the kid to leave her alone. The kid becomes belligerent, shoves Joseph away, and starts to fondle the girl. Joseph steps in and throws a solid punch to the guy's head. The kid staggers back and falls; his head crashes hard against the edge of a table. Other kids call for help. Bleeding profusely, he is rushed off to the emergency room in an ambulance. He dies before he gets to the hospital.

Joseph's actions have resulted in the death of a fellow human being. How do we rate Joseph's worth now? Do we calculate a certain number of points for his hard work, community involvement, and concern for others? How much credit do we give him for his devotion to church and family? And just how much do we subtract for his terrible lapse in judgment? Is he suddenly a horrible person? Did this one act negate his entire life? Clearly, evaluating Joseph simply as good or bad is not only impossible, but also a ridiculous oversimplification of the complexity that he really represents. Yet that's exactly what we encourage kids to do when we promote obsession with self-esteem.

Recall from Chapter 2 that the essence of self-esteem is a self-rating in which we make an emotional investment. Inevitably, the rating involves comparison with others. Am I rich enough, thin enough, perfect enough? Making these self-ratings global—which is what self-esteem advocates encourage when they push the message "I'm special"—is fraught with error and dangers. Global self-ratings require you to elevate them when you do well and lower them when you goof up or do poorly. Obviously, no one does well all of the time and in every respect. Half of the world is always below average; they must either deceive themselves or suffer low self-esteem.

Most important, this kind of self-absorption causes us to focus excessively on our flaws, faults, and triumphs. When self-absorbed children are encouraged to make global assessments, some will see themselves as better and some will see themselves as worse than others. Telling kids they're special won't change that because some will know they don't "measure up," while others will deny their flaws, resting their worth on a puffed-up and vulnerable self-esteem.

We focus on self-esteem to make kids feel better, but, in fact, the self-absorbed child is vulnerable to depression as well as anxiety. Even with some therapy, both depression and anxiety, like the common cold, are likely to come back. Why? It is self-absorption that lays the foundation for these problems. And what do you do when you go to therapy? You talk about yourself. You build your self-esteem. Some therapists make you the wonderful, exclusive center of attention for a glorious 50-minute hour without providing challenging work on your issues. In short, you become even more self-absorbed. Is it any wonder that too often therapy provides only temporary relief? Like cold medication, many therapies only relieve the symptoms you are suffering from today without ever touching their cause.

The prescriptions of the self-esteem movement are like many psychotherapies in their emphasis on raising self-esteem as the answer to emotional difficulties. Undoubtedly, raising self-esteem does make people feel better, at least for a while. The problem is that just raising self-esteem leaves people vulnerable to any diminishment of their positive self-view. And when their global ratings of themselves drop, their emotions plummet along with them.

If we want to encourage our kids to be genuinely healthy and happy, we need to start with a different foundation. In the words of Terry London, practitioner of Rational Emotive Behavior Therapy,

> What the self-esteem advocates do not understand is that it is relatively easy to get a person to temporarily "feel better" about themselves [sic] through palliative/diversionary strategies (affirmations, interpersonal "warm fuzzys," diversionary positive imagery, false accolades), but to really work toward resiliency, mental health and enjoyment of life has to be based on a deep structural change in the core schema of self revolving around unconditional self-acceptance.[6] (Emphasis added)

THE ACCEPTANCE ALTERNATIVE

Acceptance provides a prudent alternative to the misguided quest for self-esteem. By acceptance, we mean the ability to acknowledge imperfections, flaws, and foibles alongside talents, skills, and achievements. Acceptance is quite different from narcissistic self-esteem. It is not a global exaltation of the self that forces us to distort reality in order to protect our illusions. Nor is it a complacent self-satisfaction. In a sense, acceptance isn't about the "self" at all. Acceptance means becoming *self-forgetful*. It doesn't dwell on who we are in terms of how we measure up compared to others, or how others measure up compared to us. It's a fundamental attitude that endorses the reality of *oneself* in perpetual relation to *others,* without glorifying or denigrating either.

Acceptance keeps a balanced perspective on personal qualities and accomplishments, viewing them in much the same way as height or hair color—as "givens" or gifts, but not as equivalent to global self-worth. For this reason, acceptance allows us to fully appreciate the qualities and achievements of others without jealousy. Moreover, acceptance liberates us from self-absorption. It shifts our focus outward, toward a larger picture. As psychology professor June Tangney has said, "One important consequence of becoming 'unselved' is that we no longer have the need to enhance and defend an all-important self at the expense of our evaluation of others."[7]

Fostering an Attitude of Acceptance in Our Children

How do we begin to substitute acceptance for concern with self-esteem? The journey toward acceptance begins with the abandonment of global self-ratings. Children are neither good nor bad. They are humans who do good and bad things. Instead of focusing kids' attention on their *selves,* we need to teach them to evaluate their *behaviors* in terms of whether or not their actions facilitate the attainment of their goals and support their values.

For example, most kids like to stay out of trouble. If Jeremy throws a paper airplane in class, you might ask him to tell you what was good about that and then what it cost him. Jeremy might say he liked watching the airplane soar and the surprised look on the other kids' faces, but he didn't much care for the consequence he received in the form of missing recess. You could then problem-solve with him to discover a more appropriate way to get what he wants. He could fly the airplane at recess, for instance. This response encourages Jeremy to evaluate whether what he does produces the outcomes he wants, rather than adding or subtracting from his global self-esteem. When you put a child's entire self-esteem on the line, you only encourage excessive self-focus and useless comparisons with others.

This strategy works especially well with oppositional and defiant kids. These kids spend a lot of time battling authority figures. They accurately understand that many adults consider them rotten to the core. If you ask these kids why they performed some misdeed, they assume you're about to judge them and immediately slip into defensiveness. Inevitably, they will tell you, "I dunno," or "I didn't do it," or "So and so made me do it." When kids anticipate that they are about to receive a judgment, their entire self-esteem goes on the line and they feel obliged to defend their worth.

However, if you ask these kids to evaluate the positive and negative consequences of their actions instead of passing judgment on them in a global way, they will usually engage in a more productive discussion. Accepting delinquents in this manner does not mean approving their deeds or lifestyles. On the contrary, it means focusing attention on *what they do* instead of on who they are.

As an example, Dr. Smith recently had a talk with Alexander, an acknowledged gang member who had been incarcerated for the sixth time. At 16 years of age, Alexander felt fairly comfortable in the detention center. He exhibited considerable loyalty to his gang and expressed no remorse for his actions. He bragged about breaking and entering, stealing cars, and smoking dope whenever he wanted. Rather than judging his character, Dr. Smith asked him what he would like to do at the age of 21. Alexander replied that he would like to have a car, a job, and a girlfriend, and that he'd like not to be in jail. She then asked him if he would need to change his ways in order to get those things. Alexander predicted that he would change on his eighteenth birthday so he wouldn't have to serve adult time. Dr. Smith inquired whether Alexander had friends or knew others who had changed on their eighteenth birthday. She asked about his uncles, fellow gang members, and cousins. Had any of them turned their entire lives around starting on their eighteenth birthday? Alexander admitted he knew of no one who had done that. Dr. Smith left the discussion hanging at that point.

Dr. Smith didn't go home thinking she'd turned Alexander's life around, but she did believe she'd planted a seed. And she's seen some of these seemingly incorrigible kids make real changes after a series of such discussions accompanied by firm consequences for their behavior. By contrast, when people make harsh judgments of juveniles' worth, the kids inevitably dig in their heels and throw up defensive walls. These walls block out any possibility of insight, growth, or change.

Acceptance breeds the potential for insight, growth, and change, and not just for delinquents. It also clears a path for kids plagued by perfectionism, low self-esteem, depression, and other problems. Consider Billy, a fifth-grade boy. He is clumsy and flinches when trying to catch a baseball, which he usually drops. He can't bat much better. Billy worships baseball players, and he is emotionally invested in his baseball skill, or lack of it. As a result, to Billy being a poor baseball player amounts to being a total failure, and he feels lousy about himself.

What's the best thing to tell Billy? He knows he's a rotten baseball player, so there's no point in trying to sell him on the idea that he's not that bad or that he can only improve and one day he'll be the star he would like to be. Nor will it be any use to ignore Billy's feelings about baseball and try to convince him that he's special no matter what. However, while empathizing with his feelings about baseball, we can teach him to accept his limitations and to put them in perspective. We can point out that there are many roads to a happy life and that he has other qualities and potentials that are more important in the overall scheme of things. If we can get Billy to understand this idea, he may actually relax during games. He might start enjoying baseball more for the fun of it and the challenge of becoming a little better over time. Paradoxically, with less self-absorption, his skills may improve.

Thus, acceptance is not the same thing as resignation. Acceptance means preparing ourselves to deal with whatever limitations we have without obsessing about them. It allows us to cope because our entire self-worth is not at stake. We are humans with both positive and negative traits. Some things we do well, and others we do poorly. Neither fact makes us inherently better or worse than other people. At the same time, we can strive to grow and progress. The Serenity Prayer captures the spirit of acceptance:

God, grant me the serenity
to accept the things I cannot change,
courage to change the things I can,
and the wisdom to know the difference.
Living one day at a time;
enjoying one moment at a time;
accepting hardship as the pathway to peace.
Taking, as He did, this sinful world as it is,
not as I would have it.
Trusting that He will make all things right
if I surrender to His Will;
that I may be reasonably happy in this life,
and supremely happy with Him forever in the next.

—*Reinhold Niebuhr, 1926*

Regardless of our spiritual beliefs, the Serenity Prayer enhances our understanding of acceptance. It does not promise never-ending, unlimited good times and happiness. In fact, it declares hardship as the pathway to peace. The feel-good movement would hardly endorse the idea of adversity leading to tranquility. But isn't that the wisdom we find in the world's great religions and philosophies?

The Foundation of Acceptance: Self-Control

Children cannot learn acceptance without knowing how to deal with adversity and hardship. Acceptance involves the ability to affirm not only the good and bad qualities in people, but the good and bad events in life. Kids immersed in the culture of self-absorption and feeling good can't stand to acknowledge mistakes, inadequacies, failures, or negative feedback from others. They want their pleasures now, even if it means they'll get less in the long run. They don't know how to save for a rainy day. They fall apart when bad things happen to them. *Accepting reality with grace requires considerable self-control.*

To achieve self-control, children need to learn to tolerate frustration, accept delay of gratification, and master self-discipline. They can't learn these things without experiencing unpleasant feelings. Kids can't learn to tolerate frustration without feeling frustrated. They can't learn to delay gratification if they always get what they want on demand. They can't learn self-discipline without adults putting limits on them, and sometimes those limits will hurt.

How important is self-control? *A whole lot more important than self-esteem!* Researchers conducted a study of kids that established self-control as central to a child's healthy development. They brought 95 4-year-olds, one at a time, into a room with a table. On one part of the table, there was a single marshmallow, while on another part there were two marshmallows. The researchers told each child, "If you wait until I come back by myself, then you can have this one [pointing to the two marshmallows]. If you don't want to wait, you can ring the bell and bring me back any time you want to. But if you ring the bell, then you can't have this one [pointing to the two marshmallows], but you can have that one [pointing to the single marshmallow]."[8]

As you might imagine, some 4-year-olds couldn't wait and rang the bell. Others managed to delay their impulses and hung in for the two marshmallows. Now, here is the fascinating part.

A full 10 years later, the researchers contacted the parents of these kids. Astonishingly, the children who had displayed the best self-control at age 4 were stronger academically, more skillful at maintaining friendships and getting along with others, more free from social and personal problems, and better at coping with stress than the kids who couldn't delay gratification. In addition, their parents described the self-controlled kids as more verbally fluent, responsive to reason, attentive, "planful," competent, skillful, resourceful, self-reliant, trustworthy, dependable, curious, eager to learn, and concerned with moral issues.[9]

A follow-up sample of these kids even found significantly higher SAT scores for those children more able to delay gratification. Furthermore, the simple self-control task predicted ratings of cognitive and coping competence. In other words, self-control at age 4 was associated with higher school achievement, personal competencies, and moral character many years later.[10] In another study, researchers gave another delay of gratification task to 116 4-year-olds. Teachers were asked to describe the children without knowing the results of this task. They described boys who could delay gratification as deliberative, reserved, attentive, reasonable, and cooperative. They described girls who could delay gratification as competent, resourceful, and intelligent. Kids unable to delay gratification presented a different picture to their teachers. The teachers described the boys as aggressive, irritable, restless, and uncontrolled. They rated girls with poor self-control on the task as whiny, easily offended, victimized by other children, having a tendency to go to pieces under stress, and sulky.[11]

Among adolescents, the ability to delay gratification continues to relate to positive traits and even intelligence. Researchers gave 104 teenagers a choice of an immediate monetary payment or a larger delayed payment. Examiners who were unaware of how the teens responded rated all of the kids. They described kids who managed to delay their payments as more responsible, interested in intellectual matters, productive, and ethically consistent. These kids also had somewhat higher IQ scores than those less able to defer gratification.[12]

A careful reader might wonder whether other characteristics of the kids studied actually were responsible for the findings about delay of gratification. For example, perhaps intelligence is greater among those kids who delay gratification and that explains the affects on later achievement scores and positive personality traits. Or, perhaps, the tasks themselves were flawed in some way. However, additional research has consistently verified the power of delay of gratification to predict subsequent positive adjustment and school performance. This research has used a wide variety of delay tasks, multiple age groups, and kids from all walks of life: privileged to disadvantaged. The discerning reader is correct in assuming that those able to delay gratification are somewhat brighter than other kids. But experimenters can remove the effect of intelligence from predictions with a statistical formula. When both intelligence and other likely influences are removed in that way, the ability of delay skills to predict achievement and social competencies remains robust.[13]

Few psychological competencies have such powerful ability to predict important future characteristics as these simple, playful tasks asking young kids to inhibit their impulses. If you think about it, maybe these results aren't as surprising as they look at first glance. Consider how many of our kids' problems involve a failure to balance long-term versus short-term consequences. Choosing to wait for pleasure or profit versus immediate satisfaction isn't easy for either children or adults. Chocolate cake tastes good even though it adds fat and calories. Alcohol and drugs feel good for a while, yet they can destroy lives. Going on shopping sprees can buoy your mood—until the bills come in. Watching television feels better than studying for a test. At times, losing your temper can be momentarily satisfying, but it usually exacts a price on relationships in the long run.

Self-control forms the foundation of acceptance. For this reason, teaching children self-control is central to their well-being. Unfortunately, our culture has obsessed over making sure our kids feel good all the time. Frustration and delay of pleasure don't fit with this obsession.

Learning self-control is like developing muscles. Exercise hurts. As they say, "no pain, no gain." In any given exercise session, your muscles will first hurt and then give out. But if you continue to exercise them, they get stronger. It's the same with self-control. Researchers have found that, when stressed, we all have limits to our self-control. However, repeated practice with tasks requiring self-control leads to stronger ability to delay impulses and gratification.[14]

Benefits of Acceptance

Whereas the benefits of raising self-esteem are mostly unproven or illusory, the benefits of acceptance are clear. To begin with, children who accept themselves, others, and the challenges of life enjoy deeper, more fulfilling relationships. That's because they have what psychologists call a secure attachment style. The way in which people attach to others predicts both psycho logical adjustment and quality of relationships. Attachment style forms during the early years of life through the interactions between an infant and a caregiver. This style becomes an important part of the personality structure. Though attachment style can change, it frequently remains the same throughout a person's life.[15]

Three attachment styles are usually identified. Some infants seek comfort and contact with their mothers and are soothed by their mothers' presence. These infants are *securely attached*. Later in life they find it comfortable and easy to be close to others. Other babies appear indifferent to their mothers when reunited with them after an absence and do not seek comfort from them. These babies develop an *avoidant attachment* style; as adults, they keep their distance from people. A third group of infants, when reunited with their mothers, seek contact but do not comfort easily. They are described as *anxiously attached*. As adults, anxiously attached people worry a lot about their relationships.[16]

Researchers have shown great interest in the role of attachment and later adjustment. In one study, high school students completed a measure of their attachment style. The researcher found that avoidantly attached students described themselves in highly positive terms, seemingly unaware of their negative qualities. By contrast, kids with an anxious attachment style described themselves in negative terms, with little awareness of their positive traits. Securely attached kids revealed an *open acceptance* of their positive and negative attributes.[17]

Avoidantly attached kids exhibit denial and defensiveness. They can't accept negative feedback. It's likely that they view other people with the same negative traits they deny having. They can only think positively about themselves; they have few close friends. Adolescents with avoidant tendencies more often get in trouble with the law, steal, fight, argue, abuse substances, and gravitate toward narcissism. People don't like them as much, yet they have inflated self-esteem.[18]

Anxiously attached kids don't use denial and defensiveness; they all too readily accept negative feedback. They see themselves as less worthwhile than others and spend time in self-absorbed worry about rejection. They frequently suffer from depression and anxiety.[19] They have low self-esteem.

Securely attached children have many close relationships. Other kids like them. They are well adjusted and happy. They do not use denial and defensiveness and are open to both good and bad feedback. They find it easier to forgive others. They apparently have mastered acceptance.[20]

Attachment style has also been related to empathy, the ability to feel accurately the emotions of others and to understand their point of view. Children who are securely attached are better able to take the perspective of another person and experience similar emotions. The ability to empathize is related to prosocial behavior, morality, and better interpersonal adjustment. The ability to accept others as they are allows children to develop empathy.[21]

Acceptance has another benefit as well. When young people learn to accept their past, they can move from the position of victim to "coper." Victims use a difficult childhood or trauma as a crutch and excuse for lifelong misery. They obsess about the injustice of past events. Blaming others provides them a way to feel better about problems and transiently improves self-esteem. Victims do not take responsibility for their bad behavior, preferring to get sympathy from others for their pitiful circumstances. Psychologist Martin Seligman discussed various "benefits" of what he contends has evolved into a national ideology of victimology: "You identify with the underdog. . . . you can shuck off failings, blame them on other people or the establishment or racism, you feel better about yourself. Your self-esteem goes up. . . . it changes the traditional wages of failure from pity and contempt to compassion and support."[22] Unfortunately, victimhood implies helplessness. There is nothing to be done. Victims remain mired in their negative past.

Copers view their negative past events or childhoods as unfortunate, but not as life sentences. Copers recognize their own power and resources, or they develop them if they are lacking. They understand the unfairness of some occurrences, but they do not wallow in the past. Copers work hard to put the past behind and live well in the present.

Let's illustrate the difference between victims and copers with a story. Julie lives with her mother and two younger brothers. Julie's mother, Lisa, never married, and she is unemployed. The family barely gets by on assistance and food stamps. Lisa spends a good portion of her meager income on cigarettes and beer. At the end of each month, food runs scarce and Lisa becomes even more irritable. At times, for no reason at all, she hits Julie. Julie puts herself in the middle when her mother goes after her little brothers. She'd rather take the blows than see them hurt.

Julie takes care of her younger brothers when her mother gets drunk or goes to parties. Julie never invites friends home because the shabby furniture and mess embarrass her. She misses school frequently because she's worried about her mother's ability to take care of her brothers. When she's at school, she has difficulty concentrating and doesn't get good grades.

In high school, Julie starts to hang around with a bad crowd. Occasionally, Julie's English teacher sits down with her at lunch. She tries to boost Julie's self-esteem by telling her how bright she is and how much potential she is wasting. She offers to help Julie in any way she can. She pleads with Julie to change her ways and tells her she looks just like a gangster. In response, Julie complains that her teacher has no idea how bad things are at home. Her teacher argues that her own life was just as bad as Julie's and that she was able to change. Julie defiantly tells her no one can understand how awful her life is.

Every weekend Julie needs to get high to escape her negative feelings. Soon she moves from drinking and smoking marijuana to crack. She shoplifts to support her habit. When arrested for the first time, she tells her public defender about her horrible home life. Julie sees herself as a victim of her miserable environment and feels helpless to change.

Now consider an alternative outcome. In high school, Julie starts to hang around with a bad crowd. Occasionally, Julie's English teacher sits down with her at lunch. She expresses empathy about Julie's home life, but she tells Julie that she can't use that as an excuse. She offers to help Julie, but only if Julie will meet her halfway. If Julie will stop by after school and bring in her homework, she will tutor her. She points out the consequences of Julie continuing on the road she has chosen, but without a judgmental tone.

Julie slowly begins to realize that there is a different way to live. She'd heard that her teacher had a similar upbringing but managed to turn her life around. She knows it will be very difficult to learn new study habits and take control of her life—her teacher has made that clear. But Julie decides to accept help from her teacher and cope with a difficult situation.

In the first outcome, a well-intentioned teacher reaches out to Julie. She groundlessly tries to boost her confidence and offer help with no strings attached. She judges Julie's behavior by calling her an emerging gangster. Julie responds by proclaiming her victimhood.

In the second scenario, Julie's teacher reaches out with accepting empathy accompanied by clear expectations and a realistic offer of help. At the same time, she refuses to accept excuses from Julie. With this effective mentor, Julie has a chance.

Many factors influence whether a child becomes a victim or a coper in response to adversity. However, parents, teachers, or other interested adults who help children find the way to acceptance can make a big difference.

Acceptance, then, is the alternative that liberates us and our children from obsession with self-esteem. It is the way to a healthier and happier life, and to an attitude of respect and caring for others. It leads to effective coping instead of helpless victimization. It is, in short, what most of us want for our children. What we can do as parents and teachers to put our children on the path to acceptance is the subject of the next two chapters.

CHAPTER 9

PARENTING SOLID KIDS

CHAOS REIGNS ON MOST WEEKDAY MORNINGS AT THE MORRIS home. Pam wakes her 9- and 11-year-old two or three times every morning. The first time they beg to sleep a few more minutes, the next they promise to get up, and by the third time Pam has to stand next to their beds until she sees them standing up. Usually the kids complain about having to brush their teeth and wash up. Pam has to supervise their every move or they just don't do it. She helps them pick out their clothes and makes breakfast.

Today, Pam puts out orange juice and the brand of cereal declared as the favorite by the kids this week. Eleven-year-old Justine now complains to her mom that she hates that cereal.

"That was the brand you asked for," Pam replies, more mystified than scolding. "Besides, you've already poured it into the bowl."

Justine refuses to eat. Pam finds another brand of cereal and asks if this one will do. Nine-year-old Frank joins in. He doesn't want either one of the cereals and demands an egg muffin from his favorite fast-food restaurant. Pam throws up her hands and tells them if they hurry up, she'll take them out. Justine purposely goes into slow motion. Frank pinches her. Justine wails.

"Please, kids, can't you get along?" Pam begs.

Pam illustrates the permissive, or indulgent, style of parenting, one of four parenting styles identified by researchers. The other three styles are authoritarian, authoritative, and neglectful. Permissive parents like Pam are conscientious, committed, and engaged with their children. At the same time, they do not demand mature behavior, they avoid confrontation, and they can't stand to let their kids feel bad.

Let's imagine Pam as a parent with an authoritarian style. Conflict and calls for order reign on most weekday mornings at the Morris home. A shrill alarm clock awakens her 9- and 11-year-old at 6:00 A.M. sharp. The children march into the bathroom to brush their teeth and wash up while Pam makes breakfast.

Today, Pam puts out the standard orange juice and oatmeal. Eleven-year-old Justine complains to her mom that she hates oatmeal. Pam responds loudly, "When you have a job and you're living on your own, you can choose your own breakfast. In the meantime, you have exactly two minutes to finish eating!"

Nine-year-old Frank chimes in and declares he wants an egg muffin from his favorite fast-food restaurant. Pam explodes and dumps the kids' breakfasts in the sink. Justine purposely goes into slow motion. Frank pinches her. Justine wails.

Pam yanks both kids around and tells them to stop being brats. "Since you are such babies," she yells, "you'll be grounded to your rooms after school until you learn to grow up."

Like permissive parents, authoritarian parents are engaged and involved with their children. However, they are highly directive and demanding. They expect obedience without explanation. They have structured, ordered homes with many clearly laid-out rules. These parents place a high priority on discipline. When they make a command, they expect immediate, unquestioning compliance.

Now let's imagine Pam as a parent with an authoritative style. Calmness usually, but not always, reigns on weekday mornings at the Morris home. The clock radio wakens her 9- and 11-year-old at 6:00 A.M. Occasionally Pam needs to push them out of bed. Most mornings, the kids independently brush their teeth, wash up, and pick out their clothes.

Today, Pam puts out orange juice and one of their favorite cereals. Eleven-year-old Justine complains to her mom that she hates that cereal. Pam says, "I'll be happy to get another kind when I go to the store later in the week, but that's all we have for now." Justine refuses to eat. Pam ignores her, knowing she's unlikely to starve. Nine-year-old Frank chimes in and demands an egg muffin from his favorite fast-food restaurant. Pam calmly shrugs and tells them they have five minutes before they need to leave for school. Justine purposely goes into slow motion. Frank pinches her. Justine wails. Quietly but firmly, Pam tells the kids, "This way of doing things isn't going to work. I expect your cooperation when it's time to go to school. This afternoon you will both have a time-out after school to think about better ways of getting ready in the morning." When the kids get home after school, Pam remembers to calmly follow through with their consequence.

Authoritative parents are also involved and engaged with their kids, but their style differs from those of both permissive and authoritarian parents. They provide clear standards and expectations for their kids' behavior, but they use more supportive than punitive discipline. They aren't concerned just with obedience, or with their kids' feeling good. They want their children to learn cooperation, social responsibility, and how to regulate their own behavior.

The fourth style of parenting is uninvolved, or neglectful. These parents don't demand much and are not particularly engaged or involved. They would likely let the kids sleep in and make their own breakfast. They show little concern for schoolwork and leave social skills up to the children to learn on their own.[1]

Which of these parenting styles is most likely to encourage the development of acceptance in children? Which one is likely to produce the healthiest, most well-adjusted kids? And does parenting style really matter, or do kids turn out pretty much the same way regardless of what parents do? This chapter explores these questions.

DOES PARENTING STYLE REALLY MATTER?

Recently, some controversy has emerged concerning the influence of parents on their children relative to other factors that affect the way kids turn out. Judith Harris stimulated this controversy in her book called the *Nurturance Assumption*. She declared parenting to have only a minor impact when compared to biology, genetics, peers, and neighborhood.[2] So maybe it doesn't matter a great deal which style parents adopt. Or does it?

Although genetics and other aspects of the environment clearly play a role in kids' development, extensive research definitively demonstrates that parenting matters. The way parents raise their children helps create either hollow kids or solid kids. For example, the way mothers relate to their babies at 6 months predicts later aggression. Mothers who are intrusive, less aware of their infants' emotional state, and hostile have children who at age 3 are noncompliant, negative, and hyperactive. By first grade, these kids show more anxiety, depression, and acting-out problems than other kids. By the third grade, teachers describe them as more aggressive.[3]

Aggressive children usually start acting up during preschool and continue to be aggressive throughout their school years. In one study, kids in preschool with conduct disorders had parents who were more authoritarian and less authoritative. In other words, aggressive preschoolers tended to have parents who demanded instant obedience without explanations.[4]

Another study, this one of 1,230 mothers and their first-through fifth-grade children, demonstrated that parenting style makes a difference for elementary students. The kids of authoritative parents showed healthier adjustment, less maladaptive behavior, and greater social competence than children of authoritarian parents.[5]

Parenting style continues to influence the adjustment of adolescents. Numerous studies of thousands of adolescents have demonstrated that teens from authoritative families have more adaptive approaches to achievement, more social competence, higher grades, less substance abuse, and better psychological adjustment than kids from other families. By contrast, adolescents from authoritarian families were reasonably conforming and obedient but had lower self-esteem, poor social skills, and more depression. Those with neglectful parents demonstrated the least amount of social competence and the most emotional and behavioral problems. Teens with permissive parents showed high self-esteem and good social skills, but poor academic performance, more substance abuse, and more school misconduct.[6]

By now it should come as no surprise that higher self-esteem among the teens was associated with other, less desirable, characteristics. And concern for raising self-esteem tends to go hand in hand with permissive parenting. Like many psychologists, we see an epidemic of permissive parenting in this country. Parents coached by the self-esteem and feel-good movements appear increasingly afraid to set expectations, limits, and discipline. As with so many things in life, however, taking the easy way out in the short run by giving in to kids' demands can lead to disaster in the long run. Children of permissive parents don't experience the consequences of their behavior. Moreover, they learn to manipulate their parents and others.

Permissive parenting does work in one way; it develops high self-esteem. And that's unfortunate, because poor behavior and schoolwork tend to accompany inflated self-esteem. Furthermore, recall the risk that extremely high self-esteem poses in terms of fragility and the propensity to deflate in the face of failure. Of course, that's not what permissive parents mean to encourage. Why, then, have so many parents been seduced into a permissive style of parenting? We think a major explanation is that, for a variety of reasons, parents feel more guilt than ever before. To begin with, divorce rates have soared. In 1999, 32% of children lived with one parent as compared to 22% in 1980. Many of these parents feel terrible about their kids' having to grow up without two parents. Parents also feel guilty because they more frequently farm their kids out to daycare. Today more than half of all children from birth to third grade (about 54%) attend some type of childcare program.[7] Parents worry that their kids suffer from loneliness and deprivation while away from them. Additionally, many parents move away from extended families, thus distancing their kids from grandparents and other relatives.

Parents also feel guilty because they work longer hours than ever before. The average American workweek lasts four hours longer than in 1980; in 2000, workers put in an average of 47 hours per week.[8] Many professionals routinely work 70 or 80 hours per week.[9] The term "24/7" has sprung up from the technology revolution. Even at home, many of us stay connected to work through our e-mail, cell phones, personal digital assistants (PDAs), and computers. Parents thus end the day exhausted, with little emotional energy to give to their kids. Some children turn to TV and video games as surrogate parents. Parents fret over the effects of this disconnection. And they worry about the resulting tenuous relationship with their kids.

The self-esteem traffickers exploit parental guilt by scaring parents and offering a simplistic solution. Parents better watch out: If their kids feel bad about themselves, they'll do poorly in school, abuse drugs, and misbehave. But just pump up self-esteem and everyone can feel better.

For all these reasons, many parents strive to do everything they can to keep their kids happy, lest their children suffer any needless distress. Because expectations, limits, and discipline upset children in the short run, these parents try to minimize their use of such strategies. Parents also fear that the weakened relationship with their offspring won't withstand the temporary resentment caused by discipline. Instead, they try to become their kids' best friends. In the process, they strive to eliminate failure, unhappiness, sadness, anxiety, and anger from their kids' lives.

Instead of protecting children, these efforts backfire. In the words of psychologist Dr. Martin Seligman,

> *Children need to fail. They need to feel sad, anxious, and angry. When we impulsively protect our children from failure, we deprive them of learning. . . . By cushioning feeling bad, it has made it harder for our children to feel good. . . . By circumventing feelings of failure, it made it more difficult for our children to feel mastery. By blunting warranted sadness and anxiety, it created children at high risk for unwarranted depression. By encouraging cheap success, it produced a generation of very expensive failures.*[10]

Parenting style, then, does matter. And it makes a difference not only to kids' adjustment, but to something else parents should be concerned about: their children's values and moral behavior.

THE TWIN TOWERS OF MORALITY:
EMPATHY AND SELF-CONTROL

Twelve-year-old David runs across the playground at the sound of the tardy bell. As he tears toward the school, he notices a crowd forming around two boys and makes an immediate detour to join the flock. The noisy kids call out, daring the boys to fight. The class bully, Stephen, pushes David's friend Josh, who falls to the ground. Josh feels humiliated, and tears run down his face. Someone pulls Josh to his feet. Kids shout for him to fight back. Stephen pushes him again. David can feel Josh's shame. Josh is much smaller than Stephen and not as tough.

David never gets into fights, but he can't stand to see Josh ridiculed. Though scared, he steps into the circle and firmly tells Stephen to back off and pick on someone his own size. Stephen pushes David. Although angered, David tells Stephen the teachers are on their way, and they shouldn't be stupid and get into trouble. David challenges Stephen to a one-on-one basketball game after school.

David possesses empathy. He feels and understands the emotions of others. He wants to do whatever he can when people close to him are hurt. What kept David from punching Stephen when he was pushed? Another boy with empathy might well have done so. David also possesses a high degree of self-control. These two qualities, empathy and self-control, are what we call the twin towers of morality.

Empathy is a complex emotion. It requires taking another person's perspective, experiencing another's emotions, and making an appraisal. Emotions can be contagious. Even 2-year-olds will respond with tears when their playmates get hurt. And they sometimes offer an upset child a favorite toy or their own bottle.

How important is empathy? Researchers have found that children who empathize with others are more cooperative, socially competent, and prosocial (that is, likely to help and reach out to others).[11] Popular children have been found to have better ability to take another perspective and show empathy than their rejected peers.[12] Empathy allows children to make adaptive responses to interpersonal conflict and not rely on aggression.[13] Furthermore, lower levels of empathy have been found in children with behavior problems and lower moral regulation.[14]

Yet, empathy alone doesn't produce prudent and moral behavior. In the previous chapter, we discussed the need for self-control as a precursor for the development of acceptance. Additionally, some argue that self-control is the core psychological trait that allows virtuous, moral behavior. Virtue requires both a desire to be moral and the ability to carry out those intentions. Most immoral behavior involves a failure to control one's impulses. Consider the seven deadly sins. Gluttony involves excessive consumption and pleasures. Sloth is laziness and lack of discipline. Lust, greed, and envy all involve too much desire, which in the absence of self-control lead to immoral behavior. Anger without self-control results in violence. Pride, the seventh deadly sin, causes people to feel more deserving, entitled, special, and self-absorbed. Those with excessive "pride" put themselves above others and fail to restrain their own personal desires.[15]

As we reviewed earlier, children with good self-control (those who were able to delay gratification) at age 4 were well-adjusted as teens. They did better academically and socially more than a decade later. By the same token, poor self-control leads to disaster. Juvenile delinquents show poor self-control in their illegal activities. They also show poor self-control in other areas, such as risk taking, sexual behavior, and schoolwork.

Permissive parenting is the antithesis of what it takes for learning self-control. Young children need structure and limits set on their behavior. These external controls come before the emergence of internal self-control. Permissive parents fail to provide this essential guidance.

This point is illustrated by a study in which researchers asked preschoolers to refrain from touching a beautifully wrapped present. Children who failed to resist (in other words, could not delay gratification) had mothers who utilized a permissive parenting style. Kids who successfully resisted had mothers with an authoritative parenting style.[16] Other research has shown that the adolescent children of permissive parents get more tickets, are more often caught speeding, and have more motor vehicle accidents than other teens.[17]

No kid will exhibit a good sense of morality without empathy and self-control. To develop these qualities, they need a clear set of standards and expectations for their behavior as a guide. Parents can teach their kids standards, expectations, empathy, and self-control. Arguably, such instruction is the primary goal of parenting. But it's not just a matter of what we *say* to our kids. It's also a matter of what we *do* ourselves.

RAISING SOLID KIDS: MODELING

Most parenting experts focus on telling you how to motivate your children through applying various types of praise and punishment in response to their behavior. We will shortly share some thoughts with you along those lines. But first we want to discuss modeling, a more powerful tool than mere manipulation of consequences.

Modeling essentially means teaching by example. Children learn most of their behavior, values, and attitudes through observation. But kids don't imitate everyone and everything they see. Why do they mimic some people and not others? Several factors go into their choices. They copy models to whom they feel attached, those with high status, and those they see rewarded for their actions. Kids look to parents as their most influential models. If you want your kids to turn out well, you need to demonstrate the values, behavior, and self-control you want to see in them.

Observe children closely, and you can usually infer quite a bit about their home lives. For example, imagine Madison plays alone in the kitchen area in his preschool classroom. He picks up a plastic dish and throws it at the table. His teacher hears him shouting at the doll seated at the table. "You're a stupid, lazy drunk," he shouts. He shakes the doll and tells it to get a job or get out. He is so engrossed in his drama that his face swells with anger.

The teacher approaches Madison and kneels beside him. She gently puts her hand on his shoulder and Madison jerks back, startled. She asks him if things are all right at home. Madison doesn't respond. The teacher knows where Madison learned the script for his horrible play. He learned it through modeling.

Psychologist Albert Bandura pioneered research on the effects of modeling on kids. In a classic experiment, an adult hit, kicked, and yelled at an inflated doll while observed by one group of preschoolers. Another group of kids did not see the aggressive adult. Later, the preschoolers went into the room with the doll one at a time. Those who had viewed the aggressive adult beat up the doll in a similar manner.[18] The results of this study, and many like it, underscore the powerful influence of modeling. If you want your kids to learn impulsiveness, aggression, and arrogance, just act that way. By the same token, if you want your kids to learn self-control, then you must act accordingly.

For example, parents can model anger management rather than aggression. These days, an all-too-common occasion for anger and aggression is driving. Especially in this age of road rage, it's not such a good idea to lose control and make obscene gestures at a driver who cuts in front of you in traffic. More generally, parents can use this situation to model anger management by expressing their irritation but keeping cool. They can verbalize some of their ways of controlling anger, such as counting slowly to 10, taking a few deep breaths, or telling themselves out loud that things like this happen all the time and don't amount to a big deal.

Similarly, parents can model self-control in response to frustration. For example, while waiting more than 10 minutes in line at a grocery store with her young daughter, Marissa feels impatient. However, rather than showing irritation, she uses the occasion to teach her child frustration tolerance and coping strategies. She explains that, although it's frustrating, waiting for things happens a lot. She suggests that she and her daughter use the time to watch people, talk with each other, make future plans, daydream, or grab a magazine to read from the rack.

Daily life is full of opportunities to model self-control and effective coping behaviors. Household chores, for instance, present a good opportunity to model a strategy for getting yourself to do unpleasant tasks. Parents can say out loud that they will first vacuum and straighten up the house before they sit down and do something more pleasurable such as read a book. Or they can say, "Let's wash the car together before we go out for ice cream." Consistently demonstrating how to set priorities by putting less favored but essential tasks before more enjoyable activities not only models self-control but teaches kids useful strategies they can imitate.

Consider persistence, another crucial component of self-control. Again, daily life provides the curriculum for this learning. For many people, figuring out how to assemble a bicycle represents something of a challenge. Talking out loud as the child observes can model persistence. When William puts together a bicycle for his son, he feels apprehensive, knowing he's not very mechanically inclined. Other parents might try to cover up their anxiety in order to appear all-knowing, or give up too easily and get a neighbor to assemble the bicycle, or kick the bicycle and blame the stupid instructions when things go wrong. William chooses a different path. He tells his son that chores like these aren't easy for him, but he believes persistence will prevail. When he can't get some of the parts to fit together after several tries, he comments that he feels a little frustrated, but he just needs to try another way. After two hours, he tells his son he needs a break, but he'll get back to it tomorrow. The next day, he models persistence and frustration tolerance again. When he finally finishes the task, William remarks that it was tough, but it feels great to work on something difficult until it gets done.

Parents can also model the other twin tower of morality, empathy. It starts by taking every opportunity to point out how other people feel and expressing understanding of and concern for their situation. When driving past a person holding a sign asking for donations, Serena talks to her son, Brad, about how lonely and sad that man must feel and wonders how he ended up that way. She tells him it makes her feel sad to see people in that condition. When Brad comes home from school the next day and tells his mother about a friend's parents who are getting divorced, Serena expresses sympathy for all the family members. She remarks that his friend must feel especially upset and suggests they invite him over to spend the night sometime soon.

Finally, parents can help their children by modeling acceptance of self and others. Parents do not need to model perfection; kids will look up to them no matter what. They can acknowledge their own mistakes openly, without defensiveness, and they can show how to take pride in a job well done without becoming arrogant and conceited. And they can resist making global judgments about other people.

We are always modeling how to act, whether we're aware of it or not. Our kids will learn from what we do more than from what we say. For example, Kalene's dad is a renowned physicist. He routinely watches television while spouting a continuous commentary concerning the stupidity of politicians, the laziness of the poor, and the moral degeneration of movie stars. No one in the house dares argue with him, as his opinion reigns supreme. He never admits to mistakes or shortcomings of any kind. At school, Kalene imitates her dad's behavior by passing judgment, usually negative, on her classmates. Although she is bright, other kids don't like her. Taking after her dad, she dismisses them as know-nothings. No one ever told her to act this way. They didn't have to.

RAISING SOLID KIDS: METHODS OF INFLUENCE AND DISCIPLINE

The self-esteem movement urges parents to notice and applaud every conceivable action their kids make. What a beautiful picture you drew! You're a wonderful dancer! Great job of picking up your room! You sure cleaned up your plate well! You're the best runner in the whole first grade! I can't believe how nice you were to your brother! I'm so proud of you for taking out the trash; you're a very good boy!

This advice originates in a huge body of research showing that rewarding behavior tends to result in more of that behavior in the future. It makes sense that if you want children to do more of something, you should praise them. It works! Children find approval and praise from their parents quite rewarding. It's cheap and easy to do; what could be wrong with that?

Well, two things. First, praising a behavior you want to see repeated is quite different from lavishing praise and attention on kids no matter *what* they do in the name of boosting their self-esteem. Second, as with everything else in life, you can overdo a good thing. Praise loses meaning when it is tossed around like confetti. Some parents virtually follow their children around the playground, complimenting them on their teeter-tottering. As we remarked earlier in this book, praising kids for trivia not only dilutes the meaning of praise but also contributes to puffing up an empty self-esteem that isn't anchored by anything real.

It's also important to distinguish praise for effort and achievement (what kids do) from praise for ability or talents (what kids are, or what parents would like them to be). For example, most parents believe that praising children for their intelligence will make them feel confident and increase their motivation to learn. In fact, in one recent survey 85% of parents endorsed the idea that when kids do well on a task, it's a good idea to praise their ability.[19] Although that assumption sounds reasonable, studies have conclusively contradicted it. In one experimental study, researchers divided elementary school children into three groups. The first group completed 10 problems and received no feedback on their performance. The second group was told that they had done a good job and that they must be very smart. The third group was told that they had done a good job and that they must have worked hard. In other words, the second group received praise for their intelligence or ability, while the third group received positive feedback about their effort.

Following the initial task, the researchers gave the kids a chance to choose another set of problems. The group praised for their ability picked the easiest problems, those that they believed they could effortlessly complete. These kids showed less persistence, less enjoyment, and worse performance on the subsequent task than children praised for effort or children receiving no feedback. In contrast, the group praised for effort chose more challenging problems because they thought they could learn more from them. Moreover, they enjoyed the task more and persisted at it longer than kids in the other two groups.[20]

Another series of studies should help mute parents' unrestrained use of praise as well. Researchers praised 5- and 6-year-old children in one of three ways. They praised one group of kids for how well they completed a task. They called this type of praise "outcome praise." They praised the children in a second group for the effort they made on the task, which they called "process praise." Finally, they used "person praise" in a third group by telling the kids "You're a good girl," or "I'm really proud of you." They then gathered three more groups of children and criticized them in three ways: outcome, process, and person.

The results were startling. When asked to do another task, kids who received either person criticism *or* person praise showed poor persistence, more self-blame, and more helpless responses than kids in the other groups.[21]

For many years, parents have heard advice that they shouldn't criticize a child as a whole, but focus on specific behavior. For example, when a girl spills her milk, it's not a good idea to call her clumsy, a personal and global judgment. Or if a boy receives a bad grade on his report card, everyone knows you shouldn't call him stupid. What most people don't know is that globally *praising* the whole child, or his or her ability, does not improve motivation either; instead, it detracts from it.

The lesson? *For both praise and criticism, talk about the deed, not the doer.* Not only will you have more of the kind of influence on kids' behavior that you intend, but you'll teach a valuable lesson about acceptance. When you rate kids as a whole, you cause them to focus on themselves and increase their anxiety about their performance, which simply worsens their performance and persistence. Children then believe they are good only when they do well and bad every time they do poorly. By contrast, when you focus on deeds and reinforce kids for their efforts, you encourage them to persist and work harder. Kids who are praised in this way concentrate more on the process of learning and working than on the outcome. They learn, grow, and accomplish for the joy of doing. *They don't worry about their self-esteem because they don't connect their fundamental worth to their deeds.*

By the same token, when kids' efforts go in the wrong direction, parents must intervene. Kids thrive on limits and reasonable discipline. They need to learn that their behaviors have consequences. When parents enforce rules, kids usually rebel or feel bad for a while. That can be unpleasant for both them and their parents, but those bad feelings play a useful role in teaching.

Permissive parents try to prevent their kids from experiencing bad feelings. But hands-off parenting simply doesn't work.

A recent survey by the National Center on Addictions and Substance Abuse surveyed teens and categorized three groups of parents: hands-on, hands-off, and half-hearted. Hands-on parents monitor their kids' TV and Internet viewing, have curfews, know where their kids are after school and on weekends, usually have dinner with them, provide clear messages about marijuana use, and monitor their school performance. Hands-off parents demonstrate consistent failure to provide rules and monitor behavior and schoolwork. Half-hearted parents fall in between the two types.

Only one-fourth of teens in the survey reported having hands-on parents. Nearly one-fifth had hands-off parents, and that group had about four times the risk of substance abuse as kids of hands-on parents. Perhaps the most interesting result of this study, however, concerns the relationship teens reported having with their parents. You might suppose that rebellious adolescents would value having hands-off parents. Judging from their behavior, many parents seem to think that "hands-off" is the way to get along with their adolescent children. In fact, however, almost three times as many teens with hands-on parents said they had an excellent relationship with their dads and more than twice as many stated they had an excellent relationship with their moms as those with hands-off parents. Those with half-hearted parents fell in between the other two groups.[22]

Hands-on parents demonstrate that they are involved with their children. Moreover, they don't fear disciplining their kids. Discipline, however, should change depending on the child's age. For very young children, parents need to set limits largely for health and safety purposes. Reasoning with toddlers simply wastes words and energy.

As children get older, misbehavior provides an opportunity for parents to instill values by briefly explaining the moral basis of the transgression. This explanation works better if it is kept quite brief and *does not take the place of consequences for misdeeds.*

For example, when 4-year-old Jose grabs a toy from his sister, his mother can tell Jose that he made his sister cry, that making someone cry is not a nice thing to do, and that kids shouldn't grab things without asking first. She then instructs him that he needs to take a prompt five-minute time-out for his behavior. Notice that the mother is not calling Jose a bad boy. She simply tells him the problem with his behavior by pointing out the effect he had on his sister.

As children become capable of greater moral understanding, explanations can become more sophisticated. When 8-year-old Susan hits her playmate, her dad tells her that hurting another person is wrong and that we should treat others as we expect to be treated ourselves. He also points out that her playmate feels bad and tells her firmly that she should apologize. Again, the father focuses on the bad behavior and its consequences. He does not make a global statement about his daughter's self-worth. Research has shown that parents who regularly explain values and the effects of misbehavior on others have children who display greater empathy and sympathy than other kids. As we said before, kids with higher levels of empathy get along better with others.

These kids also feel a little more guilt.[23] But, contrary to what seems to be the popular view, guilt isn't always a bad thing. Guilt feelings produce upset about a behavior that may have caused harm. These feelings include an uncomfortable knowledge of having done wrong. Because guilt temporarily lowers self-esteem, the self-esteem movement abhors it. In recent years, however, many psychologists have determined that moderate amounts of guilt lead to increased empathy as well as greater self-control. Guilt pushes kids to repair the damage. It motivates kids to apologize and make amends. When guilt flares up, it activates concern for others and desire to improve one's relationships.[24]

When parents are uncomfortable with the idea of causing guilt feelings, they may be confusing guilt with shame. Whereas guilt arises from specific behaviors, shame involves a more global evaluation of the entire self that can be painful and even devastating. Shame emerges when parents make global judgments of their children: "You are a bad boy." "You're always careless." "You don't care about anyone but yourself." "You'll never amount to anything." A child consumed by shame feels helpless and dejected. That is because shame is self-absorbed and self-directed. It often motivates a desire to hide or escape rather than make amends. Like other self-absorbed emotions, shame has been linked to poor adjustment.[25]

Children learn to correct their behavior without devastating feelings of shame when parents focus on the deed and not the doer and follow brief explanations with swift, inescapable consequences. But these consequences must be administered in a calm, matter-of-fact manner. Parental anger, hostility, and yelling will not make consequences work better. Harshness and excessive negativity simply exacerbate the experience of shame.

Although we have emphasized explaining why behavior is wrong, we also want to stress keeping those explanations brief. Parents often make the mistake of responding to a misdeed by talking too much and seeking agreement through prolonged reasoning with their kids. Discussions about values with your kids at the dinner table may be appropriate. However, when you discipline kids, reasoning with them implies an egalitarian relationship. Kids need your leadership. As family psychologist John Rosemond has observed, "A child must learn to obey legitimate authority before he can learn self-control."[26]

RAISING SOLID *AND* HAPPY KIDS

Most parents want to see their children turn into happy, productive adults. So do we. As we have emphasized, though, fostering our kids' happiness doesn't mean sparing them every sort of bad feeling. To become the adults we hope they will be, kids need to learn self-control, frustration tolerance, and empathy.

They acquire these qualities through parental modeling, limit setting, and discipline and by learning from the consequences of their actions. Occasional bad feelings *facilitate* the process.

There is another side to this coin, however. To achieve happiness and well-being, kids don't need unconditional approval. They *do* need unconditional love and acceptance. Understanding the difference between approval and acceptance is crucial to implementing a style of parenting that is authoritative without being either authoritarian or permissive.

A recent study of young adult students looked at their well-being, as measured by positive psychological functioning in the following areas: self-acceptance, positive relations with others, environmental mastery, purpose in life, and personal growth. In addition, the researchers measured young adults' anxiety, loneliness, and depression. They found that the extent to which the students felt *accepted* by their parents strongly predicted well-being. Well-adjusted students believed that their parents loved and valued them more so than did the poorly adjusted students.[27]

Accepting parents manage to discipline with love. They provide a sanctuary of support. When their children face trouble, they may show disapproval for what their kids did, but they never withdraw their love. In the midst of discipline and consequences, accepting parents continue to treasure their children, and they show it. In so doing, they model what acceptance is all about.

CHAPTER 10

TEACHING
SOLID KIDS

THE YEAR WAS 1977; THE PLACE WAS A SOUTHFIELD, MICHIGAN, hospital. A doctor told the distressed couple that labor had progressed too far; medicine had no way to stop the births from proceeding. The couple's identical twins were 13 weeks premature. The doctor said the first twin had about a 25% chance to live. Unfortunately, the second twin had *no chance at all* of survival.

Allison, born first, weighed just two pounds, six ounces, and cried out weakly upon arrival. Nurses whisked her away to the neonatal unit and put her on a respirator as a precaution. Sara, born breech, weighed an ounce less. She did not cry; in fact, she failed to breathe. Doctors immediately put her on a respirator and sent her to neonatal intensive care.

Within 48 hours, Allison needed no help to breathe. Sara remained on the respirator. Nurses allowed the parents to stay with the babies as much as they wanted. Allison gained weight rapidly and was clearly beating the odds. But Sara still could not breathe on her own. Even with the respirator, her heart often stopped beating. Her mother prayed for Sara's life—in spite of the doctors' prediction of likely cerebral palsy, blindness, and severe mental disabilities. Sara's mother knew that she could *accept* and cherish a child with limitations.

After more than a month, one of Sara's lungs collapsed. Doctors told the parents she would not survive for long because the respirator would cause more lung complications. They encouraged the parents to consider taking her off life support. "At least you have one live baby," they said. But the parents saw how Sara struggled against the invasion of tubes. It took a team to hold her down when they needed to find a new vein. She was just too alive to abandon.

After 70 days, Allison went home. Hope for Sara dimmed because of her continued dependence on the respirator. On the seventy-first day, her parents decided to give Sara a chance to breathe with the help of an oxygen tent, knowing she would soon die if left on the respirator. Somehow, she survived.

The twins began public school at the age of 5. Developmentally, Allison seemed perfectly normal; Sara had some minor problems with speech. The girls' parents insisted on placement in different classrooms so that teachers would not compare the identical twins to each other. In first grade, Allison learned to read easily, but Sara struggled. The parents worked intensively on beginning reading skills with Sara at home.

In second and third grade, spelling became a daily frustration for Sara. Allison brought her words home on Monday and could spell them all with one or two practices. She could also spell the bonus words. She never really needed to study. But Sara did. Her mom would have Sara read each word out loud, spell it out loud, and then copy it. They repeated this process over and over each night. Usually by Thursday evening, Sara knew most of her spelling words. On Friday at breakfast, the twins would go over their words again. Sara would study while on the bus and standing in line before the bell rang. Sometimes, she would get an A on her test; other times, the spelling would just seem to disappear. By Monday, last week's words were forgotten and she'd start with a new list.

Sara also went to after-school tutoring in addition to working with her parents. She struggled throughout elementary school, working much harder than her twin. Sometimes she'd cry and ask why school was so hard for her and so easy for her twin sister. She said it wasn't fair, and she was right. Her parents grieved with her but relentlessly kept pushing. They drilled the idea into her head that she would simply have to study much harder than other kids. They refused to give her an out by calling her disabled.

Yet Sara clearly had a learning disability. By middle school, she couldn't keep up in reading. Her teachers referred her for an evaluation. The committee suggested full-time special education. The parents disagreed and requested merely one hour a day of special education in the area of language arts. Meanwhile, they continued their arduous spelling, math, and reading drills at home.

The school team thought the parents expected too much from their daughter. They worried that Sara's self-esteem would suffer in regular education, and they had concerns about the pressure put on her by her parents. Were her parents pushing her too hard?

Indeed, Sara struggled—all the way through school. Today, Allison and Sara, Dr. Smith's daughters, both enjoy a normal, full life and work as nurses. Sara, who once despised reading, enjoys reading a range of popular novels.

Sara became a solid kid, filled not with hollow self-esteem, but with acceptance. Recall that acceptance involves insight and awareness of both positive and negative qualities of the self and others. Acceptance includes the ability to deal with both blessings and plagues. Accepting such vicissitudes of life requires considerable self-control, the foundation of acceptance. Self-control fosters growth, change, courage, and serenity.

Finding the road to acceptance did not come easily for Sara or her parents. You can imagine how difficult it was to watch her identical twin sister sail through some classes that she barely survived. Not surprisingly, sometimes Sara's motivation slipped. As an adolescent, she would say she didn't have to study and beg to go out with her friends. Her parents understood and empathized with her frustrations, just as they pressed her to focus on her future goals. Sara courageously learned to tolerate frustration and delay gratification.

Acceptance, accompanied by strongly encouraging effort and self-control, is essentially what we believe both parents and educators need to foster. Teaching acceptance requires a delicate balancing act. It requires loving acceptance of the child, accompanied by firm limits on objectionable behavior. It calls for acceptance of limitations and weaknesses, but only after prodigious efforts to find where those limits truly lie. Accept the child, but not sloth and lackadaisical effort. Remember: *Acceptance is not resignation.* Children can deal with high expectations and demands, as well as frustrations and disappointments, as long as they feel accepted.

Chapter 6 reviewed the evidence that the self-esteem movement has attempted to sustain a state of feeling good through refusing to accept failure at all costs and encouraging kids to feel special and successful, regardless of their actual performance. Remember that research has demonstrated clear disadvantages to seeing yourself as better than you really are. *Denial of weaknesses and failures does not foster a realistic self-appraisal, nor does it lead to acceptance.*

In this chapter we apply these ideas to key aspects of education, showing how we believe schools and educators can cultivate acceptance in our kids—*not by eliminating failure,* but rather through practicing honesty, limit setting, high standards for academics and behavior, and encouragement of children to achieve to their fullest potential, whatever that turns out to be. You will see how employing *realistic* self-appraisals, combined with vigorous encouragement for intensified efforts, can increase kids' self-control, acceptance, and accomplishments.

These goals can be reached, however, only by altering the feel-good approach to educational standards, classroom practice, school discipline, special education, and teacher education. Of course, schools reflect the broader culture of our time. In criticizing current educational practices, we do not place the blame on individual teachers, administrators, or parents. The culture of feeling good holds primary responsibility for the cracks in our schools' infrastructure. Nevertheless, in order to make repairs, all of us—parents, educators, and concerned citizens—must join together and make our voices heard at the voting booth, PTA gatherings, and school board meetings.

EDUCATIONAL STANDARDS

Chapter 6 described how the feel-good movement, along with its intransigent "deny all failures and avoid all bad feelings" stance, has contributed to a lowering of standards in our schools in the form of grade inflation and shady testing practices. But there is another problem besides the lowering of standards. How can we obtain a realistic appraisal and understand our children's strengths and weaknesses if we have access only to contrived, inflated data? Only with honest, accurate information can parents and teachers guide children to *accept* wherever they are today while encouraging them to *develop further* through high expectations and demands.

How honest are we being? In Chapter 6 we reported on the widespread cheating that has occurred in many testing efforts to date. Cheating ranged from reviewing actual test questions with students before the test to using outdated tests, and even, incredibly, to erasure and correction of wrong answers. Many parents, educators, and politicians have joined in a call for rigorous, nationwide assessment of our schoolchildren's performance. However, you might worry how accurate such a testing program will be, given the rampant deception in testing efforts to date.

The situation is reminiscent of the problems addressed by former president Jimmy Carter in his work with the Democracy Program. As you may know, this program uses teams of observers to monitor elections in emerging democracies to ensure fairness.[1] When it comes to educational testing, perhaps we need to adopt strategies similar to those promoting honest, free elections in places like Liberia, Guyana, and East Timor. If we do implement national testing, the incredibly high political and emotional stakes will create huge pressures for school districts to demonstrate their competence. The temptation to publish stellar results will no doubt lead at least a few into chicanery. In these circumstances, we should take our cue from the Democracy Program and insist on monitoring of the testing process by disinterested observers.

Current grading practices represent another blatant example of dishonest messages and false appraisals. In our earlier critique of education, we noted that over a third of our college freshmen report having obtained a 4.0 grade point average in high school. The problem is not just that grades have lost meaning; rather, *inflated grades encourage inflated self-perceptions and intolerance of frustrations and failures.* It's time for us all to demand that educators change the set point. A's should reflect excellence. When kids fail to achieve good grades, parents and teachers must urge them to work harder. And teachers deserve support from administrators in facing irate parents and students who demand grades for nothing. Schools need to quit using grades to make all our kids feel good.

Incessant worry about making all students feel good does not develop self-control; it does not encourage acceptance.

When kids waltz through school with fraudulent, pumped-up grade point averages, what have we taught them about how to deal with frustration?

TEACHING MATTERS

When we apply the feel-good principle to teaching, chaos erupts. The child-centered classroom allows virtually no one to fail. This method embraces raising self-esteem and enabling children to feel good. The approach emphasizes making learning fun and engaging, more than difficult and challenging. But self-control, the foundation of acceptance, does not spring from constant entertainment. Child-centered classrooms rob our children of the opportunity to learn about self-discipline, delay of gratification, frustration tolerance, and, ultimately, acceptance.

You need to know, too, that the wolf of child-centered teaching sometimes appears in grandma's clothing. Various labels such as progressive, humanistic, and mastery learning disguise what amounts to essentially the same thing.[2]

One of the latest tags put on child centered teaching is "constructivist education." What is constructivist education? This is what a recent constructivist textbook for college education majors has to say. You may have to read this quote more than once; we did. "Teaching is not a process of imparting knowledge, because the learner cannot know what the teacher knows and what the teacher knows cannot be transferred to the learner. We believe that teaching is a process of helping learners to construct their own meaning from the experiences they have by providing those experiences and guiding the meaning-making process."[3]

This quotation typifies the sad state of teacher education today. If teachers don't impart knowledge, what exactly will they do? The alternative to "imparting knowledge" is "facilitating learning," which sounds so good, but study after study says it just doesn't work as well as teacher-directed approaches.

As you may recall, these studies have found higher achievement scores for children in teacher-directed classrooms than for those taught in child-centered classrooms. Constructivism is simply child-centered education, thinly veiled.

Progressive, humanistic, child-centered thinking is rampant in teacher education, but it is supported mostly by ideology. We all need to make an appeal for schools to return to programs identified as effective.[4] Schools need to put teachers back in charge of the classroom. Teachers as leaders must feel free to challenge and, yes, even frustrate their pupils. Learning is not always fun. Often it requires boring repetition, torturous struggle through complex concepts, and tremendous self-discipline. The muscle of self-control only develops from regular exercise. The classroom that challenges students and both demands and expects diligent work is far more likely to produce solid, accepting kids.

DISCIPLINE

Children learn self-control first through limits, expectations, consequences, and demands imposed by parents and teachers. In the preceding chapter, you read about three primary parenting styles. *Permissive* parents, who set few limits, tend to have children with high self-esteem and good social skills, but poor academic performance, more substance abuse, and more school misconduct. *Authoritarian* parents, who set rigid, harsh limits, tend to have children with poor social skills and more depression. These kids conform and obey authority, yet many of them ultimately become aggressive and act out. *Authoritative* parents, who provide clear expectations and standards without harshness, tend to have kids who are highly socially competent, academically successful, and better psychologically adjusted than kids with the other types of parents.[5] Clearly, kids raised by authoritative parents have superior self-control and acceptance.

Inspired by the self-esteem and feel-good movements, student-centered education generally avoids strict discipline policies. In essence, teachers who use this method are much like permissive parents. This philosophy eschews the use of established behavior management principles. Some educators assumed that making the classroom environment interesting to the students would minimize the need for discipline. Children would somehow naturally learn to cooperate because of their natural desire to be good citizens.[6] That philosophy doesn't work, and it doesn't foster self-control.

With feel-good–inspired, student-centered education, the teacher's role changed from respected intellectual authority to facilitator or tour guide. The resulting decrease in status encouraged unhappy students and their parents to challenge teachers. These challenges caused many educators to start ignoring petty misbehavior on the part of students. Discipline didn't seem worth the effort.

Unfortunately, overlooking minor behavioral disruptions such as disrespectfulness, tardiness, and bullying leads to more of the same in an accelerating spiral of negative behavior. Research supports the relationship between tolerating these small misbehaviors in schools and the ultimate eruption of more serious school violence. When schools let their students talk back, come in late, and forget homework without meaningful consequences, they invite an escalation culminating in violence.[7] In other words, schools better sweat the small stuff.

Too many of our kids have suffered the excruciating reality of school shootings, which have taken the lives of our children and traumatized a generation. In recent years, these shootings have occurred in rural and suburban schools, thereby shattering previous perceptions of immunity. Naturally, demands swelled for immediate action to quell the violence and restore a sense of safety.

The response? A swing to the opposite extreme: a policy of "zero tolerance." Like the authoritarian parent, zero tolerance is harsh and punitive, and it expects unquestioned compliance. Since 1994, for instance, federal policy has dictated a mandatory one-year expulsion for the possession of firearms on school grounds. Admittedly, it's hard to argue with that idea. However, too often, schools have used zero brains in taking the concept too far.[8]

Examples of this zero-brains approach abound. Consider 8-year-old Hamadi Alston, who took advantage of his teacher's absence, stood up on his desk pointing a folded piece of paper, and threatened his classmates. He said, "I'm going to kill you all." He and his friend Jaquill Shelton were playing cops and robbers. The boys were suspended and taken to police headquarters, where police charged the boys with making *terrorist threats*. After *five hours* of questioning, police released them to their parents, but charges remained in place.[9] In Hudson, Ohio, a third-grade student writing for a school fortune cookie project was suspended for writing the fortune, "You will die an honorable death."[10] Elsewhere, two 5-year-old students played cops and robbers and used their fingers as pretend guns. They were suspended. A 9-year-old was mandated to get therapy after he threatened to "shoot" a classmate with a spitball. In Los Angeles, the board of education prohibited R.O.T.C. cadets from using dummy rifles in their drills.[11] Two 10-year-old boys mischievously spiked their teacher's drink with soap and were suspended and later charged with a *felony*.[12] Finally, a 6-year-old boy who wanted to dress up as a firefighter for Halloween was suspended from school because his costume included a plastic ax.[13]

We all want to see an end to violence in our schools, but do you seriously believe that the mindless approach of overly zealous zero tolerance will get us there? Of course, schools need to say they will not tolerate violence, nor allow *real* weapons in school. However, zealous zero tolerance smacks of authoritarian parenting. We need to call for a more thoughtful response. Consider that authoritarian parents have kids who often become disorderly and aggressive. Paradoxically, in response to excessive, harsh limits, they do not learn self-control. They do not learn acceptance. We can only speculate that authoritarian schools will fare no better than authoritarian parents.

Thus, much like *authoritative* parents, schools need to establish clear guidelines and limits for unacceptable behavior. For example, after careful weighing of the evidence, swift suspensions and legal actions for intentionally bringing weapons into school make sense and do not represent zero brains. But kids who inadvertently leave a key chain with a nail file on it in their car should not be subjected to arrest and suspension. Schools should consistently employ a balance of positive and negative consequences. Behavior management technologies based on results from numerous studies have existed for decades. Proven strategies involve behavior monitoring, reinforcement, and strict classroom management.[14] All of these are consistent with a basic stance of acceptance.

Neither lack of discipline, nor harsh, unbridled discipline will instill self-control in our youth. Let's encourage our schools to look toward research findings for reasoned, thought-out solutions. Knee-jerk responses to emotionally charged catastrophes will not create solid kids.

SPECIAL EDUCATION: VICTIMS VERSUS COPERS

Previously, we told you about the escalating reliance on special education in our schools. Incredibly, today about 12% of our kids are called disabled. Much of the motivation for this increased dependency on special education appears to derive from what probably sounds like a repetitive theme by now—a desire to prevent children from feeling bad and experiencing any kind of failure. Furthermore, it does so by invoking "innate ability" as the primary cause of learning difficulties. In the process, it provides kids with a global label ("learning disabled") that facilitates what amounts to a total capitulation to their presumed limitations.

This approach subtly seduces kids stuck with this label into victim thinking. Such thinking may temporarily fluff up their self-esteem by preventing failure and providing excuses, but it also shackles them with reduced expectations and limits both their horizons and their achievements.

Think back to Dr. Smith's daughter Sara. One alternative for Sara would have been to take on victim thinking and resign herself to the idea of having a disability. That certainly would have made life much easier for her in the short run. She could have followed the short-term feel-good approach by embracing the ideal excuse for poor performance, her learning disability. Does it seem likely she would have worked and accomplished as much this way? If she and her parents had completely bought into her so-called limited innate abilities, wouldn't she have had less reason to work hard?

In fact, research to date has failed to find that labeling young children disabled and assigning them to special education provides any advantage for most kids. Shockingly, the longer they remain in special education, the farther behind their peers they fall.[15] Unfortunately, the label simply focuses attention on a presumed lack of ability as opposed to the need for increased effort. The alternative? Earlier intervention that emphasizes extra help and *extra effort.*

Dr. G. Reid Lyon, at the National Institute of Child Health and Human Development, has summarized data from five prevention studies designed to deliver early, extra help. These studies targeted at-risk readers and successfully reduced the number of those eligible for special education *by 70%.* Dr. Lyon suggested that this approach could cut the frequency of reading disability from the 12-to-18% range down to 2 to 5½%. Notice what this implies about so-called innate abilities. Dr. Lyon's data indicate that *large numbers of children need never receive a label of learning disabled.* Furthermore, Dr. Lyon contends, "Poor instruction causes L.D." (learning disabilities).[16] In other

words, our failure to provide appropriate kinds of early instruction, along with increased demands for at-risk children,
actually causes much of what we have learned to think of as
"learning disabilities."

Rather than increase expectations and demands while
adding early, intensive intervention efforts when needed, schools
today place kids in special education after they've experienced
numerous failures. Most remain there throughout the balance of
their school careers. That's because reading remediation after
the third grade, when most kids are identified, tends to be much
less successful than earlier intervention. This explains why more
than 70% of children identified as reading disabled in the third
grade *remain* reading disabled in the twelfth grade, despite all
the special assistance.[17]

You might wonder where schools will get the money for
making early interventions. Look at it this way: Eliminate 70%
of special education students from the pool, and you'll find
more than enough money to fund the necessary staff and training to do the job. The most recent estimate of total special education costs puts the tab at $34.8 billion dollars per year.
Disturbingly, this estimate may or may not approximate reality.
That's because the last formal accounting of special education
costs occurred in 1987–1988.[18]

The Department of Education's Center for Special Education Finance's Web site directs visitors to view the most frequently asked questions. One of these questions asks, "Where
can I get more recent data on special education costs? Most of
the data on your site are 10 years old." The response was that
the government ceased collecting these data in 1987–1988 because they were *too difficult to compile.* How can collecting
these data present a more formidable task than tracking the
gross national product, the consumer price index, or the national debt?[19] Why would the Department of Education fail to
demand accountability? We honestly don't know, but we do

know the net effect: shielding the feel-good solution, special education, from scrutiny.

Close scrutiny may very well reveal that special education has cost too much and produced too little. It has grown out of control due to well-intentioned concerns. No one likes to see kids struggle, fail, and feel bad. So, rather than demand more effort and work, schools refer more and more kids to special education to protect their feelings. Although special education has given parents, teachers, and administrators an easy out, it has turned too many kids into victims and failed to prod them to succeed. *By eliminating special education in the elementary grades (at least for the majority who have mild learning delays) and replacing it with early screening and intensive prevention efforts, we can turn more of our students into copers and fewer into victims.*

TEACHING AS A TRUE PROFESSION

If we want our schools to educate solid kids, we need teachers who are well-trained, highly respected professionals. But teachers today can look forward to a life of chronically low pay, disrespect from students and parents, and few opportunities for advancement. No wonder our nation anticipates an alarming shortage of qualified teachers. We simply cannot expect to implement rigorous standards and testing, teacher-led classrooms, tightened discipline, and effective early interventions without true professionals to deliver them.

As in business, teachers should have an opportunity to acquire financial rewards for their efforts. For example, Connecticut requires teachers to pass an exam in their subject area and work with a mentor during their first year. Teachers are evaluated during their first three years, and those who don't foster learning effectively are let go. Yes, this practice makes some new teachers feel bad when they don't make the grade. But consider the advantages. Teachers in Connecticut can earn up to $80,000 per year. Connecticut now ranks first in the nation in reading. Teachers remain in the profession longer, and shortages don't exist. In fact, schools in Connecticut receive three applications for every opening.[20]

Unfortunately, many colleges of education appear woefully ill-equipped to handle the task of training truly professional teachers. Only very recently, Congress has forced colleges of education to divulge the number of their graduates who flunk state teacher certification exams.[21] The results are not encouraging. For example, in 1998, after graduation from colleges of education, 50% of prospective teachers in Massachusetts flunked the teacher certification exam. This outcome is especially ominous when you consider that the National Education Test consists mostly of middle school math problems and reading at the level of the *National Geographic*.[22]

Colleges of education should overhaul their curriculums to include methods of evaluating scientific research. Teachers must know how to determine the effectiveness of new ideas, textbooks, and methods of teaching. They have eagerly swallowed too many myths and fads for too long. The self-esteem movement would never have succeeded in permeating our schools so pervasively if teachers had subjected it to critical evaluation.

The professionalization of teaching extends beyond teacher preparation to the way educators are treated once they enter practice. Schools cannot possibly train, recruit, and retain teachers who possess sophisticated critical thinking skills until they reward teachers with respect, support, and income. But rewards must also be associated with expectations. Almost miraculously, many excellent, dedicated, and well-educated teachers work in public schools today. However, society must muster the courage to weed out or retrain educators who lack the necessary talent and skill to teach our young. Our children deserve true, highly regarded professionals to lead them.

RETURNING TO THE BASICS:
EDUCATIONAL REFORM

You've heard the clamor for educational reform. We hope you'll join us in that movement. But before you buy into the next dazzling solution or quick fix, remember the slogan "Let the buyer beware." Self-esteem, whole language, and child-centered education all promised so much and sounded so good. The ideas even appealed to common sense. But after reading about the research that exposes their shortcomings and risks, how do you feel about them now?

Research must guide any approach to educational reform. Some of that research might be correlational in nature, but such studies require backup from long-term predictive as well as experimental studies. Before jumping on the next bandwagon, let's demand to see the evidence.

Obviously, the suggestions in this chapter do not constitute a blueprint for comprehensive school reform. That's a book in and of itself. However, we hope we've challenged you to reconsider some of the popular educational practices in our schools today.

Together we can travel the road toward educating solid kids. Schools can't accomplish that goal until they renew their focus. The self-esteem movement has distracted schools from their primary mission. Curriculums have been broadened to include a host of strategies designed to supposedly improve emotional well-being, teach morality, and instill values. These curriculums consume considerable time sorely needed for academic instruction. Worst of all, they don't work—and they carry a significant risk of increasing self-absorption, the last thing our kids need.

What children actually need in order to lead productive, successful, happy, and moral lives is the ability to delay gratification, tolerate frustration, and become more self-forgetful. Once they master these abilities, they will have the foundation for morality and values instilled by family and faith. Solid kids can accept life's challenges, obstacles, and failures, and they have the stamina and resolve to overcome them to the limits of their true abilities. Ironically, schools foster these characteristics most effectively *not* by trying to raise self-esteem, but rather by concentrating on what they are best designed to do: with high expectations and firmness, teach reading, writing, and arithmetic.

EPILOGUE: CONCLUDING THOUGHTS AT THE MALL

Our youth now love luxury. They have bad manners, contempt for authority; they show disrespect for their elders, and love chatter in place of exercise. They no longer rise when elders enter the room. They contradict their parents, chatter before company, gobble up their food, and tyrannize their teachers.

—Socrates, fifth century B.C.

We sit once again at the food court in the mall, sipping smoothies and reviewing our ideas for concluding this book, realizing, as the quote from Socrates illustrates, we're obviously not the first authors to carp about the younger generation. Dual cell phones ring simultaneously at a table nearby. Both of us turn to notice a group of young people, spiked, pierced, and tattooed, dressed in black gothic attire; they look similar to the kids we interviewed nine months earlier. We watch as one of the them sweeps their huge pile of litter off the table, scattering it over the floor. All laughing, they saunter away.

We feel a touch of angst at the sight of these kids; they appear to us the epitome of hollow, lost children. To quell our distress, we decide to engage in a little "feel-good" therapy and head for the Cookie Warehouse at the other end of the food court. We indulge in a couple of sinful treats and return to our discussion.

We glance around and agree that not all of the young people at the mall look like our gothic group. The two teens who served us cookies were polite and clean-cut. And both of us have met many other teens who exhibit exemplary behavior along with solid values. Realizing this makes us feel a little better.

Yet as many good kids as there are out there, the evidence presented throughout earlier chapters shatters the comforting illusion everyone wants so much to believe: the myth that raising self-esteem will spare our kids from needless suffering. The facts say that in greater numbers than ever before, our children have succumbed to the very ills the self-esteem movement hoped to cure. Instead of raising a generation of emotionally healthy children, our culture has inadvertently unleashed upon the world far too many hollow kids who lack the fundamentals of knowing who they are and what they can accomplish. Kids who are destructive not only to themselves, but also to those around them. Kids who frenetically rush to fill up on good feelings in a constant quest for momentary highs. What they get is a rush of exhilaration that quickly dissipates, leaving a hollow soul aching for the next high.

Unlike Socrates and other critics of younger generations, we don't blame the kids. The promises of the self-esteem traffickers first tempted adults, who naively submitted to *the seductive power of positive thinking*. The adult generation eagerly embraced the self-esteem message and its companion feel-good principles, without realizing the corrosive effects of *feeling too good*. With the very best of intentions, parents, teachers, and mental health practitioners innocently longed for kids to feel good. And everyone went too far.

Our discussion stretches out for over an hour and a half and we decide to get up and stimulate our thoughts with a couple cups of coffee from the Coffee Shack. When we sit down, we ask ourselves, "How was everyone so easily duped?" The self-esteem entrepreneurs promised relief from serious problems like depression, anxiety, aggression, drug abuse, teenage pregnancy, and underachievement. They pledged to deliver a quick, painless fix, and they aroused fears by warning of the consequences of not following the self-esteem remedy. When emotions run high, people become susceptible to the sellers of snake oil.

The fields of both education and mental health have fallen prey too many times to easy answers for difficult problems. Discarded prescriptions, found ineffective and impotent, litter schools and therapists' offices. We yearn for this trash to be thrown away and for teachers, parents, and mental health practitioners to become more discerning consumers. Everyone needs to look at evidence and effectiveness, rather than be conned by clever packaging.

As we continue our discussion, we whimsically ponder whether we should package an anti-self-absorption remedy—something like "Ten Days to Losing Your Self-Absorption." We could promote a series of books, talk shows, and workshops to rid the world of this latest scourge. Indeed, self-absorption contributes significantly to a host of maladies. What an opportunity to enrich ourselves, by trafficking the anti-self-absorption message!

Alas, we'd have to deceive the public into believing that self-absorption causes all our problems and then package a quick, simplistic solution complete with mantras (such as "I will focus on others more than myself"), exercises (such as "Write down ten things you like about someone else"), and books (such as *The Seven Pillars of Acceptance*). We just can't find it in our hearts to do it. You see, self-absorption can't be blamed for the miseries of war, poverty, or abuse. And many complex, interacting factors play a part in the emergence of emotional and learning difficulties: genetics, nutrition, media, poverty, ineffective parenting, peer influence, trauma, and so on.

Nevertheless, the problem of self-absorption warrants redress. At least a small part of the solution lies in old-fashioned common sense. Dr. Elliott reminisces that when he began practice 25 years ago, if somebody complained of feeling blue or sad, therapists or friends would have likely proffered advice along these lines: "Distract yourself. Get involved in some fun activities. Work on connecting with other people. Try to focus on things that make you feel grateful. Join a church group or volunteer for a good cause. You can tough it out, but you have to work hard at this."

Dr. Smith notes how many of today's professional workshops, as well as advice from all too many friends and therapists, stand in contrast to that approach. Today's recommendations might include: "Nurture yourself. Take a weekend to pamper and renew yourself. Make a list of all your wonderful qualities. Write an autobiography in which you sell yourself to the world. Stand in front of the mirror and chant, 'I like me.'"[1]

These examples capture the influence of the self-esteem movement. Our society has turned from a focus on connections, relationships, and the external world to obsessive preoccupation with internal self-worth. Everyone hoped the internal focus would lead to greater happiness. It hasn't worked.

A survey in 1957 asked people if they were happy. Thirty-five percent declared themselves "very happy." The same question was posed in 1998, and the number who endorsed "very happy" actually declined slightly, to 33%. Paradoxically, during those same years, adjusting for inflation, personal income doubled. So did the divorce rate. And to recap, suicide among our youth tripled and violent crime quadrupled; depression and anxiety among children and adolescents skyrocketed.[2]

So, if focusing on self-worth doesn't increase happiness, what does? Most people assume financial success leads to increased happiness. It appears that poverty does relate to unhappiness. However, surprisingly, once basic needs (such as housing, clothing, and food) have been met, happiness does not rise with affluence. Americans have far more dishwashers, computers, clothes dryers, microwave ovens, and gadgets of all sorts than decades ago yet report no increases in happiness. Furthermore, lottery winners report a temporary state of happiness that largely evaporates in months that follow.[3]

So, if neither focusing on self-worth nor accumulating piles of cash leads to happiness, what does? Psychologists have increased their study of happiness and well-being in the past 10 years. Mostly, they've discovered that the antitheses of self-absorption lead to a sense of well-being.

We decide to make a list of what research really tells us goes into happiness as a conclusion to the book. That's because, since pursuing self-esteem obviously doesn't lead to happiness, you might just be wondering what does. Writing on a napkin, we first recall findings that show happy people *forgive* others. Although they may experience anger at times, they do not hold grudges or dwell on their own bad fortune. They do not offend easily and don't take things too personally. Forgiveness appears to benefit the forgiver. For example, college students who were vengeful and less forgiving ruminated more and experienced less life satisfaction than those who found it easier to forgive. And self-absorbed individuals engage in greater amounts of rumination.[4]

Second, *gratitude* appears to lead to increased well-being. A colleague of ours reported the following story. After a tornado, he volunteered to counsel two couples who had lost their homes along with most of their possessions. The first couple dwelled on the horror and the loss. They felt despondent and hopeless. Even though insurance covered most of their material losses, they bemoaned the hassles and work they would have to endure. The second couple also felt sad but mainly talked about how grateful they were that both survived without injury. They talked about some of their neighbors who were less fortunate than they were. This couple recovered quickly from their loss.

The role of gratitude has been cited by many experts as important to well-being and has also been put to the test experimentally. Researchers assigned a group of people to write about their hassles once a week. They asked another group to write about anything they wanted to and a third group to write about events that had led them to feel grateful. After 10 weeks, the participants in the gratitude group reported feeling better about their lives, more optimism, and fewer physical complaints and even exercised more than those in the other two groups.[5]

The third factor that appears to contribute to happiness and well-being also requires a lack of self-absorption. Self-centered narcissists have few friends. But *friendships and belonging* provide a host of benefits. People with social support have better health, improved ability to cope with adversity, and greater happiness. Happy people also do more volunteer work, contribute to charity, and involve themselves in various types of community work.[6]

Fourth, *marriage* usually seems to improve happiness and well-being. Psychologist David Myers reviewed numerous studies that collectively demonstrated married people experience greater life satisfaction than others. In this case, the data are largely correlational, so we don't know for sure whether happier people marry or if marriage creates more happiness. However, most researchers believe that the intimacy, support, and companionship of marriage generally reduce loneliness and increase emotional well-being.[7]

Fifth, *religion and spirituality* have demonstrated a relationship to happiness and well-being. People with faith cope more effectively with adversity and live longer than others. Religious people often practice together, which provides relationships and additional social support. Faith also provides a sense of meaning and a crucial focus on something bigger than the self.[8]

Sixth, and finally, *self-control* deserves mention as a likely contributor to happiness and well-being. Self-control overcomes selfish impulses. It allows people to delay immediate gratification and pursue more satisfying, long-term goals. Forgiveness, gratitude, social connectedness, marriage, and religion all require considerable self-control.[9]

As we conclude our list, we wonder whether the self-esteem movement will ever, like Narcissus, wither and die. Will parents and educators truly learn to raise more solid, fulfilled kids who have a sense of purpose and well-being? Is there any hope?

We mull over the question and mindlessly collect our debris into a pile on the table. As we do, the rising clamor for educational reform comes to mind as a source of hope. Both states and the federal government have promised renewed efforts at toughening standards. Many voices have also called for teaching character and morality. But will the reformers succumb to new, easy, quick fixes? Will anyone take the time and effort to root out the fraudulent myths from programs that have shown substantiated promise? Gloomy thoughts start to overtake us.

Amidst cookie crumbs and cold coffee, the napkin with our list of what contributes to happiness lies inadvertently wadded up in the pile of trash. A teenager comes up to our table. We notice his single gold earring and bleached hair. He's wearing the required khakis and blue shirt of the mall clean-up crew. He smiles at us and asks if we're okay, and did we know the mall closed 30 minutes ago? We tell him no; we were so absorbed in our discussion, we didn't notice. He offers us another cup of coffee and tells us they leave the coffee on for the night shift. We decline the offer, thank him, and get up to leave. As we walk away, he calls out and rushes up to us with the wadded-up napkin. He noticed we'd been writing on it and it looks important. He asks if we want it. Yes, we do.[10]

NOTES

Chapter 1

1. For an excellent discussion of changes in values and various cultural plagues, see D. Meyers, *The American Paradox: Spiritual Hunger in an Age of Plenty* (New Haven, Connecticut: Yale University Press, 2000).
2. G. Cooper, "Survey Suggests a Rise in Apathy Among College Freshman," *The Harold Sphere*, January 28, 1998.
3. From www.teen.com, a Web site for American teenagers that routinely surveys teens on issues that are important to them. This survey was created February 17, 2001.
4. B. Wildavsky, "At Least They Have High Self-Esteem: Students Slack Off but Still Get Top Grades," *U. S. News & World Report*, 7 February 2000.
5. L. Sax, A. Astin, W. Korn, and K. Mahoney, *The American Freshman: National Norms for Fall 1999,"* Los Angeles: Higher Education Research Institute, UCLA.
6. P. Lewinsohn, P. Rohde, J. Seeley, and S. Fischer, "Age-Cohort Changes in the Lifetime Occurrence of Depression and Other Mental Disorders," *Journal of Abnormal Psychology* 102 (1993): 110–120.
7. Martin Seligman, *The Optimistic Child* (Boston: Houghton Mifflin Company, 1995), 38.
8. Timothy Egan, "Where Rampages Begin: A Special Report; from Adolescent Angst to Shooting Up Schools," *The New York Times*, 14 June 1998.
9. For a variety of statistics about the current condition of our youth and society, see William Bennett, *The Index of Leading Cultural Indicators* (New York: Broadway Books, 1999).

10. Center for Disease Control regularly studies trends in youth risk behavior. Results of their comprehensive surveys can be downloaded from the Internet at http://www.cdc.gov/nccdphp/dash/yrbs/index.htm

11. T. Achenbach and C. Howell, "Are American Children's Problems Getting Worse? A Thirteen-Year Comparison," *Journal of the American Academy of Child and Adolescent Psychiatry* 32 (1993): 1145–1154.

12. J. Twenge, "The Age of Anxiety? Birth Cohort Change in Anxiety and Neuroticism, 1952–1993," *Journal of Personality and Social Psychology* 79 (2000): 1007–1021.

13. G. Wilson, K. Heffernan, and C. Black, "Eating Disorders," in *Child Psychopathology*, edited by E. Mash and R. Barkley (New York: The Guilford Press, 1996), 541–571.

14. The College Entrance Examination Board maintains a Web site with a variety of research and information available on the SAT which it administrates. www.collegeboard.org

15. There has been much controversy about the meaning of SAT scores. However, most agree that overall they have decreased. For a discussion of these issues, see David Myers, *The American Paradox: Spiritual Hunger in an Age of Plenty* (New Haven, Connecticut: Yale University Press, 2000); Anjetta McQueen, *Math Scores Dip, Grades Outpace Test Scores*, Associated Press, 2000 [cited 31 August 2000]. Available from http://wire.ap.org/APnews/; William Bennett, *The Index of Leading Cultural Indicators* (New York: Broadway Books, 1999). Also, Seymour Itzkoff wrote in *The Decline of Intelligence in America*, (Westport CT: Praeger, 1994) about the overall decline in SAT scores, as cited in, C. J. Sykes, *Dumbing Down Our Kids: Why America's Children Feel Good About Themselves but Can't Read, Write, or Add.* (New York: St. Martin's Griffin, 1995).

16. Howard Snyder, "Juvenile Arrests 1999," *The Juvenile Justice Bulletin* (Washington, DC: Office of Juvenile Justice and Delinquency Prevention, 2000).

17. This extensive report can be downloaded from the Internet. It not only covers rates of violence, but causes and protective factors. "Youth Violence: A Report of the Surgeon General." Rockville, MD: U.S. Department of Health and Human Services, Centers for Disease Control and Prevention, National Center for Injury Prevention and Control, Substance Abuse and Mental Health Services Administration, Center for Mental Health Services, National Institutes of Health, and National Institute of Mental Health, 2001.

18. Adapted from M. Sickmund., H. Snyder, and E. Poe-Yamagata, *Juvenile Offenders and Victims: 1997 Update on Violence* (Washington, DC: Office of Juvenile Justice and Delinquency Prevention, 1999).

19. William Bennett, *The Index of Leading Cultural Indicators 2000*. Available at www.empower.org/ilci2001.htm.

20. News, Cable Network, *Dylan Bennett Klebold and Eric David Harris* (www.cnn.com/SPECIALS/columbine.cd/Pages/SUSPECTS_TEXT.htm) CNN, 2000 [cited 2000].

21. E. Kramarow, H. Lentzner, R. Rooks, J. Weeks, and S. Saydah, *Health and Aging Chart Book. Health, United States, 1999* (National Center for Health Statistics, 1999 [cited 27 August 2000]). Available from www.cdc.gov/nchs/data/hus99.pdf.

22. William Damon, *Greater Expectations: Overcoming the Culture of Indulgence in our Homes and Schools* (New York: Free Press Paperbacks, 1995), 69. Damon's book is a wonderful review of declining standards in our schools.

23. APA, *PsychInfo* 2000 [cited 2000]. Available from www.apa.org/. PsychInfo is a comprehensive database of psychological journals from 1887 to the present.

24. Steven Ward, "Filling the World with Self-Esteem: A Social History of Truth-Making," *Canadian Journal of Sociology* 21, no. 1 (1996): 1–23.

25. William James,. *The Principles of Psychology,*. authorized ed., 2 vols., Vol. 1 (New York: Dover Publications, 1950).

26. Abraham H. Maslow, "Self-Esteem (Dominance-Feeling) and Sexuality," *Psychological Bulletin* 37 (1940): 504; Maslow, "Self-Esteem (Dominance-Feeling) and Sexuality in Women," *Journal of Social Psychology* 16 (1942): 259–294.

27. Thomas H. Leahey, *A History of Psychology*, 3rd ed. (Englewood Cliffs, New Jersey: Prentice Hall, 1992). Leahey provides a complete history of the major theories of psychology. Stout, *The Feel-Good Curriculum*. Stout discussed Maslow's influence on our schools of education.

28. P. Botheme, *Alfred Adler: A Biography* (New York: A. P. Putnam's Sons, 1946); Adler, *Problems of Neurosis* (New York: Harper Torchbooks, 1964).

29. Carl R. Rogers, *Freedom to Learn* (Columbus, Ohio: Merrill, 1969).

30. Carl R. Rogers, *A Way of Being* (New York: Houghton Mifflin Company, 1980), 203.

31. Morris Rosenberg, *Society and the Adolescent Self-Image* (Princeton, New Jersey: Princeton University Press, 1965).

32. APA, *PsychInfo* 2000.

33. William H. Fitts and William T. Hamner, "Self Concept and Delinquency," *Studies on the Self Concept, Monograph I* (1989), 96; Milton E. Rosenbaum and Richard Decharms, "Direct and Vicarious

Reduction of Hostility," *Journal of Abnormal and Social Psychology* 60 (1960), 105–111.

34. S. H. Nagler, "Fetishism: A Review and a Case Study," *Psychiatric Quarterly* 31, 1957, 713–741.

35. Norman Vincent Peale, *The Power of Positive Thinking* (New York: Fawcett Crest, 1952), 1.

36. John P. Hewitt, *The Myth of Self-Esteem: Finding Happiness and Solving Problems in America* (New York: St. Martin's Press, 1998). See Hewitt for one of the first critiques of the self-esteem movement.

37. Nathaniel Branden, *The Psychology of Self-Esteem* (New York: Bantam Books, 1969).

38. Nathaniel Branden, *Honoring The Self: Self-Esteem and Personal Transformation* (New York: Bantam Books, 1985).

39. Ibid., 105.

40. Ibid., 140–141.

41. John Vasconcellos, "Preface," in *The Social Importance of Self-Esteem*, edited by Andrew Mecca, Neil Smelser, and John Vasconcellos (Berkeley: University of California Press, 1989), xxi. See this book for an amazing contradiction between a book title and its contents.

42. Neil Smelser, "Self-Esteem and Social Problems: An Introduction," In *The Social Importance of Self-Esteem*, edited by Andrew Mecca, Neil Smelser, and John Vasconcellos (Berkeley: University of California Press, 1989), 15.

43. Hewitt, *The Myth of Self-Esteem*; The National Association for Self-Esteem, 2000 [cited 2000]. Available from www.self-esteem-nase.org.

44. Stout, *The Feel-Good Curriculum*; Damon, *Greater Expectations*; Hewitt, *The Myth of Self-Esteem*.

45. Myers, *The American Paradox*; Deb Riechmann, *SAT Scores Point to Possible Grade Inflation at High School*, Associated Press Online, 1998 [cited 8 July 2000]. Also, see The College Board Web site for recent statistics on the SAT, www.collegeboard.org.

46. David Mills, *Overcoming "Self-Esteem:" Why Our Compulsive Drive for "Self-Esteem" Is Anxiety-Provoking, Socially Inhibiting, and Self-Sabotaging* (REBT Institute, 2000 [cited 27 August 2000]), 4. Available from http://REBT.org/essays/.

Chapter 2

1. William James, *The Principles of Psychology*, authorized ed., 2 vols., Vol. 1 (New York: Dover Publications, 1950), 310. William

James was a psychologist ahead of his times in many areas of psychology. This reference is helpful for anyone interested in psychological theory.

2. Nathaniel Branden, *Honoring the Self: Self-Esteem and Personal Transformation* (New York: Bantam Books, 1985), 7.

3. S. Taylor and J. Brown, "Illusions and Well-Being: A Social Psychological Perspective on Mental Health," *Psychological Bulletin* 103, 1988, 193–210.

4. D. Cartwright, *Personal Communication* (1991), as cited in C. R. Colvin and J. Block, "Do Positive Illusions Foster Mental Health? An Examination of the Taylor and Brown Formulation," *Psychological Bulletin* 116, no. 1 (1994): 3–20.

5. Colvin, "Do Positive Illusions Foster Mental Health;" J. Shedler, M. Mayman, et al. "More Illusions," *American Psychologist* 49, no. 11 (1994): 974–976.

6. J. Shedler, M. Mayman, et al., "The Illusion of Mental Health," *American Psychologist* 11, no. 48 (1993): 11. This article stirred considerable controversy in the field of psychology. Nevertheless, the weight of the evidence supports the authors' conclusions regarding difficulties with the self-report of mental health and the way it can be confounded by denial and repression.

7. Colvin, "Do Positive Illusions Foster Mental Health?"

8. Steven Vannoy, *The Ten Greatest Gifts I Give My Children* (New York: Simon & Schuster, 1994), 164.

9. Ibid., 45.

10. Jean Clarke, *Self-Esteem: A Family Affair* (Center City, Minnesota: Hazelden, 1998), 8.

11. Ibid., 9.

12. Charles H. Elliott and Laura L. Smith, *Why Can't I Be the Parent I Want to Be?* (Oakland, California: New Harbinger Publications, 1999). This book discusses how parents' self-views affect both their children and their parenting; Charles H. Elliott and Maureen K. Lassen, *Why Can't I Get What I Want?* (Palo Alto, California: Davies-Black Publishing, 1998); Charles H. Elliott and Maureen K. Lassen, "A Schema Polarity Model for Case Conceptualization, Intervention, and Research," *Clinical Psychology: Science and Practice* 4, no. 1 (1997): 12–28. This article presents a review of data supportive of this type of structure for a variety of self-views known as schemas. Surprising convergence among several theoretical typologies is also revealed.

13. Elliott and Lassen, "A Schema Polarity Model;" Elliott and Lassen, *Why Can't I Get What I Want?*

14. Ian Gotlib and Elena Krasnoperova, "Biased Information Processing as a Vulnerability Factor for Depression," *Behavior Therapy* 29, no. 4 (1998): 603–617.

15. Romin Tafarodi, "Paradoxical Self-Esteem and Selectivity in the Processing of Social Information," *Journal of Personality and Social Psychology* 74, no. 5 (1998): 1181–1196.

16. Mario Mikulincer, "Attachment Style and the Mental Representation of the Self," *Journal of Personality and Social Psychology* 69, no. 6 (1995): 1203–1215; Mark Baldwin, "Relational Schemas and the Processing of Social Information," *Psychological Bulletin* 112, no. 3 (1992): 461–484.

17. R. Ingram, "Self-Focused Attention in Clinical Disorders: Review and a Conceptual Model," *Psychological Bulletin* 107, no. 2 (1990): 156–176.

18. S. Nolen-Hoeksema and J. Morrow, "A Prospective Study of Depression and Posttraumatic Stress Symptoms after a Natural Disaster: The 1989 Loma Prieta Earthquake," *Journal of Personality and Social Psychology* 61 (1991): 115–121.

19. S. Nolen-Hoeksema, "The Role of Rumination in Depressive Disorders and Mixed Anxiety/Depressive Symptoms," *Journal of Abnormal Psychology* 109, no. 3 (2000): 504–511.

20. S. Lyubomirsky and S. Nolen-Hoeksema, "Self-Perpetuating Properties of Dysphoric Rumination," *Journal of Personality and Social Psychology* 65, no. 2 (1993): 339–349; S. Lyubomirsky and S. Nolen-Hoeksema, "Effects of Self-Focused Rumination on Negative Thinking and Interpersonal Problem Solving," *Journal of Personality and Social Psychology* 69, no. 1 (1995): 176–190; J. Wood, J. Saltzberg, et al., "Self-Focused Attention, Coping Responses, and Distressed Mood in Everyday Life," *Journal of Personality and Social Psychology* 58, no. 6 (1990): 1027–1036; J. Roberts, E. Gilboa, et al., "Ruminative Response Style and Vulnerability to Episodes of Dysphoria: Gender, Neuroticism, and Episode Duration," *Cognitive Therapy and Research* 22, no. 4 (1998): 401–423; S. Nolen-Hoeksema, "The Role of Rumination in Depressive Disorders and Mixed Anxiety/Depressive Symptoms," *Journal of Abnormal Psychology* 109, no. 3 (2000): 504–511. These studies on self-absorption and rumination pull together research of three different types: correlational, predictive, and experimental. Although predictive studies are, in a sense, correlational studies, they represent a more elaborate form. They come closer to establishing causation by demonstrating that one variable leads to another at a distal point in time. As a composite, these studies demonstrate a high degree of consilience, which is a

term referring to consistency of results among varied types of evidence and fields.

21. J. Canfield and H. C. Wells, *100 Ways to Enhance Self-Concept in the Classroom: A Handbook for Teachers and Parents* (Englewood Cliffs, New Jersey: Prentice-Hall, 1976); S. McDaniel, *Project Self-Esteem: A Parent Involvement Program for Improving Self-Esteem and Preventing Drug and Alcohol Abuse, K–6* (Rolling Hills Estates, California: Jalmar Press, 1990).

22. *Diagnostic and Statistical Manual of Mental Disorders, 4th ed.* (Washington, D.C.: American Psychiatric Association, 1994).

23. C. Randall Colvin, Jack Block, and David C. Funder, "Overly Positive Self-Evaluations and Personality: Negative Implication for Mental Health," *Journal of Personality and Social Psychology* 68, no. 6 (1995): 1161. This article reports on the three studies about overly positive self-esteem.

24. Delroy L. Paulhus, "Interpersonal and Intrapsychic Adaptiveness of Trait Self-Enhancement: A Mixed Blessing?" *Journal of Personality and Social Psychology* 74, no. 5, (1998): 1197–1208.

Chapter 3

1. Howard Markel, "CASES: Anorexia Can Strike Boys, Too," *New York Times,* 25 July 2000.

2. Rebecca Zak, "Centerfolds Talk About Battling Bulimia," *Daily Trojan* [University Wire], 30 November 2000.

3. Kim Hubbard, Anne-Marie O'Neill, and Christina Cheakalos, "Out of Control Weight-Obsessed, Stressed-Out Coeds are Increasingly Falling Prey to Eating Disorders," *People,* 12 April 1999.

4. Nathaniel Branden, *The Six Pillars of Self Esteem* (New York: Bantam, 1994).

5. Nellie Williams, "Professors: Media Images Lead to Eating Disorders," *Observer,* 15 February 2000.

6. Alan Mozes, *Miss America May Set Unhealthy Weight Standard* (Health Front) [Fox News.com], 2000 [cited 23 March 2000]. Available from http://www.foxnews.com/health/032300/missamerica.sml.

7. Jill S. Zimmerman, "An Image to Heal: Influence of Models as a Cause of Eating Disorders," *The Humanist* 57 (Jan–Feb 1997): 20–26.

8. Ibid.

9. Williams, "Professors: Media Images Lead to Eating Disorders."

10. *Harvard Eating Disorders Center: Information About Eating Disorders* [Internet], Harvard Eating Disorders Center, 2000 [cited 9

December 2000]. Available from http://www.hedc.org/info.html. The Harvard Eating Disorders Center maintains a comprehensive Web site with facts and research about eating disorders.

11. YRBSS: *1997 Youth Risk Behavior Surveillance System* [Dietary Behaviors] (Centers for Disease Control and Prevention, 1997 [cited 1997]). Available from http://www.edc.gov/nccdphp/dash/yrbs/natsum97/sudi97.htm.

12. *Diagnostic and Statistical Manual of Mental Disorders*, 4th ed. (Washington, D.C.: American Psychiatric Association, 1994).

13. Ibid.

14. Some experts feel that the binge-eating/purging type of anorexia actually belongs on a continuum with the two types of bulimia. See D. Gleaves, M. Lowe, B. Green, M. Cororve, and T. Williams, "Do Anorexia and Bulimia Nervosa Occur on a Continuum? A Taxometric Analysis," In *Behavior Therapy*, edited by J. Gayle Beck (New York: AABT, 2000), 195–218.

15. G. Terence Wilson, Karen Heffernan, and Carolyn Black, "Eating Disorders," in *Child Psychopathology*, edited by Eric J. Mash and Russell A. Barkley (New York: The Guilford Press, 1996), 541–571; P. J. Cooper and C. G. Fairburn, "Confusion over the Core Psychopathology of Bulimia-Nervosa," *International Journal of Eating Disorders* 13, no. 4 (1993): 385–389; Richard Allan Gordon, *Eating Disorders: Anatomy of a Social Epidemic*, 2nd ed. (New York: Blackwell, 2000).

16. A. R. Lucas, C. M. Beard, W. M. O'Fallon, and L. T. Kurland, "50-Year Trends in the Incidence of Anorexia Nervosa in Rochester, Minnesota: A Population-Based Study," *American Journal of Psychiatry* 148 (1991): 917–922, as cited in Gordon, *Eating Disorders: Anatomy of a Social Epidemic*.

17. Gordon, *Eating Disorders: Anatomy of a Social Epidemic*.

18. Claudia Kalb, "When Weight Loss Goes Awry," *Newsweek*, 3 July 2000, 46.

19. WebMD. Pulse (Heart Rate) [Internet] 2001 Available at: http://mywebmd.com/content/asset/adam_test_heart_rate

20. "Facts About Eating Disorders" (Highland Park, Illinois: National Association of Anorexia Nervosa and Associated Disorders, 2000).

21. WebMD, *What Are Eating Disorders* (Health) [Internet], 2000 [cited 2001]. Available from http://my.webmd.com/content/article/1680.50411.

22. Ibid.

23. D. P. Krowchuk, S. R. Kreiter, C. R. Woods, S. H. Sinal, and R. H. DuRant, "Problem Dieting Behaviors Among Young Adolescents," *Archives of Pediatrics and Adolescent Medicine* 152, no. 9 (1998): 884–888.

24. "BodyWise: The Problem of Eating Disorders Is a Mental Health as Well as a Physical Health Issue," in *The BodyWise Eating Disorders Information Packet for Middle School Personnel*, (Washington, D.C.: U.S. Department of Health and Human Services Program Support Center, 1999).

25. Gordon, *Eating Disorders: Anatomy of a Social Epidemic*. See Gordon for a comprehensive overview about the etiology, biological consequences, and treatment of eating disorders.

26. P. K. Keel, J. E. Mitchell, et al., "Long-Term Outcome of Bulimia Nervosa," *Archives of General Psychiatry* 56 (1999): 63–69.

27. "Facts About Eating Disorders."

28. K. S. Kendler, C. MacLean, M. Neale, R. Kessler, A. Heath, and L. Eaves, "The Genetic Epidemiology of Bulimia Nervosa," *American Journal of Psychiatry* 148, no. 12 (1991): 1627–1637.

29. Gordon, *Eating Disorders: Anatomy of a Social Epidemic*; WebMD, *What Are Eating Disorders*.

30. Tim Kasser and Richard M. Ryan, "Further Examining the American Dream: Differential Correlates of Intrinsic and Extrinsic Goals," *Personality & Social Psychology Bulletin* 22, no. 3 (1996): 280–287.

31. G. E. Akan and C. M. Grilo, "Sociocultural Influences on Eating Attitudes and Behaviors, Body Image, and Psychological Functioning: A Comparison of African-American, Asian-American, and Caucasian College-Women," *International Journal of Eating Disorders* 18, no. 2 (1995): 181–187; M. Fisher, M. Schneider, C. Pegler, and B. Napolitano, "Eating Attitudes, Health-Risk Behaviors, Self-Esteem, and Anxiety Among Adolescent Females in a Suburban High-School," *Journal of Adolescent Health* 12, no. 5 (1991): 377–384; E. J. Button, P. Loan, J. Davies, and E. J. S. SonugaBarke, "Self-Esteem, Eating Problems, and Psychological Well-Being in a Cohort of Schoolgirls Aged 15–16: A Questionnaire and Interview Study," *International Journal of Eating Disorders* 21, no. 1 (1997): 39–47; Melissa P. Mussell, Roslyn B. Binford, and Jayne A. Fulkerson, "Eating Disorders: Summary of Risk Factors, Prevention Programming, and Prevention Research," *Counseling Psychologist* 28, no. 6 (2000): 764–796; Catherine M. Shisslak, Susan L. Pazda, and Marjorie Crago, "Body Weight and Bulimia as Discriminators of Psychological Characteristics Among Anorexia, Bulimic, and Obese Women," *Journal of Abnormal Psychology* 99, no. 4 (1990): 380–384.

32. A. Meijboom, A. Jansen, M. Kampman, and E. Schouten, "An Experimental Test of the Relationship Between Self-Esteem and Concern About Body Shape and Weight in Restrained Eaters," *International Journal of Eating Disorders* 23, no. 3 (1999): 327–334.

33. A. K. Lindeman, "Self-Esteem: Its Application to Eating Disorders and Athletes," *International Journal of Sport Nutrition* 4, no. 3 (1994): 237–252.

34. P. J. Cooper and C. G. Fairburn, "Confusion over the Core Psychopathology of Bulimia-Nervosa," *International Journal of Eating Disorders* 13, no. 4 (1993): 385–389.

35. M. Dezwaan, J. E. Mitchell, H. C. Seim, S. M. Specker, R. L. Pyle, N. C. Raymond, and R. B. Crosby, "Eating Related and General Psychopathology in Obese Females with Binge-Eating Disorder," *International Journal of Eating Disorders* 15, no. 1 (1994): 43–52.

36. Fisher, et al., "Eating Attitudes, Health-Risk Behaviors, Self-Esteem, and Anxiety Among Adolescent Females in a Suburban High-School," *Journal of Adolescent Health* 12, no. 5 (1991): 377–384.

37. WebMD, *What Are Eating Disorders.*

38. K. M. Thompson, S. A. Wonderlich, R. D. Crosby, and J. E. Mitchell, "The Neglected Link Between Eating Disturbances and Aggressive Behavior in Girls," *Journal of the American Academy of Child and Adolescent Psychiatry* 38, no. 10 (1999): 1277–1284.

39. Katherine A. Halmi, Suzanne R. Sunday, Michael Strober, and Alan Kaplan, "Perfectionism in Anorexia Nervosa: Variation by Clinical Subtype, Obsessionality, and Pathological Eating Behavior," *The American Journal of Psychiatry* (November 2000); P. L. Hewitt, G. L. Flett, and E. Ediger, "Perfectionism Traits and Perfectionistic Self-Presentation in Eating Disorder Attitudes, Characteristics, and Symptoms," *International Journal of Eating Disorders* 18, no. 4 (1995): 317–326; Kathleen D. Vohs, Anna M. Bardone, Thomas Joiner, Lyn Y. Abramson, and Todd F. Heatherton, "Perfectionism, Perceived Weight Status, and Self-Esteem Interact to Predict Bulimia Symptoms: A Model of Bulimic Symptom Development," *Journal of Abnormal Psychology* 108, no. 4 (1999): 695–700; WebMD, *What Are Eating Disorders.*

40. Kendler, et al., "The Genetic Epidemiology of Bulimia Nervosa."

41. William B. Swann, *The Elusive Quest for Higher Self-Esteem* (New York: Freeman and Company, 1996). See Swann for an overview about the difficulties in changing self-esteem.

42. H. Steiger, S. Jabalpurwala, J. Champagne, and S. Stotland, "A Controlled Study of Trait Narcissism in Anorexia and Bulimia Nervosa" *International Journal of Eating Disorders* 22, no. 2 (1997): 173–178.

43. B. E. Steinberg and R. J. Shaw, "Bulimia as a Disturbance of Narcissism: Self-Esteem and the Capacity to Self-Soothe," *Addictive Behaviors* 22, no. 5 (1997): 699–710.

44. P. M. Lehoux, S. Howard, and S. Jabalpurwala, "State/Trait Distinctions in Bulimic Syndromes," *International Journal of Eating Disorders* 27, no. 1 (2000): 36–42.

45. J. Carter, A. Stewart, et al., "Primary Prevention of Eating Disorders: Might It Do More Harm Than Good?" *International Journal of Eating Disorders* 94, no. 22 (1997):167–172.

46. *Diagnostic and Statistical Manual of Mental Disorders,* 4th ed. (Washington, DC: American Psychiatric Association, 1994).

47. Stephen S. Hall, "The Troubled Life of Boys; The Bully in the Mirror," *New York Times,* 22 August 1999; Sean Swint, *Obsessing about Body Image Is Not Just for Women Anymore* [Internet], WebMD Health, 2000 [cited 21 July 2000]. Available from http://my.webmd.com/content/article/1723.59692; "How's the Old 'Body Image'?" *Washington Times,* 30 August 1999.

48. James C. Rosen, Jeff Reiter, and Pam Orosan, "Cognitive-Behavioral Body Image Therapy for Body Dysmorphic Disorder," in *Journal of Consulting and Clinical Psychology,* ed. Larry E. Beutler (Washington, D.C.: American Psychological Association, 1995), 263–296.

49. George Spellwin, *Chemical Wizardry* [Internet], 2000 [cited 2000]. Available from http://www.elitefitness.com/reports/guidesales/.

50. Richard Peters, Jan Copeland, and Paul Dillon, "Anabolic-Androgenic Steroids User Characteristics, Motivations, and Deterrents," *Psychology of Addictive Behaviors* 13, no. 3 (1999): 232–242.

51. "NIDA Announces Multimedia Public Education Initiative Aimed at Reversing Rise in Use of Anabolic Steroids by Teens" (National Institute on Drug Abuse, 2000); WebMD, *Anabolic Steroids (Systemic)* [Internet], 2000 [cited 2000]. Available from http://my.webmd.com/content/asset/uspdi.202035.

52. Susan McClelland, "The Lure of the Body Image: In Their Quest for the Beefcake Look, Some Men Try Extreme Measures," *Better Homes and Gardens,* 02-22-1999, p 38.

53. WebMD, *What You Should Know About . . . Dietary Supplements and Athletic Performance* [Internet, cited 2000]. Available from http://my.webmd.com/content/article/1671.50535.

54. Paula Gray Hunker, "Pressure to Be Perfect," *Washington Times,* 12 March 2000 [cited 2000], 29.

55. Dr. Barron, *The Barron Centers: Liposuction and Penile Enhancement* [Internet]. 2000 [cited 2000].

56. ASPS. *National Clearinghouse of Plastic Surgery Statistics* [Internet]. Plastic Surgery Information Service, 1998 [cited 1998]. Available from http://www.plasticsurgery.org/mediactr/trends92-99.htm.

57. Nora Underwood, *Body Envy: This Is In—and People Are Messing with Mother Nature as Never Before* [Internet], Maclean's, 2000 [cited 14 August 2000].
58. Dr. Barron, *The Barron Centers: Liposuction and Penile Enhancement* [Internet], 2000 [cited 2000].
59. M. Dunofsky, "Psychological Characteristics of Women Who Undergo Single and Multiple Cosmetic Surgeries," *Annals of Plastic Surgery* 39, no. 3 (1997): 223–228.
60. J. Greif, W. Hewitt, and M. L. Armstrong, "Tattooing and Body Piercing. Body Art Practices Among College Students," *Clinical Nursing Research* 8, no. 4 (1999): 368–385.
61. Carol A. Hasenyager, *Body Piercing: A New Challenge* (Ob/Gyn) [Internet], 2000 [cited July 2000].
62. M. L. Armstrong and K. P. Murphy, "Tattooing: Another Adolescent Risk Behavior Warranting Health Education," *Applied Nursing Research* 10, no. 4 (1997): 181–189; Robert P. Libbon, "Dear Data Dog: Why Do So Many Kids Sport Tattoos?" *American Demographics* 22, no. 9 (2000): 26.
63. Ibid.
64. Hasenyager, *Body Piercing: A New Challenge*; Sherice L. Shields, "Popular Piercing Opens Possibility of Serious Illness: The Hole in the Trend May Be Hepatitis, HIV Years From Now," *USA Today*, 19 July 2000 [cited 2000]; 09D.
65. Norma Wagner, "Popularity of Body Piercing Fails to Elate Emergency-Room Doctors," *The Salt Lake Tribune*, 18 September 2000 [cited in 2000].
66. David R. Drews, Carlee K. Allison, and Jessica R. Probst, "Behavioral and Self-Concept Differences in Tattooed and Nontattooed College Students," *Psychological Reports* 86, no. 2 (2000).

Chapter 4

1. G. Kaufman, L. Raphael, et al., *Stick Up for Yourself! Every Kid's Guide to Personal Power and Positive Self-Esteem* (Minneapolis: Free Spirit Publishing Inc., 2000).
2. National Association for Self-Esteem Web site reviews the self-esteem research and basically links low self-esteem to poor school achievement, crime, violence, teenage pregnancy, substance abuse, etc. Web site: http://www.self-esteem-nase.org/research.shtml
3. Jeanette Gonzalez, Tiffany Field, Regina Yando, Ketty Gonzalez, David Lasko, and Debra Bendell, "Adolescents' Perceptions of Their Risk-Taking Behavior," *Adolescence* 29, no. 115 (1994).

4. Karla Baker, Joe Beer, and John Beer, "Self-Esteem, Alcoholism, Sensational Seeking, GPA, and Differential Aptitude Test Scores of High School Students in an Honor Society," *Psychological Reports* 69, no. 3 (1991): 1147–1150.

5. John Vavrik, "Personality and Risk-Taking: A Brief Report on Adolescent Male Drivers," *Journal of Adolescence* 20, no. 4 (1997): 461–465.

6. S. Boney-McCoy, F. Gibbons, et al., "Self-Esteem, Compensatory Self-Enhancement, and the Consideration of Health Risk," *Personality and Social Psychology Bulletin* 25, no. 8 (1999): 954–965.

7. R. Emmons, "Relationship Between Narcissism and Sensation Seeking," *Psychological Reports* 48, no. 1 (1981): 247–250; J. Johanson, "Correlations of Self-Esteem and Intolerance of Ambiguity with Risk Aversion," *Psychological Reports* 87, no. 2 (2000): 534; R. Ryckman, B. Thornton, et al., "Personality Correlates of the Hypercompetitive Attitude Scale: Validity Tests of Horney's Theory of Neurosis," *Journal of Personality Assessment* 62, no. 1 (1994); Howard Tennen and Glenn Affleck, "The Puzzles of Self-Esteem: A Clinical Perspective," in *Self-Esteem: The Puzzle of Low Self Regard*, edited by Roy Baumeister (New York: Plenum Press, 1993), 241–262.

8. J. Arnett, "Heavy Metal Music and Reckless Behavior Among Adolescents," *Journal of Youth and Adolescence* 20, no. 6 (1991): 573–592; M. Fisher, M. Schneider, et al., "Eating Attitudes, Health Risk Behaviors, Self-Esteem, and Anxiety Among Adolescent Females in a Suburban School," *Journal of Adolescent Health* 12, no. 5 (1991): 377–384; D. Smith and T. Heckert, "Personality Characteristics and Traffic Accidents of College Students," *Journal of Safety Research* 29, no. 3 (1998): 163–169.

9. Laura Fitchman, Richard Koestner, David Zuroff, and Laurel Gordon, "Depressive Styles and the Regulation of Negative Affect: A Daily Experience Study," *Cognitive Therapy and Research* 23, no. 5 (1999): 483–495.

10. James Coleman, "Crime and Money: Motivation and Opportunity in a Monetarized Economy," *American Behavioral Scientist* 32, no. 6 (1992): 827–836.

11. Alice Hanley and Mari Wilhelm, "Compulsive Buying: An Exploration into Self-Esteem and Money Attitudes," *Journal of Economic Psychology* 13, no. 1 (1992): 5–8.

12. Ronald Faber, "Money Changes Everything: Compulsive Buying from a Biopsychosocial Perspective," *American Behavioral Scientist* 35, no. 6 (1992): 809–819.

13. *Diagnostic and Statistical Manual of Mental Disorders, 4th ed.* (Washington, D.C.: American Psychiatric Association, 1994).

14. Lisa Goff, "Don't Miss the Bus!" *American Demographics,* 1 August 1999 [cited 1999]; Lorrie Grant, "Like, Be Hip or Be Gone in Teen Clothes Market Stores: Go from Way Trendy to Totally Uncool Overnight," *USA Today,* 5 July 2000 [cited 2000], B 8; Ken Gronbach, "Generation Y—Not Just 'Kids,'" *Direct Marketing* 63, no. 4 (2000): 36–39.

15. Brigid McMenamin, "First Class Follies," *Forbes,* 12 June 2000.

16. Albert Crenshaw, "Students Pay Dearly for Debt; Study Finds Effects Far Beyond the Financial," *The Washington Post,* 13 June 1999.

17. Marcy Gordon, *Credit Card Cos. Come Under Fire,* Associated Press, 1999 [cited 8 June 1999].

18. John Baldwin, *Impact of Gambling-Economic Effects More Measurable Than Social Effects,* Government Accounting Office, 2000 [cited 27 April 2000]. Available from wwws.elibrary.com.

19. S. Spencer, R. Josephs, et al., "Low Self-Esteem: The Uphill Struggle for Self-Integrity," in *Self-Esteem: The Puzzle of Low Self-Regard,* R. Baumeister, ed. (New York: Plenum Press, 1993).

20. Howard Tennen and Glenn Affleck, "The Puzzles of Self-Esteem: A Clinical Perspective," in *Self-Esteem: The Puzzle of Low Self Regard,* edited by Roy Baumeister (New York: Plenum Press, 1993), 241–262. See Baumeister's book for a fascinating review of the multiple effects of low and high self-esteem.

21. Ibid.

22. Robert Cialdini, *The Psychology of Influence* (New York: William Morrow, 1984).

23. *Hooked on Pokemon: Is Pokemania Harmless Entertainment or an Addiction?* Concerned Women for America, 1999 [cited]. Available from www.cwfa.org/library/1999-12-21_ent-pokemon.html.

24. Sarah Yang, "Pokemon-ia Promoting Gambling?" *The San Francisco Examiner,* 27 September 1999.

25. Jeffrey Kassinove, *Problem Gambling: The Hidden Addiction,* Aldelphi University, 2000 [cited 2000]. Available at www.indiana.edu/~div16/preventing_problem_gambling.htm.

26. Mark Stewart, "Betting the Future: False Promise of Easy Money Tempts More, Younger Children," *The Washington Times,* 21 March 2000.

27. P. Hovarth and M. Zuckerman, "Sensation Seeking, Risk Appraisal and Risky Behavior," *Personality and Individual Differences* 14 (1993) 41-52.

28. Fredreka Schouten, "Gambling Explosion Takes Toll on Teens," *Gannett News Service,* 12 March 2000, ARC.
29. Ibid.
30. Christine Patterson, *BBB Reports 1998 Statistics for Shoplifting Program,* Better Business Bureau, 1999 [cited]. Available from www.ky-in.bbb.org/alerts/19990101.html.
31. Brent Goff and H. Goddard, "Terminal Core Values Associated with Adolescent Problem Behaviors," *Adolescence* 34 (1999): 47–60; Jack Katz, *Seductions of Crime* (New York: Basic Books, 1988).
32. Goff and Goddard, "Terminal Core Values Associated with Adolescent Problem Behaviors."
33. Anthony Cox, Dena Cox, and Ronald Moschis, "Research Note: Social Influences on Adolescent Shoplifting: Theory, Evidence, and Implications for the Retail Industry," *Journal of Retailing* 69, no. 2 (1993): 234–246; Tennen and Affleck, "The Puzzles of Self-Esteem."
34. Lloyd Johnston, Patrick O'Malley, and Jerald Bachman, "The Monitoring: The Future National Results on Adolescent Drug Use" (Ann Arbor, Michigan: The University of Michigan Institute for Social Research, 2000). The University of Michigan keeps extensive data on the drug use of adolescents.
35. Karen Zeese, *The Effective National Drug Control Strategy,* The Net Work of Reform Groups, 1999 [cited 2000]. Available at www.csdp.org/edcs/edcs.htm.
36. Johnston, "The Monitoring:The Future National Results on Adolescent Drug Use."
37. Ibid.
38. Peggy Peck, *Asian Herb Ma Huang May Trigger Psychosis, Mood Disorders,* WebMD, 2000 [cited 2000]; Arthur Whitmore, *MedWatch Safety Summaries: Ephedrine* (U. S. Department of Health and Human Services, Food and Drug Administration, 1997 [cited 2000]).
39. Joseph Donnelly, *Self-Esteem and Its Relationship to Alcohol and Substance Abuse Prevention in Adolescence,* The National Association for Self-Esteem, 2000 [cited 2000]. Available at www.self-esteem-NASE.org/journal02.shtml. The NASE posted this article as their plea for including Self-Esteem in drug prevention programs.
40. Jennifer Gonnerman, "Or DARE," *The Village Voice,* 13 April 1999.
41. Dennis Rosenbaum and Gordon Hanson, "Assessing the Effects School-Based Drug Education: A Six Year Multilevel Analysis of Project DARE," *The Journal of Research in Crime and Delinquency* 35, no. 4 (1998): 381–399.

42. Donald Lynam, Richard Milich, Rick Zimmerman, Scott Novak, T. Logan, Catherine Martin, Carl Leukefeld, and Richard Clayton, "Project DARE: No Effects at a 10-year Follow-Up," *Journal of Consulting and Clinical Psychology* 67, no. 4 (1999): 590–593.

43. Ibid., 593.

44. Andrew Mecca, Neil Smelser, and John Vasconcellos, eds. *The Social Importance of Self-Esteem* (Berkeley: University of California Press, 1989), 320.

45. Harry Kitano, "Alcohol and Drug Use and Self-Esteem: A Socio-Cultural Perspective," in *The Social Importance of Self-Esteem*, edited by Andrew Mecca, Neal Smelser, and John Vasconcellos (Berkeley: University of California Press, 1989), 294–326.

46. Rodney Skager and Elizabeth Kerst, "Alcohol and Drug Use and Self-Esteem: A Psychological Perspective," in *The Social Importance of Self-Esteem*, edited by Andrew Mecca, Neil Smelser, and John Vasconcellos (Berkeley: University of California Press, 1989). 248-293.

47. Baker, Beer, and Beer, "Self-Esteem, Alcoholism, Sensational Seeking, GPA, and Differential Aptitude Test Scores of High School Students in an Honor Society."

48. R. Ingram, "Self-Focused Attention in Clinical Disorders: Review and a Conceptual Model," *Psychological Bulletin* 107, no. 2 (1990): 156–176.

49. S. J. Ventura, "Nonmarital Childbearing in the United States, 1940–99," *National Vital Statistics Reports* 48, no. 16 (2000).

50. *Fact Sheet: Youth Risk Behavior Trends* (Center for Disease Control, 2000 [cited 2000.]) Available from www.cdc.gov/nccdphp/dash/yrbs/trend.htm.

51. Douglas J. Besharov and Karen N. Gardiner, "Trends in Teen Sexual Behavior," *Children and Youth Services Review*, no. 5/6 (1997): 341–367.

52. William Bennett, *The Index of Leading Cultural Indicators* (New York: Broadway Books, 1999); *Fact Sheet: Youth Risk Behavior Trends* (Center for Disease Control, 1999 [cited]). Available from www.cdc.gov/nccdphp/dash/yrbs/trend.htm.

53. Tamar Lewin, "Teen-Agers Alter Sexual Practices, Thinking Risks Will Be Avoided," *New York Times*, 5 April 1997.

54. Linda Feldman, Philippa Holowaty, and Bart Harvey, "A Comparison of the Demographic, Lifestyle, and Sexual Behavior Characteristic of Virgin and Non-Virgin Adolescents," *Canadian Journal of Human Sexuality* 6, no. 3 (1997): 197–209.

55. M. Schuster, R. Bell, and D. Kanouse, "The Sexual Practices of Adolescent Virgins: Genital Sexual Activities of High School Students Who Have Never Had Vaginal Intercourse," *American Journal of Public Health* 86, no. 11 (1996): 1570–1576.

56. Anne Jarrell, "The Face of Teenage Sex Grows Younger," *New York Times*, 2 April 2000.

57. Susan Crockenberg and Barbara Soby, "Self Esteem and Teenage Pregnancy," in *The Social Importance of Self-Esteem*, edited by Andrew Mecca, Neil Smelser, and John Vasconcellos (Berkeley: The University of California Press, 1989), 125–164.

58. Anthony Walsh, "Self-Esteem and Sexual Behavior: Exploring Gender Differences," *Sex Roles* 25, no. 7–8 (1991): 441–450.

59. A. Seal, Victor Minichiello, and M. Omodei, "Young Women's Sexual Risk Taking Behaviour: Re-Visiting the Influences of Sexual Self-Efficacy and Sexual Self-Esteem," *International Journal of STD & AIDS* 8, no. 3 (1997): 159–165.

60. Margaret Taylor-Seehafer and Lynn Rew, "Risky Sexual Behavior Among Adolescent Women," *Journal of the Society of Pediatric Nurses* 5, no. 1 (2000): 15–25.

61. Ingram, "Self-Focused Attention in Clinical Disorders."

Chapter 5

1. L. Smith, 2000. This example is real; however, the details have been significantly changed due to privileged communication.

2. Jody Brown compiled statistics from the FBI Uniform Crime Reports from the Bureau of Justice Statistics (16 October 2000), www.ojp.usdoj.gov/bjs/

3. Ibid.

4. *Youth Violence: A Report of the Surgeon General* (Rockville, Maryland: U.S. Department of Health and Human Services, Centers for Disease Control and Prevention, National Center for Injury Prevention and Control, Substance Abuse and Mental Health Services Administration, Center for Mental Health Services, National Institutes of Health, and National Institute of Mental Health, 2001), 153. This extensive report can be downloaded from the Internet. It not only covers rates of violence, but causes and protective factors.

5. Ibid., 7. The Executive Summary of the Surgeon Generals report contains major findings, highlights and trends.

6. H. Snyder and M. Sickmund, *Juvenile Offenders and Victims: 1999 National Report* (Pittsburgh, Pennsylvania: National Center for Juvenile Justice, 1999).

7. Loyd Ivey, *Mobile Electronics and Wireless Communications* (Consumer Electronics Association, 1999 [cited 2000]). Available from www.ce.org/market_overview/uceit_99/mobile.cfm.

8. *Where Do All These Alarm Systems Come From?* (International Association of Chiefs of Police, 2000 [cited 2000]). Available from www.theiacp.org/pubinfo/pubs/pslc/pslc5.box1.htm. Cited data from Private Security Trends, 1970–2000: The Hallcrest Report II.

9. Joe Agron and Larry Anderson, "School Security by the Numbers," *American School and University* 72, no. 9 (2000): 6–12.

10. P. Kaufman, X. Chen, S. Ruddy, A. Miller, J. Fleury, K. Chandler, M. Rand, P. Klaus, and M. Planty, "Indicators of School Crime and Safety 2000," *U. S. Department of Education and Justice.* NCES 2001–017/NCJ-184176 (2000).

11. David Myers, *The American Paradox: Spiritual Hunger in an Age of Plenty* (New Haven, Connecticut: Yale University Press, 2000). See Myers for a fascinating discussion of the many paradoxes of American wealth and despair.

12. William Bennett, *The Index of Leading Cultural Indicators* (New York: Broadway Books, 1999).

13. *OJJDP Statistical Briefing Book,* Office of Juvenile Justice and Delinquency Prevention, 2000 [cited 2000]. Available from www.ojjdp.ncjrs.org.

14. L. Kohlberg, "A Cognitive Developmental Analysis of Children's Sex Role Concepts and Attitudes," in *The Development of Differences,* edited by E. Maccoby (Palo Alto, California: Stanford University Press, 1966).

15. Centers for Disease Control Statistics, cited in Marc Miringoff and Marque-Louisa Miringoff, *The Social Health of the Nation* (New York: Oxford University Press, 1999).

16. FBI, *Uniform Crime Reports* (Criminal Justice Information Services, 2000 [cited 2000]). Available from www.fbi.gov/ucr/ucreports.htm.

17. Charles H. Elliott and Maureen K. Lassen, "A Schema Polarity Model for Case Conceptualization, Intervention, and Research," *Clinical Psychology: Science and Practice* 4, no. 1 (1997): 12–28.

18. A. Beck, *Prisoners of Hate: The Cognitive Basis of Anger, Hostility, and Violence* (New York: Harper Collins, 1999).

19. M. Seligman, *Depression and Violence* (American Psychological Association, 1998). Available from www.apa.org/releases/epidemic.html.

20. Ibid., 6.

21. T. Scheff, S. Retzinger, and M. Ryan, "Crime, Violence, and Self-Esteem: Review and Proposals," in *The Social Importance of Self-Esteem,* edited by A. Mecca, N. Smelser, and J. Vasconcellos (Berkeley: University of California Press, 1989) 165–199.

22. J. Hughes, T. Cavell, and P. Grossman, "A Positive View of Self: Risk or Protection for Aggressive Children?" *Development and Psychopathology* 9, no. 1 (1997): 75–94.

23. C. David and J. Kistner, "Do Positive Self-Perceptions Have a Dark Side? Examination of the Link Between Perceptual Bias and Aggression," *Journal of Abnormal Psychology* 28, no. 4 (2000): 327–337.

24. J. Edens, T. Cavell, and J. Hughes, "The Self-Systems of Aggressive Children: A Cluster Analytic Investigation," *Journal of Child Psychology and Psychiatry and Allied Disciplines* 40, no. 3 (1999): 441–453.

25. J. Edens, "Aggressive Children's Self-Systems and the Quality of Their Relationships with Significant Others," *Aggression and Violent Behavior* 4, no. 2 (1999): 151–177.

26. PRIDE. *Pride Questionnaire Report* in Parents Resource Institute for Drug Education, 2000 [cited]. Available from www.pridesurveys.com/.

27. D. Olweus, "Bullying at School: Long-Term Outcomes for the Victims and an Effective School-Based Intervention Program," in *Aggressive Behavior: Current Perspectives*, edited by R. Huesmann (New York: Plenum Press, 1994).

28. Hester Lacey, "Focus: Bullied to Death," *Independent on Sunday*, 22 February 1998.

29. J. Sutton, P. Smith, and J. Swettenham, "Social Cognition and Bullying: Social Inadequacy or Skilled Manipulation," *British Journal of Developmental Psychology* 17, no. 3 (1999): 435–450.

30. R. Raskin, J. Novacek, and R. Hogan, "Narcissistic Self-Esteem Management," *Journal of Personality and Social Psychology* 60 (1991): 911–918, as cited in R. Baumeister, L. Smart, and J. Boden, "Relation of Threatened Egotism to Violence and Aggression: The Dark Side of High Self-Esteem," *Psychological Review* 103 (1996): 5–33; P. Wink, "Two Faces of Narcissism," *Journal of Personality and Social Psychology* 61 (1991): 590–597, as cited in Baumeister, "Relation of Threatened Egotism to Violence and Aggression."

31. Roy F. Baumeister, *Evil: Inside Human Violence and Cruelty* (New York: W. H. Freeman and Company, 1997), 149.

32. Elijah Anderson, "The Code of the Streets," *The Atlantic Monthly* 273 (1994): 81–94.

33. Jack Katz, *Seductions of Crime* (New York: Basic Books, 1988).

34. Baumeister, "Relation of Threatened Egotism to Violence and Aggression," 22.

35. D. Long, *The Anatomy of Terrorism* (New York: Free Press, 1990), as cited in Baumeister, "Relation of Threatened Egotism to Violence and Aggression"; R. Oates and D. Forrest, "Self-Esteem and Early Background of Abusive Mothers," *Child Abuse and Neglect* 9 (1985): 89–93, as cited in Baumeister, "Relation of Threatened Egotism to Violence and Aggression."

36. Leslie Pearlman, "Hidden Fears Behind Youth Violence: Linking Self-Image and Aggression," Doctoral Dissertation, The Fielding Institute, 1999.
37. S. Jang and T. Thornberry, "Self-Esteem, Delinquent Peers and Delinquency: A Test of the Self-Enhancement Thesis," *American Sociological Review* 63 (1998): 586–598.
38. A. Goldstein, B. Harootunian, and J. Conoley, *Student Aggression: Prevention Management and Replacement Training* (New York: The Guilford Press, 1994).
39. L. Smith, "Social Skills Training for Juvenile Delinquents" (unpublished manuscript), 1999.
40. D. Hurlbert, "Sexual Narcissism and the Abusive Male," *Journal of Sex and Marital Therapy* 17 (1991): 279–292.
41. A. Groth, *Men Who Rape: The Psychology of the Offender* (New York: Plenum Press, 1979), as cited in Baumeister, Smart, and Boden, "Relation of Threatened Egotism to Violence and Aggression."
42. Baumeister, Smart, and Boden, "Relation of Threatened Egotism to Violence and Aggression."
43. D. Scully, *Understanding Sexual Violence: A Study of Convicted Rapists* (New York: Harper Collins, 1990), as cited in Baumeister, "Relation of Threatened Egotism to Violence and Aggression."
44. R. Hare, "Psychopaths and Their Nature: Implications for the Mental Health and Criminal Justice Systems," in Millon, ed., *Psychopathy: Antisocial, Criminal, and Violent Behavior*; T. Widiger and D. Lynam, "Psychopathy and the Five-Factor Model of Personality," in Millon, ed., *Psychopathy: Antisocial, Criminal and Violent Behavior*.
45. Beck, *Prisoners of Hate*.
46. J. Meloy and C. Gacano, "The Internal World of the Psychopath," in *Psychopathy: Antisocial, Criminal, and Violent Behavior*, edited by T. Millon, E. Simonsen, M. Birket-Smith, and R. Davis (New York: The Guilford Press, 1998).
47. D. Goodman, *Abraham Sentenced to Juvenile Facility,* ABC News, 2000 [cited]. Available from http://abcnews.goo.com/us/Daily/News/abraham000113.html.
48. *Boys Imprisoned for Dropping Child to His Death,* CNN News, 1996 [cited]. Available from www.cnn.com/US/Newsbriefs?01/30/96.
49. *12-Year-Old Accused in Los Angeles Murder, Rape.* CNN News, 1996 [cited]. Available from www.cnn.com/US08/02/96violent.child/index.html.
50. *Judge Refuses to Release Child Accused of Beating Infant.* CNN News, 1996 [cited]. Available from www.cnn.com/US/9605/04/abuse.hearing/index.html.

51. *Funeral Service for Teacher Fatally Shot.* CNN News, 2000 [cited]. Available from www.cnn.com/2000/US/05/30/teacher.killed.02/.

52. Timothy Egan, "Where Rampages Begin: A Special Report: From Adolescent Angst to Shooting Up Schools," *New York Times*, 14 June 1998.

53. Egan, "Where Rampages Begin;" D. Sharp, "Student Gun Violence Creeps into Small-Community Schools," *USA Today*, 3 December 1997.

54. T. Egan, "Where Rampages Begin;" B. Hewitt, J. Harmes, and B. Stewart, "The Avenger Police Say Luke Woodham, Accused of Killing Three in Pearl, Miss., May Have Been Part of a Plot That Was Larger, Stranger, and Even More Deadly," *People*, 3 November 1997; G. Witkin, M. Tharp, J. Schrof, T. Toch, and C. Scattarella, "Again," *U.S. News and World Report* , June 1, 1998.

55. J. Blankenship, "Heeding the Signs," *Northwest Education Magazine* (Spring 1998).

56. P. Belluck and J. Wilgoren, "Shattered Lives—A Special Report. Caring Parents, No Answers, in Columbine Killers' Pasts," *New York Times*, 29 June 1999; *Dylan Bennet Klebold and Eric David Harris* (CNN News, 2000 [cited]). Available from www.cnn.com/SPECIALS/2000/Columbine.cd/pages/SUSPECTS_test.htm; S. Greene and B. Briggs, "Massacre at Columbine High: Youth Underworld?" *Denver Post*, 22 April 1999.

57. M. Kernis, "The Roles of Stability and Level of Self-Esteem in Psychological Functioning," in *Self-Esteem: The Puzzle of Low Self-Regard*, edited by R. Baumeister (New York: Plenum Press, 1993), 167–219.

58. K. Kling, J. Hyde, C. Showers, and B. Buswell, "Gender Differences in Self-Esteem: A Meta Analysis," *Psychological Bulletin* 125, no. 4 (1999): 470–500.

59. H. Snyder and M. Sickmund, *Juvenile Offenders and Victims: 1999 National Report* (Pittsburgh, Pennsylvania: National Center for Juvenile Justice, 1999).

60. Baumeister, Smart, and Boden, "Relation of Threatened Egotism to Violence and Aggression."

61. F. Rhodewalt and C. Morf, "On Self-Aggrandizement and Anger: A Temporal Analysis of Narcissism and Affective Reactions to Success and Failure," *Journal of Personality and Social Psychology* 74 (1998): 672–685.

62. B. Bushman, "Threatened Egotism, Narcissism, Self-Esteem, and Direct and Displaced Aggression: Does Self-Love or Self-Hate Lead to

Violence?" *Journal of Personality and Social Psychology* 73 (1998): 219–229.

63. Baumeister, "Relation of Threatened Egotism to Violence and Aggression."

64. M. Kernis, B. Grannemann, and L. Barclay, "Stability and Level of Self-Esteem as Predictors of Anger Arousal and Hostility," *Journal of Personality and Social Psychology* 56 (1989): 1013–1022.

Chapter 6

1. J. Canfield and H. C. Wells, *100 Ways to Enhance Self-Concept in the Classroom* (Boston: Allyn and Bacon, 1994), 125.

2. Ibid., 44.

3. S. Lyubomirsky and S. Nolen-Hoeksema, "Effects of Self-Focused Rumination on Negative Thinking and Interpersonal Problem Solving," *Journal of Personality and Social Psychology* 69, no. 1 (1995): 176–190.

4. Canfield and Wells, *100 Ways to Enhance Self-Concept in the Classroom*, 45.

5. Sandy McDaniel, *Project Self-Esteem: A Parent Involvement Program for Improving Self-Esteem and Preventing Drug and Alcohol Abuse, K–6* (Rolling Hills Estates, California: Jalmar Press, 1990), 89.

6. Terri Akin, David Cowan, Gerry Dunne, Susanna Palomares, Dianne Schilling, and Sandy Schuster, *The Best Self-Esteem Activities: For the Elementary Grades* (Spring Valley, California: Innerchoice, 1990).

7. Barbara Sher, *Self-Esteem Games: 300 Fun Activities That Make Children Feel Good About Themselves* (New York: John Wiley & Sons, 1998).

8. P. Berne and L. Savary, *Building Self-Esteem in Children: New Expanded Edition* (New York: The Crossroad Publishing Company, 1996), 36.

9. H. Stevenson and J. Stigler, *The Learning Gap: Why Our Schools Are Failing and What We Can Learn from Japanese and Chinese Education* (New York: Simon & Schuster, 1992).

10. Ibid.

11. J. Chall, *The Academic Achievement Challenge: What Really Works in the Classroom* (New York: The Guilford Press, 2000); W. Damon, *Greater Expectations Overcoming the Culture of Indulgence on Our Homes and Schools* (New York: Free Press, 1995); M. Stout, *The Feel-Good Curriculum: The Dumbing Down of America's Kids in*

the Name of Self-Esteem (Cambridge, Massachusetts: Perseus Books, 2000).

12. G. Adams and S. Engelmann, *Research on Direct Instruction* (Seattle: Educational Achievement Systems, 1996); D. Carnine, *Why Education Experts Resist Effective Practices (and What It Would Take to Make Education More Like Medicine)* (Washington, D.C.: Thomas B. Fordham Foundation, 2000); L. Izumi, *Facing the Classroom Challenge* (San Francisco: Pacific Research Institute for Public Policy, 2001).

13. Stout, *The Feel-Good Curriculum*.

14. Nick Anderson and Duke Helfand, *A Long Road Back from Reading Crisis* (home) latimes.com, 1998 [cited 13 September 1998]. Available from http://latimes.qpass.com; Stout, *The Feel-Good Curriculum*.

15. *Report of the National Reading Panel: Teaching Children to Read* (National Institute of Child Health & Human Development, 2000 [cited]). Available from http://www.nichd.nih.gov/publications/nrp/findings.htm.

16. K. Anderson, "The Reading Wars," 2000. Available at www.latmes.com.

17. Barbara R. Foorman, David J. Francis, Jack M. Fletcher, Christopher Schatschneider, and Paras Mehta, "The Role of Instruction in Learning to Read Preventing Reading Failure in at-Risk Children," *Journal of Educational Psychology* 90, no. 1 (1998): 37–55.

18. L. C. Moats, *The Illusion of "Balanced" Reading Instruction*, October 2000 [cited]. Available from http://www.edexcellence.net/library/wholelang/moats.html.

19. J. K. Torgesen, "The Prevention and Remediation of Reading Disabilities: Evaluating What We Know from Research," *Journal of Academic Language Therapy* 1 (1997): 11–47; J. Chall, *The Academic Achievement Challenge: What Really Works in the Classroom* (New York: The Guilford Press, 2000).

20. *A Nation Still at Risk: An Education Manifesto*, Fordham Foundation, 30 April 1998 [cited]. Available from http://www.edexcellence.net/library/manifes.html.

21. Jay R. Campbell, Catherine M. Hombo, and John Mazzeo, *NAEP 1999 Trends in Academic Progress: Three Decades of Student Performance* (National Assessment of Educational Progress, August 2000 [cited]). Available from http://nces.ed.gov/nationsreportcard/pubs/main1999/2000469.shtml; NCES. *Learner Outcomes* [government publication], The Condition of Education 2000 [cited 2000]. Available from http://nces.ed.gov.

22. Phillip Kaufman, Jin Y. Kwon, Steve Klein, and Christopher D. Chapman, *Dropout Rates in the United States: 1998* [statistical

analysis report], National Center for Education Statistics, November 1999 [cited].

23. Campbell, Hombo, and Mazzeo, *NAEP 1999 Trends in Academic Progress.*

24. NCTM, "Curriculum and Evaluation Standards for School Mathematics," in *Dumbing Down Our Kids: Why American Children Feel Good About Themselves but Can't Read, Write, or Add,* edited by Charles J. Sykes (New York: St. Martin's Griffin, 1989).

25. Stevenson and Stigler, *The Learning Gap: Why Our Schools Are Failing and What We Can Learn from Japanese and Chinese Education* (New York: Simon & Schuster, 1992).

26. *Highlights from the Third International Mathematics and Science Study-Repeat (TIMSS-R)* [Study], 2000 [cited]. Available from http://nces.ed.gov/timss/timss-r/highlights.asp.

27. Ibid.

28. Chester E. Finn, "Why America Has the World's Dimmest Bright Kids," *The Wall Street Journal,* 25 February 1998.

29. Lee Hoffman, "Overview of Public Elementary and Secondary Schools and Districts: School Year 1998–99," *Education Statistics Quarterly* (summer 2000); G. R. Lyon, J. M. Fletcher, et al., "Rethinking Learning Disabilities," in *Rethinking Special Education for a New Century,* edited by C. Finn, A. Rotherman, and C. Hokanson (Washington, D.C.: Thomas B. Fordham Foundation and Progressive Policy Institute, 2001). [prepublication copy]

30. Ibid., 20.

31. Robert Rosenthal, *Interpersonal Expectancy Effects: A Forty Year Perspective.* ERIC: ED415460. 1997.

32. Caroline R. Nolander, "The Effect of Expectation and Tinted Overlays on Reading Ability in Dyslexic Adults," Dissertation Abstracts International, University of Arizona, 1999.

33. Lyon, "Rethinking Learning Disabilities."

34. Stevenson and Stigler, *The Learning Gap: Why Our Schools Are Failing and What We Can Learn from Japanese and Chinese Education* (New York: Simon & Schuster, 1992).

35. The College Entrance Examination Board maintains a Web site with a variety of research and information available on the SAT, which it administrates. www.collegeboard.org

36. Cited in Brent Staples, *Editorial Observer: Why Colleges Shower Their Students with A's* [Internet], The New York Times on the Web, 1998 [cited 8 March 1998].

37. Sykes, *Dumbing Down Our Kids.*

38. "More Freshmen Feel High Degree of Stress."

39. Gregory J. Cizek, "Filling in the Blanks: Putting Standardized Tests to the Test," *Fordham Report* 2, no.11 (October 1998).
40. N. Kher-Durlabhji and L. J. Lacina-Gifford, "Quest for Test Success: Preservice Teachers' Views of High Stakes Tests," in *Putting Standardized Tests to the Test*, edited by Gregory J. Cizek (Fordham Foundation, 1992); Cizek, *Filling in the Blanks*.
41. Cizek, *Filling in the Blanks*.
42. John J. Cannell, "How Public Educators Cheat on Standardized Achievement Tests: The 'Lake Wobegon' Report," *U.S.: New Mexico* (1989): 125.
43. Sykes, *Dumbing Down Our Kids*.
44. *Students and Parents—SAT Program Information—Calculators* [Internet], The College Board, 2001 [cited 28 January 2001]. Available from http://www.collegeboard.org.
45. *A Nation Still at Risk: An Education Manifesto* (Fordham Foundation, 30 April 1998 [cited]). Available from http://www.edexcellence.net/library/manifes.html.
46. Stevenson and Stigler, *The Learning Gap*; Harold W. Stevenson, "Con: Don't Deceive Children Through a Feel-Good Approach. What's Behind Self-Esteem Programs: Truth or Trickery?" *School Administrator* 48, no. 4 (1992): 23–30.
47. Justin Kruger and David Dunning, "Unskilled and Unaware of It: How Difficulties in Recognizing One's Own Incompetence Lead to Inflated Self-Assessments," *Journal of Personality and Social Psychology* 77, no. 6 (1999): 1121–34.
48. C. Rodgers and R. Dymond, *Psychotherapy and Personality Change* (Chicago: University of Chicago Press, 1954).
49. J. Bybee and E. F. Zigler. "Self-Image and Guilt: A Further Test of the Cognitive-Developmental Formulation." *Journal of Personality* 59, no.4 (1991): 733-745; R. Leahy and C. Huard . "Role Taking and Self-Image Disparity in Children." *Developmental Psychology* 12, no.6 (1976): 504-508; I. Rosales and E. F. Zigler (1989). "Role Taking and Self-Image Disparity: A Further Test of Cognitive-Developmental Thought." *Psychological Reports* 64,no.1 (1989): 41-42.

Chapter 7

1. Anemona Hartocollis, *The Big Test Comes Early: Anxious Competition to Get into Hunter Elementary*, The New York Times on the Web, 1997 [cited 15 December 1997]. This example was based on the contents of this article about parents preparing their preschoolers for admission to Hunter Elementary in New York.

2. Sidney J. Blatt, "The Destructiveness of Perfectionism: Implications for the Treatment of Depression," *American Psychologist* 50, no. 12 (1995): 1003–20.

3. C. Bull, *Perfectionism and Self-Esteem in Early Adolescence* (University of Missouri, Columbia: Dissertation Abstracts International, 1999); C. White and R. Schweitzer, "The Role of Personality in the Development and Perpetuation of Chronic Fatigue Syndrome," *Journal of Psychosomatic Research* 48 no.6 (2000): 515-524.

4. M. Mann, *The Relationship of Narcissistic Vulnerability, Shame-Proneness, and Perfectionism, to College Student Adjustment* (University of Missouri at Columbia: Dissertation Abstracts International, 1999); P. Watson, S. Varnell, et al, "Self-Reported Narcissism and Perfectionism: An Ego-Psychological Perspective and the Continuum Hypothesis," *Imagination, Cognition & Personality* 19, no.1 (2000): 59-69.

5. Linda A. Morse, "Working with Young Procrastinators: Elementary School Students Who Do Not Complete School Assignments," *Elementary School Guidance & Counseling* 21, no. 3 (1987): 221–28; Josee Rheaume, Robert Ladouceur, and Mark H. Freeston, "The Prediction of Obsessive-Compulsive Tendencies: Does Perfectionism Play a Significant Role?" *Personality & Individual Differences* 28, no. 3 (2000): 583–92; Gordon L. Flett, Kirk R. Blankstein, Paul Hewitt, and Spomenka Koledin, "Components of Perfectionism and Procrastination in College Students," *Social Behavior & Personality* 20, no. 2 (1992): 85–94.

6. Blatt, "The Destructiveness of Perfectionism," 1012.

7. Julie Boergers, Anthony Spirito, and Deidre Donaldson, "Reasons for Adolescent Suicide Attempts: Associations with Psychological Functioning," *Journal of the American Academy of Child and Adolescent Psychiatry* 37, no. 12 (1998): 1287–98.

8. Paul Hewitt, James Newton, Gordon L. Flett, and Lois Callander, "Perfectionism and Suicide Ideation in Adolescent Psychiatric Patients," *Journal of Abnormal Child Psychology* 25, no. 2 (1997): 95–101; Karen K. Adkins and Wayne Parker, "Perfectionism and Suicidal Preoccupation," *Journal of Personality* 64 (1996): 529–43.

9. David M. Dunkley and Kirk R. Blankstein, "Self-Critical Perfectionism, Coping, Hassles, and Current Distress: A Structural Equation Modeling Approach," *Cognitive Therapy & Research* 24, no. 6 (2000): 713–30; Nancy Arthur and Lois Hayward, "The Relationships Between Perfectionism, Standards for Academic Achievement, and Emotional Distress in Postsecondary Students," *Journal of College Student Development* 38, no. 6 (1997): 622–32.

10. Bettie B. Youngs, *Stress and Your Child: Helping Kids Cope with the Strains and Pressures of Life* (New York: Fawcett Book Group, 1995).

11. M. Frese, "Stress at Work and Psychosomatic Complaints: A Casual Interpretation," *Journal of Applied Psychology* 70 (1985): 314–28; S. Cohen and S. L. Syme, *Social Support and Health* (Orlando, Florida: Academic Press, 1985).

12. WebMD, *How Serious Is Long-Term Stress?* 2001 [cited 2001]. Available from http://my.webmd.com/content/article/1680.51974.

13. S. Goetz, R. H. Adler, and R. Weber, "High Need for Control as a Psychological Risk in Women Suffering from Ischemic Stroke: A Controlled Retrospective Exploratory Study," *International Journal of Psychiatry in Medicine* 22, no. 2 (1992): 119–29; M. Kukleta and E. Dungelova, "Activation States with Putative Pathogenic Impact in Patients with Ischemic Heart Disease," *Homeostasis in Health & Disease* 35, no. 1–2 (1994): 101–102.

14. A. Kowal and D. Pritchard, "Psychological Characteristics of Children Who Suffer from Headache: A Research Note," *Journal of Child Psychology and Psychiatry and Allied Disciplines* 31, no. 4 (1990): 637–49; Thomas R. Martin, Gordon L. Flett, Paul L. Hewitt, and Lester Kramcs, "Personality Correlates of Depression and Health Symptoms: A Test of a Self-Regulation Model," *Journal of Research in Personality* 30, no. 2 (1996): 264–77.

15. C. White and R. Schweitzer, "The Role of Personality in the Development and Perpetuation of Chronic Fatigue Syndrome," *Journal of Psychosomatic Research* 48, no.6 (2000): 515-524; WebMD, *How Serious Is Long-Term Stress?* 2001 [cited 2001]. Available from http://my.webmd.com/content/article/1680.51974.

16. Debra Nussbaum, *How a Speeded-up Society Trickles Down to Children: From Infancy to Academics, the Race Is On* [Internet] (The New York Times on the Web, 1999 [cited 31 October 1999]).

17. Jane Healy, "The 'Meme' That Ate Childhood," *Education Week* 18, no. 6 (1998): 56+.

18. Nussbaum, *How a Speeded-Up Society Trickles Down to Children: From Infancy to Academics, the Race Is On* [Internet] (The New York Times on the Web, 1999 [cited 31 October 1999]).

19. Edward F. Zigler, "Formal Schooling for Four-Year-Olds? No," *Annual Progress in Child Psychiatry & Child Development* 198, no. 8 (1991): 162–76; "School Should Begin at Age 3 Years for American Children," *Journal of Developmental & Behavioral Pediatrics* 19, no. 1 (1998): 38–40.

20. *Children's Time* [Internet], Institute for Social Research, date unknown [cited]. Available from http://www.isr.umich. edu/src/child-development/home.html.
21. Tony Schwartz, "The Test Under Stress," *The New York Times Magazine*, January 10, 1999.
22. Tara Bahrampour, *Urban Tactics; They Do Everything but Take the Test for You* (The New York Times on the Web, 1999 [cited 7 November 1999]).
23. Jack McCallum and Richard O'Brien, "The Razor's Edge," *Sports Illustrated* (4 November 1996), 22.
24. "Father, Son Sentenced in Buckle-Sharpening; Player Says Helmet Altered for Protection," *Minneapolis Star Tribune* (24 December 1996), 8.
25. Sunil S. Bhar and Michael Kyrios, "Cognitive Personality Styles Associated with Depressive and Obsessive Compulsive Phenomena in a Non-Clinical Sample," *Behavioural & Cognitive Psychotherapy* 27, no. 4 (1999): 329–43; A. Rothenberg, "Adolescence and Eating Disorder: The Obsessive-Compulsive Syndrome," *Psychiatric Clinics of North America* 13, no. 3 (1990): 469–88; M. M. Antony, C. L. Prudon, V. Huta, and R. P. Swinson, "Dimensions of Perfectionism Across the Anxiety Disorders," *Behaviour Research and Therapy* 36, no. 12 (1998): 1143–54.
26. Jennifer Mills and Kirk R. Blankstein, "Perfectionism, Intrinsic Vs Extrinsic Motivation, and Motivated Strategies for Learning: A Multidimensional Analysis of University Students," *Personality & Individual Differences* 29, no. 6 (2000): 1191–204.
27. Antony, Prudon, Huta, and Swinson, "Dimensions of Perfectionism Across the Anxiety Disorders."
28. Roy F. Baumeister, *Evil: Inside Human Violence and Cruelty* (New York: W. H. Freeman & Company, 1997); Rick E. Ingram, "Self-Focused Attention in Clinical Disorders Review and a Conceptual Model," *Psychological Bulletin* 107, no. 2 (1990): 156–76.
29. Karen E. Ablard, "Parents' Achievement Goals and Perfectionism in Their Academically Talented Children," *Journal of Youth and Adolescence* 26, no. 6 (1997): 651–67; G. D. Heyman and C. S. Dweck, "Achievement Goals and Intrinsic Motivation: Their Relation and Their Role in Adaptive Motivation," *Motivation & Emotion.* 16 (1992): 231–47.
30. Monica Ramirez Basco, "Cover Story: The 'Perfect' Trap," *Psychology Today* 32, no. 68 (1999): 30–34.
31. Edward Chang and Kevin Rand. "Perfectionism as a Predictor of Subsequent Adjustment Evidence for a Specific Diathesis-Stress

Mechanism Among College Students," *Journal of Counseling Psychology* 47, no.1, (2000): 129-137.

Chapter 8

1. R. F. Baumeister, *Evil: Inside Human Violence and Cruelty* (New York: W. H. Freeman and Company, 1997).
2. Leonard S. Newman, Kimberley J. Duff, and Roy F. Baumeister, "A New Look at Defensive Projection Thought Suppression, Accessibility, and Biased Person Perception," *Journal of Personality and Social Psychology* 72, no. 5 (1997): 980–1001.
3. Mario Mikulincer, "Adult Attachment Style and Affect Regulation: Strategic Variations in Self-Appraisals," *Journal of Personality and Social Psychology* 75, no. 2 (1998): 420–35; Kelly A. Brennan and Phillip R. Shaver, "Attachment Styles and Personality Disorders: Their Connections to Each Other and to Parental Divorce, Parental Death, and Perceptions of Parental Caregiving," *Journal of Personality* 66, no. 5 (1998): 835–78.
4. Rick E. Ingram, "Self-Focused Attention in Clinical Disorders Review and a Conceptual Model," *Psychological Bulletin* 107, no. 2 (1990): 156–76.
5. Albert Ellis, *REBT Diminishes Much of the Human Ego* (New York: Institute for Rational-Emotive Therapy, 1991), 7.
6. Terry P. London, "The Case Against Self-Esteem: Alternative Philosophies Toward Self That Would Raise the Probability of Pleasurable and Productive Living," *Journal of Rational-Emotive & Cognitive-Behavior Therapy* 15, no. 1 (1997): 22.
7. June P. Tangney, "Humility: Theoretical Perspectives, Empirical Findings and Directions for Future Research," *Journal of Social and Clinical Psychology* 19, no. 1 (2000): 73.
8. Walter Mischel, Yuichi Shoda, and Philip K. Peake, "The Nature of Adolescent Competencies Predicted by Preschool Delay of Gratification," *Journal of Personality and Social Psychology* 54, no. 4 (1988): 687–696. p. 691.
9. Ibid.
10. Yuichi Shoda, Walter Mischel, and Philip K. Peake, "Predicting Adolescent Cognitive and Self-Regulatory Competencies from Preschool Delay of Gratification Identifying Diagnosis Conditions," *Developmental Psychology* 26, no. 6 (1990): 978–86.
11. David C. Funder, Jeanne H. Block, and Jack Block, "Delay of Gratification: Some Longitudinal Personality Correlates," *Journal of Personality and Social Psychology* 44, no. 6 (1983): 1198–213.

12. David C. Funder and Jack Block, "The Role of Ego-Control, Ego-Resiliency, and IQ in Delay of Gratification in Adolescence," *Journal of Personality and Social Psychology* 57, no. 6 (1989): 1041–50.

13. David C. Funder and Jack Block, "The Role of Ego-Control, Ego-Resiliency, and IQ in Delay of Gratification in Adolescence," *Journal of Personality and Social Psychology* 57, no. 6 (1989): 1041-50; T. Jacobsen, M. Huss, et al, "Childrens Ability to Delay Gratification: Longitudinal Relations to Mother-Child Attachment." *Journal of Genetic Psychology* 158 no. 4 (1997): 411-426; C. Schwarz, J. Schrager, et al, "Delay of Gratification by Preschoolers: Evidence for the Validity of the Choice Paradigm." *Child Development* 54 no. 3 (1983): 620-625; R. Howse, *Motivation and Self-Regulation as Predictors of Achievement in Economically Disadvantaged Young Children* (University of North Carolina at Greensboro: Dissertation Abstracts International, 1999). M. Waugh, "A Temperamental and Developmental Model for Personality Assessment: Application to Self-Control in Middle Childhood," *Journal of Personality and Individual Differences* 5 no. 3 (1984): 355-358.

14. R. F. Baumeister and Julie J. Exline, "Self-Control, Morality, and Human Strength," *Journal of Social and Clinical Psychology Special Issue: Classical Sources of Human Strength: A Psychological Analysis* 19, no. 1 (2000): 29–42; Mark Muraven, R. F. Baumeister, and Dianne M. Tice, "Longitudinal Improvement of Self-Regulation Through Practice: Building Self-Control Strength Through Repeated Exercise," *The Journal of Social Psychology* 139, no. 4 (1999): 446–457.

15. John Bowlby, *A Secure Base* (New York: Basic Books, 1988).

16. M. Ainsworth, M. Blehar, E. Waters, and S. Wall, *Patterns of Attachment: A Psychological Study of the Strange Situation* (Hillsdale, New Jersey: Eribaum, 1978).

17. Mikulincer, "Attachment Style and the Mental Representation of the Self."

18. D. Rosenstein and H. Horowitz, "Adolescent Attachment and Psychopathology," *Journal of Consulting and Clinical Psychology* 64, no. 2 (1996): 244–253.

19. Ibid.

20. Michael C. Luebbert, "Attachment, Psychosocial Development, Shame, Guilt, and Forgiveness," (Dissertation Abstracts International: Section B., Texas A & M University, 2000).

21. Nancy Eisenberg, "Emotion, Regulation, and Moral Development," *Annual Review of Psychology* 51, no. 1 (2000): 665–97; Roberta Kestenbaum, Ellen A. Farber, and L. A. Sroufe, "Individual Differ-

ences in Empathy Among Preschoolers: Relation to Attachment History," *New Directions for Child Development* Sum, no. 44 (1989): 51–64.

22. Martin Seligman, *Depression & Violence* [Speech], American Psychological Association: National Press Club: Morning Newsmaker, 1998 [cited 3 September 1998] p. 4.

Chapter 9

1. D. Baumrind, "The Influence of Parenting Style on Adolescent Competence and Substance Use," *Journal of Early Adolescence* 11, no. 1 (1991): 56–95; Nancy Darling, *Parenting Style and Its Correlates* [ERIC Digest], 1999 [cited March 1999]. Available from http://ericeece.org/pubs/digests/1999/darlin99.html.

2. Judith R. Harris, *The Nurture Assumption: Why Children Turn Out the Way They Do* (New York: Free Press, 1998).

3. Byron Egeland, Robert Pianta, and Maureen A. O'Brien, "Maternal Intrusiveness in Infancy and Child Maladaptation in Early School Years," *Development & Psychopathology* 5, no. 3 (1993): 359–70.

4. B. L. Baker and T. L. Heller, "Preschool Children with Externalizing Behaviors: Experience of Fathers and Mothers," *Journal of Abnormal Child Psychology* 24, no. 4 (1996): 513–32.

5. Dagmar Kaufmann, Ellis Gesten, Raymond C. Santa Lucia, Octavio Salcedo, Gianna Rendina-Gobioff, and Ray Gadd, "The Relationship Between Parenting Style and Children's Adjustment: The Parents' Perspective," *Journal of Child & Family Studies* 9, no. 2 (2000): 231–45.

6. K. Aunola, H. Stattin, and J. E. Nurmi, "Parenting Styles and Adolescents' Achievement Strategies," *Journal of Adolescence* 23, no. 2 (2000): 205–22; Baumrind, "The Influence of Parenting Style on Adolescent Competence and Substance Use"; D. A. Cohen and J. Rice, "Parenting Styles, Adolescent Substance Use, and Academic Achievement," *Journal of Drug Education* 27, no. 2 (1997): 199–211; Darling, *Parenting Style and Its Correlates*; S. D. Lamborn, N. S. Mounts, L. Steinberg, and S. M. Dornbusch, "Patterns of Competence and Adjustment Among Adolescents from Authoritative, Authoritarian, Indulgent, and Neglectful Families," *Child Development* 62, no. 5 (1991): 1049–65; L. Steinberg, S. D. Lamborn, Nancy Darling, N. S. Mounts, and S. M. Dornbusch, "Over-Time Changes in Adjustment and Competence Among Adolescents from Authoritative, Authoritarian, Indulgent, and Neglectful Families," *Child Development* 65, no. 3 (1994): 754–70.

7. *Population and Family Characteristics* [Internet], 2000 [cited 2000]. Available from http://childstats.gov/ac2000/poptxt.asp.

8. *No Time to Slow Down: Can We Keep Working Harder and Harder Indefinitely?* (Outlook) [U.S. News Online], 2000 [cited 26 June 2000]. Available from http://www.usnews.com/usnews/issue/000626/26atlarge.htm.

9. Leslie A. Perlow, *The Time Famine: Toward a Sociology of Work Time* [Internet], Administrative Science Quarterly, 1999 [cited March 1999]. Available from http://www.findarticles.com/m4035/1_44/54482493/p1/article.jhtml.

10. Martin E. P. Seligman, Karen Reivich, Lisa Jaycox, and Jane Gillham, *The Optimistic Child: A Revolutionary Program That Safeguards Children Against Depression & Builds Lifelong Resilience* (Boston: Houghton Mifflin, 1995), 45.

11. N. Eisenberg and P. Miller, "The Relation of Empathy to Prosocial and Related Behaviors," *Psychological Bulletin* 101, no. 1 (1987): 91–119.

12. M. Dekovic and J. Gerris, "Developmental Analysis of Social Cognitive and Behavioral Differences Between Popular and Rejected Children," *Journal of Applied Developmental Psychology* 15 (1994): 367–386.

13. D. Richardson, G. Hammock, S. Smith, W. Gardner, and M. Signo, "Empathy as a Cognitive Inhibitor of Interpersonal Aggression," *Aggressive Behavior* 20, (1994): 275–289.

14. B. Kozeki and R. Berghammer, "The Role of Empathy in the Motivational Structure of School Children," *Personality and Individual Differences* 13, no. 2 (1992): 191–203; K. Minde, "Aggression in Preschoolers: Its Relation to Socialization," *Journal of the American Academy of Child and Adolescent Psychiatry* 31, no. 5 (1992): 853–62.

15. Roy F. Baumeister and Julie J. Exline, "Virtue, Personality, and Social Relations: Self-Control as the Moral Muscle," *Journal of Personality* 67, no. 6 (1999): 1165–1194.

16. Christian F. Mauro and Yvette R. Harris, "The Influence of Maternal Child-Rearing Attitudes and Teaching Behaviors on Preschoolers' Delay of Gratification," *Journal of Genetic Psychology* 161, no. 3 (2000): 292–306.

17. Jessica L. Hartos, Patricia Eitel, Denise L. Haynie, and Bruce G. Simons-Morton, "Can I Take the Car? Relations Among Parenting Practices and Adolescent Problem-Driving Practices," *Journal of Adolescent Research* 15, no. 3 (2000): 352–67.

18. Albert Bandura, Dorothea Ross, and Sheila A. Ross, "Vicarious Reinforcement and Imitative Learning," *Journal of Abnormal Child Psychology* 67, no. 6 (1963): 601–607.

19. C. M. Mueller and C. S. Dweck, "Implicit Theories of Intelligence: Relation of Parental Beliefs to Children's Expectations," (Poster session presented at Head Start's Third National Research Conference, Washington, D.C., 1996).

20. C. M. Mueller and C. S. Dweck, "Praise for Intelligence Can Undermine Children's Motivation and Performance," *Journal of Personality and Social Psychology* 75, no. 1 (1998): 33–52.

21. Melissa L. Kamins and C. S. Dweck, "Person Versus Process Praise and Criticism Implications for Contingent Self-Worth and Coping," *Developmental Psychology* 35, no. 3 (1999): 835–47.

22. The National Center on Addiction and Substance Abuse, "National Survey of American Attitudes on Substance Abuse VI: Teens," New York: Columbia University , 2001.

23. N. Eisenberg, *Emotion, Regulation, and Moral Development* [Internet]. Annual Review of Psychology, 2000 [cited 2000]. Available from http://www.findarticles.com/cf_0/m0961/2000_Annual/61855640/print .jhtml.

24. Baumeister and Exline, "Virtue, Personality, and Social Relations;" Tamara J. Ferguson, Hedy Stegge, Erin R. Miller, and Michael E. Olsen, "Guilt, Shame, and Symptoms in Children," *Developmental Psychology* 35, no. 2 (1999): 347–57.

25. June P. Tangney, "Moral Affect: The Good, the Bad, and the Ugly," *Journal of Personality and Social Psychology* 61, no. 4 (1991): 598–607; June P. Tangney, Patricia F. Wagner, Deborah Hill-Barlow, Donna E. Marschall, and Richard Gramzow, "Relation of Shame and Guilt to Constructive Versus Destructive Responses to Anger across the Lifespan," *Journal of Personality and Social Psychology* 70, no. 4 (1996): 797–809.

26. John Rosemond, *Raising a Nonviolent Child* (Kansas City: Andrews McMeel, 2000).

27. Aaron P. Turner, Irwin G. Sarason, and Barbara R. Sarason, "Exploring the Link Between Parental Acceptance and Young Adult Adjustment," in *Cognitive Therapy and Research*, 25, no.2 (2001): 185–99.

Chapter 10

1. Carter Center, 2001 [cited 2001]. Available from http://www.carter-center.org/elections.html.

2. C. J. Sykes, *Dumbing Down Our Kids: Why America's Children Feel Good About Themselves but Can't Read, Write, or Add* (New York: St. Martin's Griffin, 1995).

3. David H. Jonassen, Kyle L. Peck, Brent G. Wilson, and William S. Pfeiffer, *Learning with Technology: A Constructivist Perspective* (Upper Saddle River, New Jersey: Merrill, 1998), 3.

4. Jeanne S. Chall, *The Academic Achievement Challenge: What Really Works in the Classroom?* (New York: The Guilford Press, 2000).

5. B. L. Baker and T. L. Heller, "Preschool Children with Externalizing Behaviors: Experience of Fathers and Mothers," *Journal of Abnormal Child Psychology* 24, no. 4 (1996): 513–532; D. A. Cohen and J. Rice, "Parenting Styles, Adolescent Substance Use, and Academic Achievement," *Journal of Drug Education* 27, no. 2 (1997): 199–211; Nancy Darling, *Parenting Style and Its Correlates* [ERIC Digest], 1999 [cited March 1999]. Available from http://ericeece.org/pubs/digests/1999/darlin99.html; D. Baumrind, "The Influence of Parenting Style on Adolescent Competence and Substance Use," *Journal of Early Adolescence* 11, no. 1 (1991): 56–95.

6. Chall, *The Academic Achievement Challenge*.

7. Russell J. Skiba and Reece L. Peterson, "School Discipline at a Crossroads: From Zero Tolerance to Early Response," *Exceptional Children* 66, no. 3 (2000): 335–46.

8. Ibid.

9. Reginald Roberts and Jeffery C. Mays, "Boys, 8, Charged in Paper Gun Incident," *The Star-Ledger*, 21 March 2001.

10. Mark Eissman, *Zero Tolerance: Does It Protect or Harm Kids?* 2000 [cited 20 April 2000]. Available from http://apbnews.com/safetycenter/family/2000/04/20/zerotolerance0420_01.html.

11. David Stolinsky, "Zero Tolerance, Zero Sense," *The American Enterprise* 12, no. 3 (2001): 11–12.

12. Vanessa Dea, "Lawyers' Group Pans 'Zero Tolerance' Rules," *Education Week* 20, no. 24 (2001): 3.

13. John Leland, "Zero Tolerance Policies Change Life at One School" (Living) *New York Times,* 2001 [cited 8 April 2001]. Available from http://www.nytimes.com/2001/04/02/living/08HIGH.html.

14. Skiba and Peterson, "School Discipline at a Crossroads;" "Youth Violence: A Report of the Surgeon General" (Washington, D.C.: Department of Health and Human Services, 2001).

15. G. R. Lyon, J. M. Fletcher, S. E. Shaywitz, and B. A. Shaywitz, "Rethinking Learning Disabilities," in *Rethinking Special Education for a New Century*, edited by C. Finn, A. Rotherman, and C. Hokanson

(Washington, D.C.: Thomas B. Fordham Foundation and Progressive Policy Institute, 2001).

16. Ibid., 43.

17. Lyon, "Rethinking Learning Disabilities."

18. Jay G. Chambers, Thomas B. Parrish, Joanne C. Lieberman, and Jean M. Wolman, "What Are We Spending on Special Education in the U.S.?" *CESF Brief*, no. 8 (1998).

19. *Where Can I Get More Recent Data on Special Education Costs? Most of the Data on Your Site Are 10 Years Old* (Center for Special Education Finance, 1999 [cited 9 September 1999]). Available from http://csef.air.org/faq3-10.html.

20. W. C. Symonds, A. T. Palmer, et al., "How to Fix America's Schools," *Business Week*, (03/19/2001): 66–80.

21. "Teacher Colleges Stew over Accountability Rules," *USA Today* (11 April 2001 [cited 2001]), A14.

22. Gannet News Service, "Most States' Teacher Tests Are Too Easy, Report Says," *The Salt Lake Tribune*, Salt Lake City, 28 May 1999.

Epilogue

1. D. Mills, *Overcoming "Self-Esteem:" Why Our Compulsive Drive for "Self-Esteem" Is Anxiety-Provoking, Socially Inhibiting, and Self-Sabotaging* (New York: Rational Emotive Behavior Therapy Institute, 2000). We thank Mills for the ideas that inspired our thoughts on this matter.

2. D. Myers, "The Funds, Friends, and Faith of Happy People," *American Psychologist 55*, no. 1 (2000): 56–67; D. Myers, *The American Paradox: Spiritual Hunger in an Age of Plenty* (New Haven, Connecticut: Yale University Press, 2000).

3. M. Argyle, *The Psychology of Happiness* (London: Methuen, 1986); M. Csikszentmihalyi, "If We Are So Rich, Why Aren't We Happy?" *American Psychologist 54* (1999): 821–827; Myers, "The Funds, Friends, and Faith of Happy People"; Myers, *The American Paradox*.

4. M. McCullough, C. G. Bellah, et al., "Vengefulness: Relationships with Forgiveness, Rumination, Well-Being, and the Big Five," *Personality and Social Psychology Bulletin 27*, no. 5 (2001): 601–610; J. Maltby, A. Macaskill, et al., "Failure to Forgive Self and Others: A Replication and Extension of the Relationship Between Forgiveness, Personality, Social Desirability, and General Health," *Personality and Individual Differences 30*, no. 5 (2001): 881–885.

5. R. Emmons and C. Crumpler, "Gratitude as Human Strength: Appraising the Evidence," *Journal of Social and Clinical Psychology* 19 (2000): 56–69, as cited in M. McCullough, S. Kilpatrick, et al., "Is Gratitude a Moral Affect?" *Psychological Bulletin* 127, no. 2 (2001): 249–266.

6. Myers, "The Funds, Friends, and Faith of Happy People"; Myers, *The American Paradox*; G. Easterbrook, "Psychology Discovers Happiness," *The New Republic*, 03/05/2001.

7. Myers, "The Funds, Friends, and Faith of Happy People;" Myers, *The American Paradox*.

8. Ibid.

9. R. Baumeister and J. Exline, "Virtue, Personality and Social Relations: Self-Control as the Moral Muscle," *Journal of Personality* 67, no. 6 (1999): 1165–1194.

10. Smith and Elliott. Note: We hope the readers forgive our poetic license in this concluding story. Though we often did our research at local malls and coffee shops, and jotted down our ideas on napkins, this last story represented wishful thinking.

INDEX